Dynamics of
Social Welfare Policy

Dynamics of Social Welfare Policy

Right versus Left

Gardenia Harris, Bernard Ivan Tamas, and Nancy S. Lind

ROWMAN & LITTLEFIELD PUBLISHERS, INC.
Lanham • Boulder • New York • Toronto • Plymouth, UK

ROWMAN & LITTLEFIELD PUBLISHERS, INC.

Published in the United States of America
by Rowman & Littlefield Publishers, Inc.
A wholly owned subsidiary of The Rowman & Littlefield Publishing Group, Inc.
4501 Forbes Boulevard, Suite 200, Lanham, Maryland 20706
www.rowmanlittlefield.com

Estover Road
Plymouth PL6 7PY
United Kingdom

British Library Cataloguing in Publication Information Available

Library of Congress Cataloging-in-Publication Data:
Harris, Gardenia, 1961–
  Dynamics of social welfare policy : right versus left / Gardenia Harris,
Bernard Ivan Tamas, and Nancy S. Lind.
    p. cm.
  ISBN-13: 978-0-7425-5949-3 (cloth : alk. paper)
  ISBN-10: 0-7425-5949-1 (cloth : alk. paper)
  ISBN-13: 978-0-7425-5950-9 (pbk. : alk. paper)
  ISBN-10: 0-7425-5950-5 (pbk. : alk. paper)
  1. United States—Social policy—1993– 2. Social problems—United States. 3.
Social service—United States. I. Tamas, Bernard Ivan. II. Lind, Nancy S., 1958– III.
Title.
  HN59.2.H373 2007
  320.60973—dc22   2007005907

Printed in the United States of America

♾™ The paper used in this publication meets the minimum requirements of
American National Standard for Information Sciences—Permanence of Paper for
Printed Library Materials, ANSI/NISO Z39.48-1992.

Gardenia Harris dedicates this book to her great grandmother, Irene Coleman, and her uncle Robert Thomas.

Bernard Ivan Tamas dedicates this book to his nephew Henry Tamas.

Nancy Lind dedicates this book to her parents, Robert and Camille Lind, and her godchildren: Brian Sroda, Mitchell Lind, and Jensynn Lesinski.

This book is dedicated to future generations who will be able to understand philosophical differences between liberals and conservatives and who may be dedicated to working toward change for those less well-off.

Contents

Acknowledgments

We are indebted to our department chairpersons, Jamal Nassar and Wanda Bracy, who encouraged us to develop this project. We are also indebted to Art Pomponio, our editor at Rowman & Littlefield, and Asa Johnson, his editorial assistant, who have provided prompt responses to our many questions throughout the process. We especially appreciate the contributions of graduate student Vanda Rajcan, who directed a research team of undergraduate students, including Kalen Tjarks, Ashley Velon, Michelle Cross, Renee Gudeman, Elizabeth Boratto, Kelli Evans, Dana Fogarty, Katie Echeverria, and Kyle Schneider.

Introduction

The majority of social work practice occurs in bureaucratic environments such as state-sponsored organizations and private social service agencies. Agency and organizational activities are largely determined by policies that spell out the mode of intervention, the resources available, and the persons eligible to receive services. In fact, the goals that social work can accomplish are so dependent on social, ideological, and economic forces that the National Association of Social Workers (NASW) code of ethics identifies the "promotion of the general welfare of society" as one of its six ethical responsibilities. More specifically, this ethical standard directs social workers to

1. act to prevent and eliminate discrimination
2. ensure that all people have access to the resources, services, and opportunities they need
3. act to expand choice and opportunity for all people
4. promote conditions that encourage respect for diversity
5. advocate for changes in policy and legislation to improve social conditions and to promote social justice, and
6. encourage informed participation by the public in shaping social policies and institutions

The unique attention paid to shaping institutions and policies to improve clients' status is one factor that distinguishes social work from other helping professions. If the source or solution of the problem lies within the community, institution, or society, inattention to these areas violates ethical standards and inadvertently "blames victims" for situations over which they have little control. Casework and therapy alleviate clients' symptoms and pain, but do not rectify social and economic injustices.

In planning interventions, social workers must determine whether clients' problems are the result of individual or family factors that are amenable to direct intervention, or whether the problems are caused by oppressive social or institutional arrangements that are best addressed at the macro level. The "dual nature of social work practice" refers to the need to attend to both individual and societal factors that contribute to client problems. Thus, social workers must become adept at shifting their focus between psychological and political perspectives when assessing and addressing clients' needs.

Social work students often underestimate their capability to effectively advocate in the political arena. It is essential that social work students recognize that the individual, family, and group skills they are acquiring are readily transferable to the political realm. In fact, social workers are among the best-equipped professionals to engage in social advocacy on behalf of their clients. Although policy makers have developed expertise in specialized areas, few policy makers interact with social work clientele on a personal level. Policy makers' lack of intimate knowledge and experience in regard to social work clients' situations generally translates into a lack of understanding of the origins of and solutions to client problems. However, as experts on their clients' situations, social workers can utilize their interpersonal communication and persuasion skills to educate and influence policy makers.

At no time in U.S. history has the American electorate been so divided in terms of its political affiliation. Currently, the majority political party in both the U.S. House of Representatives and the U.S. Senate holds only a slight majority. Similarly, many state legislatures are nearly evenly split between Democrats and Republicans. Therefore, social workers who seek to shape social welfare policy must be able to collaborate with both conservatives and liberals to craft policies that are favorable to social work clients. Knowledge of policy makers' ideologies and values is indispensable to social workers who hope to persuade legislators to support their positions. To obtain bipartisan support for their proposals, advocates need to frame issues so they meet both liberal and conservative objectives.

Social workers are agents of change. To enact this change, they need to be knowledgeable about the public policy issues that confront their clientele. Social workers need to empower their clientele and lobby alongside them to create public policies that do not disadvantage people in society who are already less powerful. Empowerment, however, takes knowledge, and it is thus incumbent on social workers to understand the historical events that lead to various issues of policy and to differentiate between the opinions of liberals and conservatives on these issues. Social workers, in turn, can share this information with their clientele and together they can collectively enact change.

As a student of social work, it is your responsibility to engage in grassroots advocacy and to make your voice heard in Washington, D.C., and at your state capitols. Your professional organization, the National Association of Social Workers, is already fighting hard to have their voices heard in Washington and, as an incoming social worker, you need to be prepared to join this fight. Members of Congress are often the leaders who hold the policy-making ability in their hands to enact policies that are representative of all people, regardless of race, gender, sexual orientation, or socioeconomic status. Influencing social policies is so critical to the jobs of social workers that the NASW annually develops a legislative agenda for each session of Congress and alerts members to the issues where a social worker's involvement is key. NASW remains concerned about a range of issues that influence the quality of life for people both nationally and globally. Many of the issues highlighted in this text already have the backing of the NASW but are still a long way from full implementation. Highlighting the social work policy issues debated by the U.S. Congress, a brief overview of the 108th and 109th Congresses follows.

The legislative agenda for the 108th Congress, January 2003–December 2004, supports a national economic policy that includes universal access to full employment, opportunities to accumulate financial assets, and access to unstigmatized financial support for those in need. Toward this end, NASW supports policies improving Temporary Assistance to Needy Families (TANF) resources and eliminating racial and ethnic discrimination in access to these programs. Similarly, NASW supports programs to protect and improve the Social Security system, to raise the federal minimum wage, and to require equal pay for equal work.

The legislative agenda for the 109th Congress, January 2005–December 2006, continues to advocate for a national health insurance program, including both physical and mental health services. The NASW opposes legislation designed to further fragment an already decentralized health care system. Another high priority for NASW is to support Medicaid, Medicare, and the State Children's Health Insurance Program. Within the realm of Medicare, for example, NASW supports the reimbursement of social workers who provide mental health counseling in nursing homes.

The criminal justice system is also often viewed as skewed against the interests of poor or minority citizens. NASW sees part of its obligation as protecting these classes of individuals. To this end, they advocate proposals such as the Violence Against Women Act and measures to end family violence. They wish to further protect the interests of gays, lesbians, and transgendered people through passage of the Hate Crimes Prevention Act.

NASW continues to support a strong role for federal involvement in the child welfare system, particularly promoting policies in the best interests of children. This includes the use of qualified staff in counseling children as well as reduced workloads for the caseworkers. Many children find themselves disadvantaged by the educational system and thus NASW promotes the enhancement of opportunities for all children. The No Child Left Behind Act, for example, does not make exceptions for schools populated by a majority of highly disadvantaged children, which leaves the original bill unfair and ineffective. NASW supports legislation to amend this law in the name of fairness. The integrity of the Head Start program is supported by NASW, as well as efforts to ensure that religious-based hiring does not eliminate qualified teachers from the program.

Housing needs remain a major concern for a large segment of society. The politics of exclusion leave the most stigmatized segments of society, those with drug and alcohol addictions and those suffering from mental illness, out of most government housing programs. Social workers often find themselves working to find affordable housing even for full-time employees, let alone those suffering from the above afflictions. Another segment of society often priced out of the housing market is the elderly. For seniors who cannot afford to remain in their own homes, either from financial frailty or physical frailty, the only options often become residing in supported housing or living in an assisted community. However, these are often high-cost options. Living in public senior housing facilities financed by the Department of Housing and Urban Development becomes a reality for many of these individuals.

While civil rights remains an important policy issue for all citizens, social workers find themselves struggling to protect the civil rights of the homeless and lesbians, gays, and transgendered people. For social workers, it is imperative to understand the implications and consequences of offering civil rights protections to these groups. Many of these groups have had to take their issues to court to get protection against discrimination. Social workers often have to counter misinformation that is provided about these groups of people, and legislators are certainly not immune to this misinformation.

The current globalization of society, the intertwining of the actions of the United States and other nations, requires that social workers broaden their horizons and view social justice issues within a global framework. Social workers can benefit from knowing how the issues in their community have played out in other communities, whether domestically or abroad. One need only turn to the United Nations Declaration of Human Rights (1948) to recognize the principles germane to alleviating poverty and social injustices in the world. The protection of the rights of all individuals is paramount.

This book provides current and future social workers with a framework for change. It examines ten key issues confronting social work professionals and places them in their larger context. The introduction to each chapter identifies the genesis of the issue or the reasons that the issue became a dominant theme in the policy-making agendas of Congress. The second and third sections of each issue provide actual arguments written and spoken by elected officials, both in the U.S. Congress and the presidency, and with both liberal and conservative viewpoints. By providing the actual text of the arguments, we allow students to critically evaluate each side of the debate for themselves and use the information to empower both themselves and their clients to bring about change. We are also not interpreting and biasing the political viewpoints of the legislators, as we are allowing each to speak for himself or herself. In the arguments selected, we tried as much as possible to allow liberal and conservative opinions to represent polarized views on the issues. In general, the liberal perspectives represented here believe that society can be changed for the better and that government can be used as an instrument for this change. The conservative perspective is not necessarily resistant to change, but instead believes that change should come more through free market forces and less through government intervention.

1

Poverty

According to the U.S. Census Bureau, the number of people living in poverty increased for four consecutive years from 2000 to 2004. In 2004, 12.7 percent of the American population lived in poverty (U.S. Census Bureau, www .census.gov/hhes/www/poverty/poverty04hi.html). Children are particularly vulnerable, with nearly one in every five children living in poverty.

Conservatives and liberals propose dramatically different strategies for combating poverty, largely due to dissimilar assumptions regarding the nature and causes of poverty and the role the federal government should play in addressing social problems. Conservatives attribute poverty to individual and cultural factors such as lack of motivation, poor self-discipline, low educational attainment, and dysfunctional intergenerational modeling. They believe that permissive government welfare programs encourage dependency and discourage recipients from seeking work. As a result, conservatives favor policies designed to hold individuals accountable for their situations and seek to develop the participants' work ethic. Income maintenance programs have been increasingly targeted for funding cuts in conservative efforts to balance the budget. Conservatives have also been instrumental in the development of policy components that include a more prominent role for nongovernmental sources, including faith-based organizations and privately run charities.

In contrast, liberals believe that poverty is largely caused by social and structural forces beyond the control of the individual. They contend that discrimination and economic policies to control inflation, unequal educational opportunities, and an unfair economic structure disadvantage particular groups within the labor market. The lack of apparent motivation on the part of the poor is seen as an understandable reaction to the recognition that many of the jobs available to them will not keep them out of poverty. Liberals believe that the government is obligated to ensure that all of its citizens have basic necessities and the opportunity to participate fully in the free market economy. Liberals generally support proposals for expansion of income maintenance and prefer to balance the budget by raising taxes on the rich and reducing programs such as defense spending.

TEMPORARY ASSISTANCE FOR NEEDY FAMILIES

The Personal Responsibility and Work Opportunity Reconciliation Act (PRWORA) of 1996 (P.L. 104-193) transformed the AFDC program to a new block grant called Temporary Assistance for Needy Families (TANF). The PRWORA ended the entitlement to cash welfare benefits by placing a five-year lifetime limit on the receipt of TANF benefits. States were also required to implement stringent work requirements for a larger proportion of beneficiaries than ever before. Although the block grant structure gives states more flexibility, it also caps funding levels based on 1994 expenditures, regardless of subsequent changes in states' level of need.

Liberals and conservatives agree that self-sufficiency should be a major goal of TANF, but their different assumptions regarding the nature and causes of poverty lead them to support different strategies for reducing welfare dependency. Conservative explanations of welfare dependency focus on individual and lifestyle factors. Stringent work requirements and time limits are intended to attack "the culture of poverty" that leads to welfare dependency. On the other hand, liberals' emphasis on structural and societal causes of dependency results in cries that work requirements be supplemented with training and job preparation that prepares participants for better-paying jobs.

Debate over 1996 welfare reauthorization focused on conservative proposals to increase work requirements from thirty to forty hours per week, while limiting client participation in education and job training to a maximum of sixteen hours per week. Much of the debate centered on divergent definitions of self-sufficiency. Conservatives emphasized reduction of welfare rolls, while liberals focused on helping people out of poverty and assisting them in finding better-paying jobs. Liberals highlight research that shows that persons who leave welfare rolls often continue to live in poverty and may be unable to afford sufficient food. Liberals express concern that program participants are not receiving the type of training and education needed to obtain jobs that provide a living wage. They consider the increases in work requirements to be unrealistic and believe the government is obligated to do much more to get people off welfare than establish stringent standards. In contrast, conservatives charge that programs that do not emphasize work coddle beneficiaries and that the provision of cash assistance with no strings attached serves as a work disincentive, which results in failure to develop the work skills necessary to succeed in the labor market.

CONCENTRATION OF WEALTH

Despite unprecedented economic prosperity, the United States is increasingly characterized by a disturbing concentration of wealth and poverty, accompanied by a reduction in the size of the middle class. Census Bureau figures indicate that over the last thirty years, the income of the richest Americans increased by 30 percent while the income of the poorest Americans shrank by 21 percent. During this same period, middle-class Americans experienced a modest 2 percent gain in income. The gulf between the rich and the poor is even wider when the distribution of wealth is taken into account. Analysts identify the elimination of high-wage manufacturing jobs, the accompanying growth in service jobs, the decline of labor unions, robust stock market returns, and tax cuts primarily targeted to those in the highest tax bracket as contributors to the growing income disparity.

Conservatives maintain that in an affluent society, the income gap is not the best indicator of overall well-being. Instead, the degree of social equality provides a better picture of resources available to members of society. The high level of social equality that is characteristic of the United States allows even the poorest members of society to engage in similar activities as the rich such as dining out, attending entertainment events, and purchasing consumer goods. Conservative proponents of "trickle-down" economic theory maintain that prosperity for people at the top of the social hierarchy benefits all members of society by increasing the overall standard of living. They contend that implementation of policies geared to matching worker skills with available or projected job openings is necessary to reduce the income gap.

Liberals have been strident in their claims that some Americans have been left out of economic recovery. They fear that a reversal in prosperity will exacerbate the existing gulf. Liberal analysts attribute the income gap to the erosion of worker rights and power, which has resulted in a loss of real income (income adjusted for inflation), reduced worker rights and protections, and less antidiscrimination enforcement. Many liberals contend that the government is obligated to do more to ensure that the distribution of income is more equal. Some liberal advocates have even proposed a tax on "new wealth" to reduce the amount of wealth that is transferred from generation to generation.

FOOD STAMPS

The source of the historically strong bipartisan support for the Food Stamp Act lies in the voucher structure of the program, as well as the fact that it benefits several major constituent groups in the process. Liberals support the program because of its ability to improve low-income households' opportunity to purchase nutritious food for their families. Conservatives are aware that the increased purchasing power directly benefits a key conservative constituency, business owners who profit from the low-income customers. In addition, the receipt of food stamps frees up some of the meager income of the poor to purchase nonfood items from business owners. Despite its broad-based support, budget pressures have resulted in Republican proposals to reduce funding for food stamp programs. These proposals have been met with fierce Democratic objections.

Congress has allocated significant time and resources to the reduction of fraud and waste in the program. Oversight activities have uncovered a high error rate in benefit calculations in which funds are either over- or underallocated to individuals. Both conservatives and liberals support the use of Electronic Benefit Transfers (EBT debit cards) to reduce fraud and waste in the program. Other strategies for policing fraud include surveillance and undercover investigations.

HOMELESSNESS

Homelessness emerged as a political issue in the 1980s. The McKinney-Vento Act, enacted in 1987, is a major federal legislative vehicle for addressing homelessness. The Act creates over twenty programs administered by nine federal agencies. Critics maintain that the large number and variety of programs subsumed under the Act result in inefficiency.

Current estimates of the number of homeless people in the country range from several hundred thousand to several million; however, there is general consensus that the problem is getting worse. Obtaining an accurate count of the homeless population is complicated by differing definitions of homelessness, problems locating them, and local maneuvering to obtain higher counts for funding purposes. Although the chronically homeless constitute only 10 to 20 percent of the homeless population, they absorb nearly half of the resources devoted to assisting the homeless. In response, the Bush Administration has pledged to eradicate chronic homelessness within ten years. Under the Good Samaritan Initiative, the Bush Administration proposed targeting $70 million for housing and assistance to care for the chronically homeless. Liberals responded that insufficient funds were allocated to do the job and that all segments of the homeless population must be helped.

Conservatives support the expenditure of federal resources to address homelessness as long as the resources are spent efficiently. However, they are concerned that programs that provide "handouts" to participants encourage unproductive behavior and serve as disincentives to work. They believe that programs that require constructive behavior on the part of recipients in exchange for the benefits they receive are more effective in combating the main causes of homelessness, including mental illness, substance abuse, and job skill deficits. Conservatives believe that families and local communities should serve as the first line of response to persons experiencing a homeless crisis. Private sector interventions are considered to be superior to governmental interventions because, compared to the government, the private sector is better equipped to show compassion and make judgments about what participants need.

In contrast, liberals cast homelessness as a "human rights" issue in that all citizens have a right to basic necessities, including housing. They attribute the problem of homelessness to economic and policy factors beyond individuals' control. They cite the lack of available jobs, refusal to raise the minimum wage, more restrictive TANF requirements, and the lack of affordable housing due to loss of single-room occupancy housing (SRO), urban renewal, and gentrification (conversion of run-down buildings to expensive offices or homes).

CONCLUSIONS

Policy analysts have long observed that U.S. policy toward providing assistance to the poor swings from compassion and generosity to restrictiveness and harshness and back again. In part, this fluctuation represents the expression of competing ideologies held by policy makers and the general public about the causes of and solutions to poverty. During periods when conservative philosophies prevail, poverty reduction strategies are more likely to emphasize individual accountability, stricter work requirements, reduced government expenditures, more restrictive provision of benefits, and increased reliance on the private sector. On the other hand, periods of liberal domination are more likely to result in a greater emphasis on job training, education, job creation programs, expansion of government expenditures, and benefits based on the view that society is obligated to assist those less fortunate.

TEMPORARY ASSISTANCE FOR NEEDY FAMILIES

In 1997, Temporary Assistance for Needy Families (TANF) was introduced as a successor to the Aid to Families with Dependent Children program.

Commonly known as welfare, this federal program currently gives grants to states to run their own programs. Under TANF, individuals may collect only sixty months' worth of benefits within their lifetime, and they must prove an attempt to find employment. The main goal of the program is to transition recipients from the welfare system to the workforce.

Rep. James McDermott argues for the liberal side that it is the federal government's responsibility to fund welfare programs like TANF. He believes that Republicans have attempted to shift this burden to state governments by passing unfunded mandates that states must abide by if they wish to receive federal grant money. He also argues that the program requires more assistance, such as childcare funding and job training, in order to aid the poor in finding work adequate to support themselves and their families.

On the Republican side, Rep. Walter Herger argues that the House has passed bills that would adequately fund current programs, and yet the Senate has rejected them. He claims that past measures have largely succeeded, and that Congress should continue to support these programs. He also believes that the most important factor of the welfare program is moving citizens into the workforce.

Liberal Viewpoint

James McDermott (D-WA). Mr. Speaker, these are going to be the two classic glass-half-empty/glass-half-full speeches because the chairman has told you the good things that have happened, and there are some. But, today, we have two bad choices in front of us. The first is to support this band-aid approach that has temporarily continued the funding for TANF and the child care development block grants for yet another three months. The other alternative is to abandon our most vulnerable citizens until the Republican majority accepts its responsibility to chart a new course that provides a helping hand, not a slap on the wrist.

Now, I deplore these kind of crossroads at which we stand. Ten times in the last three years we have stood right here, as we do today, the lives and welfare of the disadvantaged hanging in the balance. At a time like this, America should shine. Instead, the Republican majority strains the needs of our most vulnerable citizens to the breaking point.

Ten temporary extensions over three years should send the House a clear and unmistakable message. We need to treat America's disadvantaged as first-class citizens by charting a new course for the long-term reauthorization of the TANF program.

On this Republican watch, the House has taken up hopelessly divisive bills that have drawn the condemnation of mayors, governors, welfare directors, religious leaders, and poverty experts. Time and again, the Republicans have tried to terminate federal responsibility by replacing state flexibility with unfunded mandates and changing the focus of welfare reform from real jobs to make-work. Nothing good comes from this approach.

Instead, this wrong path has led to legislative gridlock. Those who suffer most are those who most need our help. The disadvantaged need our compassionate ideas and commitment to promote reforms that will help them leave welfare and actually escape poverty. This goal is particularly important when you consider that an additional 4.3 million Americans have fallen into poverty over the last three years for which we have data. In 2003 alone, almost another eight hundred thousand children fell into poverty. Now, that should be a rallying cry, driving us to act.

But, instead, the Republicans use the misfortune of some Americans to suggest that poverty is rising because welfare recipients are not working hard enough. That is just wrong. It is callous and cold-hearted. The problem is not the unwillingness of people on welfare to work. The problem is too many of those leaving welfare are not finding work, or they are finding jobs that do not lift them out of poverty. We could, of course, help by providing more child-care assistance, job training, and a higher minimum wage, but the Republican leadership and the president have resisted such reforms. Instead, the Republicans try to sell the same worn-out threadbare suit of clothes again.

It happened again in March when the majority unveiled their "new" three-year-old idea from the Ways and Means Subcommittee on Human Resources. Nothing has happened since. Nothing, leaving many to believe the Republican leadership intends to include the welfare legislation as part of the upcoming budget reconciliation bill rather than considering it as a separate measure. Such a process will make it harder to provide the necessary investments in child care because Republicans know the budget reconciliation process is meant to cut programs, not improve them. And that is just fine by the Republican leadership because they do not believe working families deserve any more help for child care. Like so much from their leadership, the rhetoric does not match the reality.

According to data from their own HHS, Health and Human Services Department, only about a quarter of the children who are eligible for childcare subsidies under state eligibility criteria actually receive assistance. This fraction drops to roughly one out of seven, if you use the federal eligibility standard for daycare assistance. The data does not lie. We are falling short in helping low-income families meet the challenges of raising a family and at the same time going to work.

President Bush's response to this problem is to make it even worse. His proposed 2006 budget shows the number of people receiving child assistance will decline—decline by three hundred thousand over the next five years. So the administration is proposing even greater work requirements for welfare recipients at the same time that the president proposes cutting child care. So much for a helping hand.

My friends on the other side of the aisle suggest their bill is modestly more generous on child care than the administration's budget. However, that Republican package, in reality, underfunds child care assistance by $10.6 billion over the next five years. That is their calculation.

Republicans want to outsource federal responsibility to the states without a dime more to address a $10 billion deficit. That leads nowhere except forcing states to face deep cuts in child-care assistance for the working poor.

Mr. Speaker, there is a better way. We have proposed legislation that gives the states the flexibility and the funding needed to move welfare recipients into real jobs and out of poverty. It is the right thing to do, and this is the right time to do it. And with that hope, I support this temporary extension of the current law. I will not abandon disadvantaged Americans at the very time they need us most.

The Congressional Record. June 29, 2005: H5372–H5376.

Conservative Viewpoint

Walter W. Herger (R-CA). Mr. Speaker, this will be the tenth extension of these programs since the original authorization of the 1996 welfare reform law expired in 2002. That law produced remarkable results. Work among welfare recipients doubled. The poorest single-mother families reported a 67 percent increase in their real earnings between 1995 and 2002. Single mothers' real wages continued to increase during the 2000–2004 period, despite the 2001 recession and terrorist attacks.

Despite predictions of welfare reform opponents that the 1996 welfare bill would increase poverty, the number of children in poverty fell by more than one million. The black and Hispanic child poverty rates hit record lows. Welfare caseloads fell 60 percent to their lowest levels since 1965. Welfare funds stayed constant, and child care funds grew, even as caseloads plummeted. Taxpayer resources per family on welfare more than doubled from $7,000 per year to $16,000 per year today.

In 2002 and 2003, the House passed comprehensive welfare reform legislation that would have extended these programs for a full five years. That legislation also included modest adjustments designed to encourage and support more work, higher incomes, stronger families, and less poverty. These House-passed bills offered up to $4 billion over five years and added child care funding to support more work.

Unfortunately, our friends in the Senate did not follow suit, and so we have been forced to come to the floor with repeated short-term extensions.

Mr. Speaker, it is important that we continue these programs, and I urge all members to support this legislation. But while we mark time, we are missing out on many ways to help even more low-income parents and families leave welfare for work. We must do more to encourage states and local communities to support strong, healthy families.

The subcommittee I chair has, once again, approved legislation that tracks the comprehensive welfare reform bill of the House that the House passed before. I expect in the coming months the full committee on Ways and Means and this House will once again act on comprehensive welfare reform legislation as part of the budget reconciliation process. Regardless of the process, our goals remain the same: to encourage and support more work, less poverty, and stronger families.

Mr. Speaker, I believe this process of continued extensions of welfare programs is finally nearing an end. I look forward to working with our members to get this done so more families can know the dignity of collecting paychecks instead of welfare checks.

In the meantime, I urge support of the legislation before us that continues these welfare programs in their current form.

The Congressional Record. June 29, 2005: H5372–H5376.

CONCENTRATION OF WEALTH

There has always been a divide between the upper and lower classes in America. In recent years, this gap has only grown wider. The move to an information society, paired with the increase in the number of manufacturing jobs being outsourced to other countries, has left the blue-collar working class with fewer job opportunities and without the skills needed for the kind of jobs being created. Both parties agree that something must be done to level the playing field, but the solution is not as obvious.

On the liberal side, Rep. Martin Sabo (D-MN) believes that the solution lies in making corporations more responsible for their workers' well-being. This includes sharing corporate wealth more equitably through increased wages and benefits as well as profit-sharing measures. He also proposes a more equitable tax code to divide the burden of government costs more fairly. Some of these proposals may disrupt the economy, though, by creating wage floors and leading companies to charge higher prices to offset lost profits.

For the conservatives, Rep. Gerald Weller (R-IL) suggests cutting taxes. Citizens with more disposable wealth are more likely to contribute to local economies, which in theory creates new jobs and benefits those with lower incomes. Lower taxes would also give low-income Americans more money to spend on luxuries they might not otherwise be able to afford. However, decreased taxes would lead to a cutback in government services, which tend to give greater benefits to lower-income citizens than what they pay.

Liberal Viewpoint

Martin O. Sabo (D-MN). Mr. Speaker, for many years, I have been speaking about the growing income gap in America. Due to the Republican presidential race, this issue has finally been catapulted into the forefront of the nation's consciousness. In fact, it is hard to open a newspaper op-ed page or turn on a television news program without hearing something about declining worker wages, increased layoffs, and increasing corporate profits and CEO pay. I am grateful that people have started to pay attention to this important problem. I fear, however, that as the Republican race winds down, the issue of the income gap will no longer be in vogue, and the media will turn its attention to something new.

We cannot squander this opportunity. The income gap is a growing problem that, if not addressed, threatens to undermine our nation's prosperity and calls into question the type of nation we want America to be. We must take advantage of the attention now being paid to the problems facing working Americans.

Thanks in part to the deficit reduction measures we passed in 1993, the American economy today is in good shape. We enjoy strong growth combined with low unemployment and low inflation. The stock market is also reaching record highs, as are profits of many American companies. This should seem like good news for the average American family, for in the past, Americans at all income levels shared in our nation's prosperity. Today, however, stock prices and corporate profits rise while the incomes of middle-class American families stagnate or drop.

If stagnating wages were the only problem that working Americans had to face, things might not be so bad. However, in recent years our nation has also seen unprecedented worker layoffs in corporate America. Of course, it is understandable that such upheavals may occur as our economy becomes more technology-based and integrated into global markets. What is difficult to understand, however, are the tremendous bonuses and pay increases enjoyed by the very CEOs who lay off thousands of employees.

The United States has prided itself on being a nation of the middle class—one in which, if you work hard and adhere to the rules, you can expect to do well enough to support yourself and your family. Alarmingly, this is no longer true for an increasing number of Americans.

In the decades following World War II, American workers shared in the successes of their employers. Over the past twenty years, however, only high-income Americans have moved ahead economically. Between 1977 and 1990, for instance, the average after-tax income of the wealthiest 1 percent of our population increased by 67 percent, after adjusting for inflation. During this same period, the average after-tax income of the bottom fifth decreased by nearly 27 percent.

This is not a problem that affects only the poor. Every year, thousands of Americans are laid off from well-paying middle class jobs, to be left with a choice between a new job that pays less or the unemployment line. Clearly, this trend cannot continue.

America's level of income inequality is already higher than that of any industrialized nation. Our middle class is evaporating, and we are well on the road to becoming a nation divided between a few very rich and many who simply struggle to get by. None of us, in the words of Labor Secretary Robert Reich, will "want to live in a society sharply divided between winners and losers."

Leaders in government and business must begin to address this problem, which will have social consequences that far outweigh any economic impact. We must correct policies that exacerbate the income gap and develop new ones that help to close it. Several of my Democratic colleagues have developed proposals to reduce the income gap by encouraging responsible corporate citizenship, boosting worker wages, and making our Tax Code more equitable. I commend them for these efforts, and call upon all of my colleagues to take action to restore working Americans' faith in the economy.

The widening income gap lays before us the question of what kind of country we want to be: one sharply divided between the rich and poor, or one in which all citizens can benefit from a strong economy. I believe that our choice is clear. America has always been the land of opportunity. We should work together for policies that do not favor any income group, but enable all Americans to share in our nation's strength and prosperity.

The Congressional Record. March 19, 1996: E388.

Conservative Viewpoint

Gerald C. Weller (R-IL). Over the last seven years that we have had a Republican majority in the Congress, we have been working to balance the budget and also to lower taxes for working families. Unfortunately, the previous administration, the Clinton-Gore administration, vetoed time and time again our effort to lower taxes for working Americans.

Fortunately, the voters of our nation this past year and a half ago in November of the year 2000 elected a president who feels the same way the majority of this House does—that is, the taxes are too high, families are struggling, and of course, we need to find ways to bring fairness to the Tax Code.

I was very proud of the president's leadership because he noted in January of last year, and January 2000 when he became president, that the economy was in a downturn. The president inherited a weakening economy and he says we have got this huge surplus, all this extra tax revenue that the federal government is collecting because taxes are too high and we are not spending it all, thanks to the fiscal responsibility of this House. So why do we not take a portion of that surplus, that extra tax revenue, and give it back to working families? Provide an across-the-board tax cut that helps every working family, bring about tax fairness by eliminating the marriage tax penalty, wiping out the death tax, increasing opportunities for retirement savings and saving for a college education?

The president was successful. President Bush's leadership, with the leadership of the gentleman from Illinois (Mr. Dennis Hastert) and Committee on Ways and Means chairman, the gentleman from California (Mr. William Thomas), this House led the effort to lower taxes, and in June of this past year, the president signed into law what has become known as the Bush tax cut. Unfortunately, because of the arcane rules of the Congress, the tax cut was temporary, which meant it has to expire in the year 2011.

When it expires, it is going to mean a big tax increase for millions of working families across this country. That is really what this vote is about on Thursday is whether or not we continue to keep taxes lower for working families, whether or not we continue to have tax fairness or do we bring back an unfair Tax Code that punishes married couples and takes away the family farm and family businesses and makes it harder to save for retirement or a college education, essentially imposing a tax increase on working Americans. That is what this vote is going to be this week.

I would note that one of the arguments the president made when he talked about the need to cut taxes is that the president stated that we need to get the economy moving again, and if workers have a little extra spending money in their pockets, they are going to be able to meet the family needs, go to the grocery store, make some improvements to their home, fix the car, maybe have a family vacation the first time ever.

The president said that if his tax cut was signed into law, the economy would get better, and frankly, it was working. Economists tell us that by Labor Day of this past year, Labor Day 2001, the economy was on the rebound and the Bush tax cut was the primary reason that the economy was on the upswing. Of course, every one of us knows what occurred on September 11 and the terrible tragedy of that attack on our nation and its economic impact, with almost one million Americans having lost their jobs.

Well, the Bush tax cut is continuing to work and the economy is beginning, according to economists, to get on the rebound again, and tonight we want to talk about what was in the Bush tax cut. I would note, as I stated earlier, that the Bush tax cut did a number of good things to help working families. It provided for marginal rate reductions, reducing the tax rate for every American who pays taxes, creating a whole new tax rate structure. In fact, we created a new lower tax rate for the lowest income Americans, lowering their taxes from 15 percent to 10 percent, helping low-income taxpayers. We also, of course, repealed the death tax, a tax that has historically taken a majority of the family business away from families who inherit the family business from the founder, and that has caused so many businesses to go out of business, and some of my colleagues are going to talk about that. We doubled the child tax credit from $500 to $1,000, helping families with children better afford their children's needs.

We increased retirement savings, increasing the amount one can contribute to their IRA from $2,000 to $5,000, what one can contribute to their 401(k) from $10,500 to $15,000, and for working moms and empty nesters, we allowed those over 50 to make up missed contributions to their IRA and 401(k), essentially what we call catch-up contributions. . . .

Of course, part of the debate of who benefits from tax relief is who gets it, and there is always some who say, oh, we cannot cut taxes because those who pay taxes will get it. We should not help those who pay taxes because apparently they are rich. Well, let me note who it is that benefited from the Bush tax cut.

Under the president's tax plan that was signed into law and this Congress supported and that we are going to make permanent or vote to make permanent this week, over 100 million individuals and families pay lower taxes. Forty-three million married couples see their taxes reduced on average by more than $1,700 a year. Thirty-eight million families with children will receive an average tax cut of almost $1,500. Eleven million single moms with children will be able to keep on average $77 more to care for their children. Thirteen million seniors will see their taxes reduced on average by $920, and 3.9 million taxpayers, including 3 million taxpayers with children, will have their taxpayer liability for the federal tax burden completely eliminated.

Think about that. Almost 4 million taxpayers under the Bush tax cut, those at the lower end of the economic area, pay no more taxes, thanks to the Bush tax cut. Small business owners and entrepreneurs will receive a big chunk of this tax relief. Whenever my colleagues argue about who is going to get the rate reduction and what that means, they have to recognize that the vast majority of small businesses, almost 80 percent, pay in the top rate, and we lowered their rate to 35 percent.

The Congressional Record. April 16, 2002: H1312–H1318.

FOOD STAMPS

There are very few who would argue against providing food to those who cannot afford it. However, debates still continue to rage regarding the best and most efficient way to administer the program, eligibility requirements, and the division of responsibility among local, state, and federal governments. Conflicts also arise between parties on the amount of money that should be spent on food stamps and other welfare programs. Should the money be spent on welfare or defense, or more importantly, a tax cut?

The Democrats argue for streamlining the process of collecting benefits, eliminating bureaucratic "red tape." In addition to saving time for recipients, this could reduce the administrative costs of the system. It can also allow current recipients to move out of the system, as they are able to spend more time working, and thus, earning money.

On the other side, the Republicans believe in cutting costs by enforcing stricter eligibility standards. Investigating and reducing fraudulent practices, such as counterfeit stamps, can also save money by eliminating improper payouts. The Republicans argue that these funds could then be used for other programs or to prevent an increase in taxes.

Liberal Viewpoint

President William J. Clinton. Every day, 7 million of our fellow Americans rely on food stamps for proper nourishment. These food stamps allow parents to give their children the necessities while getting their own feet on the ground. But as they return to work and struggle to make ends meet, many don't realize they're still eligible for food stamps. And in some states, parents who do sign up for food stamps have to fill out paperwork as often as once a month, and leave the workplace in order to do so.

Now, this simply should not be the case. So today I'm announcing new steps to remove some of the barriers facing working Americans and to help the families get the food they need.

First, it would allow states to provide recipients with an automatic three-month food stamp benefit as they make the transition from welfare to work. This gives new workers stability in what can be a trying time. Second, we're eliminating unnecessary bureaucracies by allowing recipients up to six months to report income changes, reducing the amount of time they spend in food stamp offices. Third, if we want people to work, they need to be able to get to work. Today's action will make it easier for food stamp recipients to own a dependable car without having to sacrifice proper nutrition for their children. This builds on the steps we took in the agriculture appropriation bill I signed last month. Finally, to ensure that the families who need assistance get it, we are requiring states to let recipients know that they're still eligible for food stamps when they start to work again.

Supporting hard-pressed working families is the right policy for America. It's also the smart thing to do. It encourages millions of people to take responsibility to strengthen their families, as well as our economy. I urge our nation's governors to implement these steps so that all working families get the nutritional benefits they need and deserve. And again I call on Congress to restore food stamp benefits to hard-working legal immigrants and to raise the minimum wage for all working families this year. No family working full-time and playing by the rules should have to raise children in poverty. In the coming weeks, Congress still has the chance to honor and award work by raising the minimum wage for our hardest-pressed working families.

Public Papers of the President: William J. Clinton. November 18, 2000: 2904–2905.

Conservative Viewpoint

Mario Diaz-Balart (R-FL). Mr. Speaker, as part of the Washington Waste Watchers, I want to highlight, once again, the waste in the federal government.

Over the last four years, the Department of Agriculture spent over $5 billion in food stamp improper payments. This could have paid for over a year of food stamps for over 3 million low-income Americans.

Improper payments alone last year could have paid for a year of food stamps for close to eight hundred thousand low-income Americans, Mr. Speaker. And yet our friends the Democrats still want to raise your taxes to pay for more of this?

Mr. Speaker, Democrats are worried about spending more money to protect our troops and to provide for America's long-term security, but they have no problem in spending money to give benefits to ineligible recipients. We have to get our priorities right, Mr. Speaker.

Let us fight waste, fraud, and abuse. We ask our friends in the other party to help us in our long-term security and not do anything to not fund our troops abroad.

The Congressional Record. October 16, 2003: H9486.

HOMELESSNESS

Homelessness is a serious problem that affects thousands of American citizens. However, it can also be very difficult to remedy due to its many disparate causes: mental illness, drug addiction, extended unemployment, and a shortage of affordable housing can all contribute in varying degrees. Thus, a variety of programs have been established over the years in an attempt to combat each of these issues. While most politicians agree that efforts to help the homeless are necessary, there is disagreement over the best way to conduct and fund such programs.

Rep. Rick Renzi (R-AZ) proposed a bill that would bring several programs working to alleviate homelessness together under the broader umbrella of the Department of Housing and Urban Development (HUD). This consolidation would save money by reducing administrative costs, standardizing eligibility requirements, and streamlining the distribution of grant money. However, it could also decrease the ability of individual programs to concentrate on a specific aspect of homelessness.

The Democrats, represented by former president William J. Clinton, argue that the lack of funding is the primary deficiency within homeless programs. Increasing funding toward federally funded programs as well as organizations will help achieve the elimination of homelessness. Clinton argues that the organizations already have success with dealing with their clientele, but an increase of funding would enhance their opportunities and reach a broader population. Even though the funding increases would generate a tax hike, Clinton fully believes that they are worth it. By eliminating homelessness, many other social issues are addressed as well.

Conservative Viewpoint

Rick Renzi (R-AZ). This afternoon I am introducing legislation, by request of the Bush Administration, designed to combat homelessness nationwide.

The Homeless Assistance Consolidation Act of 2006 would consolidate three competitive homeless assistance programs within the Department of Housing and Urban Development—Supportive Housing, Shelter Plus Care, and Section 8 Single Room Occupancy—into a single program aimed at alleviating homelessness in this country.

Consolidation of these programs would provide more flexibility to localities, fund prevention of homelessness, and dramatically reduce the time required to distribute grant funds to groups combating homelessness.

The legislation would streamline the three programs into one competitive program with a single set of eligibility requirements and would provide incentives for communities to carry out permanent housing activities with supportive services for the homeless.

I believe that this legislation is a good starting point for the House of Representatives in crafting a bill that would help achieve the goal of alleviating homelessness in my home state of Arizona, and the country.

I look forward to working with my colleagues in the House, the Senate, the Administration, and most importantly, individuals and groups throughout the country who have dedicated themselves to fight homelessness, to craft legislation in the coming months which will authorize the funding and provide the tools needed by advocates of the homeless.

In the past, Congress has provided HUD significant funding over the years to distribute to groups to fight homelessness. Millions of individuals and families are, or have in the past, faced homelessness. They deserve our help, and I am committed to fighting on behalf of the homeless, and I am hopeful that this legislation will further this most important effort.

The Congressional Record. March 29, 2006: E458.

Liberal Viewpoint

President William J. Clinton. Good morning. This weekend we not only celebrate the first Christmas of the new millennium; we also celebrate an America blessed with the gift of unprecedented prosperity and progress.

We're in the midst of the longest economic expansion in our nation's history, with record surpluses, more than 22 million new jobs, the lowest unemployment in history, and the lowest Hispanic and African American unemployment ever recorded.

We have strengthened the cornerstone of the American dream along the way: the chance to own a home. Today, we have the highest homeownership in our nation's history with record levels of minority homeownership. And more Americans than ever are celebrating that gift this holiday season.

Over the last eight years, Vice President Gore and I have worked hard to give nearly 10 million more families the opportunity to own their own homes by cutting red tape, speeding up loans, making financing available for families who were too often locked out of the market, creating more opportunity and choice for families who live in assisted housing.

In the last three years, our administration has secured nearly two hundred thousand new housing vouchers to help hard-pressed families find decent and affordable housing. I want to especially thank our HUD Secretary, Andrew Cuomo, for his extraordinary commitment to making affordable housing accessible to citizens who need it most.

Today, we're introducing new measures to more fully integrate public housing, so families from different social and economic walks of life have the chance to live in diverse communities. In addition to expanding opportunity for more Americans, this will also help to break down destructive barriers of race and class.

We're also taking action to increase loan limits from the Federal Housing Administration by nearly 9 percent to help more working families to own their first home. Since 1993, the FHA program has given more than 4 million Americans that chance. We have made real progress.

But too many Americans still will be spending this Christmas without a roof over their heads. That's why we've helped to move thousands of families off the street. Yet, there still are more than a half million men, women, and children whose only home every night is a neighborhood shelter or a park bench.

In this time of unparalleled prosperity, we must do more to help them. Today, I'm pleased to announce $1 billion in new grants to help more than two hundred thousand homeless people along the path to self-sufficiency. This is the largest amount ever dedicated to helping homeless Americans rebuild their lives.

The grants will fund proven successful programs like Continuum of Care, which helps homeless families with transitional and permanent housing, drug treatment and medication, job training, and child care. It also funds efforts like the Emergency Shelter Grants program, which provides for transitional housing and helps communities maintain emergency shelters.

Taken together, these grants are a gift that will give back to us in many ways. They will empower communities to employ innovative solutions to helping homeless adults and their children, people like Juanita Price, a recovering drug addict who once spent her nights in abandoned buildings and hollowed-out cars. Thanks to the Continuum of Care program, Juanita found the support she needed and turned her life around. Today, she's got a steady job, an apartment, and she's studying to be a nurse at Howard University here in Washington, D.C.

There are lots and lots of people like Juanita who could use a helping hand. Today we're lending that hand by giving more homeless Americans the tools they need to succeed, so that this Christmas they can find warmth inside a home, not from the top of a steam grate.

It is said in the Scripture: "I will appoint a place for my people so they may dwell in a place of their own and move no more." Today, in this season of hope and giving, we should redouble our efforts to ensure that every American can have a place of his or her own.

The steps we're taking now will create new opportunity for the homeless, for hard-pressed working families, and for those struggling to buy their first home. I can't think of any better way to celebrate this holiday season.

Public Papers of the President: William J. Clinton. January 1, 2001: 3174–3176.

SELECTED READING

Temporary Assistance for Needy Families

Pardue, Melissa G. "Sharp Reduction in Black Child Poverty due to Welfare Reform." *Heritage Foundation Backgrounder,* no. 1661 (June 12, 2003).

"TANF at a Glance." DHR Office of Communications. May 2000. www2.state.ga.us/Departments/DHR/tanfg.html.

"The New Welfare Law: Temporary Assistance for Needy Families." September 2, 1997. www.opencrs.com/document/96-902.

Concentration of Wealth

Bunch, Sonny. "Spike's Storm." *Weekly Standard*. August 21, 2005.

Danziger, Sheldon, and Sandra K. Danziger. "Poverty, Race, and Antipoverty Policy before and after Hurricane Katrina." *Du Bois Review* 3 (1): 23–36.

Fischer, Will, and Barbara Sard. *Bringing Katrina's Poorest Victims Home: Targeted Federal Assistance Will Be Needed to Give Neediest Evacuees Option to Return to Their Hometowns.* Center on Budget and Policy Priorities. November 2, 2005. http://www.cbpp.org/11-2-05hous.htm.

Rector, Robert. "Poverty and Inequality." The Heritage Foundation. 2006. www.heritage.org/research/features/issues/issuearea/Poverty.cfm.

Schweber-Koren, Raphael. "Eight Big Lies about Katrina." September 9, 2005. www.alternet.org/katrina/25227.

Zeleza, Paul T. "The Political Weath of Hurricane Katrina." *The Black Commentator*. 2005. www.blackcommentator.com/150/150_zeleza_katrina.html.

Food Stamps

"An Advocate's Guide to the Disaster Food Stamp Program." Food Research and Action Center. 2006. www.chn.org/povertyinfo.html.

Delson, Jennifer. "Aid Program Finally Speaks Their Language." *Los Angeles Times* Metro Desk, October 13, 2006, Part B, p. 3.

Jones, Jeffrey M. "Food Stamps: The Never-Ending Story." *Hoover Digest*. 2006. www.hooverdigest.org/061/jones.html.

Mehta, Shreema. "Critics Note Weaknesses of Food Stamps as Hunger Spreads." *The New Standard*. May 18, 2006.newstandardnews.net/content/index.cfm/items/3189.

Weisman, Jonathan. "Food Stamp Cuts Are on Table." *Washington Post*. November 3, 2005. www.washingtonpost.com/wp-dyn/content/article/2005/11/02/AR2005110203007.html.

Homelessness

Freese Jr., Paul. "So-Called Reforms in Welfare Will Add to Ranks of Homeless." *Los Angeles Business Journal*. February 10, 2003. www.findarticles.com/p/articles/mi_m5072/is_6_25/ai_97920339.

Hayward, Steven. "The Shocking Success of Welfare Reform." *Policy Review*, January/February 1998.

"Policy and Advocacy." People's Emergency Center. 2006. www.pec-cares.org/Policy%20and%20Advocacy.htm.

Vatlov Phillips, Sue. "Families Still Poor and Experiencing Homelessness." National Housing Institute. 2006. www.nhi.org/online/issues/118/WN&V.html.

White, Jerry. "Welfare Cuts Increase Hunger and Homelessness." *World Socialist Web Site*. March 6, 1998. www.wsws.org/news/1998/mar1998/welf-m06.shtml.

2

Taxation and the Economy

There is likely no area of public policy where liberal and conservative ideas diverge more than taxation and economic policy. Liberal and conservative views of taxation and economic policy are derived from competing economic theories that suggest vastly different implications for how policy should be carried out. Thus, the intense conflict over taxation and economic policy is effectively a debate about the correctness of Keynesian theory versus free-market economic theory. The major disagreements center on the extent to which government intervention and taxation are advantageous to the economy.

Liberals, adherents of Keynesian philosophy, believe the government should be actively involved in economic activities and should aggressively act to stabilize the economy by spending and taxing strategically and printing and circulating money. Liberals believe it is desirable and necessary for the government to redistribute income and resources from the wealthy to the less fortunate.

In contrast, conservatives are proponents of free-market economic theory, which assumes that unregulated economic activity guided by self-interest, competition, individual ownership, and the profit motive is most beneficial to economic growth. Thus, government intervention in economic matters is strongly discouraged, unless it is absolutely necessary to prevent an impending crisis.

TAXATION POLICY

Conservatives believe the U.S. tax code detracts from economic growth in a variety of ways. Conservatives believe in the principle that increased taxes on something results in less of it and thus contend that taxes on work, upward mobility, savings, and investment discourage Americans from engaging in these activities. Conservatives frown on progressive policies that tax the rich at higher rates, considering these policies an unfair form of punishment inflicted on successful people who behave productively. Taxes, they believe, result in Americans paying higher prices for goods and services as businesses pass the cost of their taxes down the line of production to consumers. Opportunities for employment are also restricted because taxes on corporations lead some firms to move their plants overseas to avoid the taxes. Conservatives maintain that U.S. tax policy disadvantages American-made products in the global marketplace. Therefore, they support the elimination of the tax component in U.S. prices to encourage more corporations to build plants in America.

Liberals, on the other hand, have more positive views of taxation and have fewer reservations about taxing individuals and corporations to fund government services and activities. Liberals further contend that many wealthy individuals have succeeded, at least in part, due to resources and opportunities provided directly or indirectly by the government. Thus, they are morally obligated to help those less fortunate achieve a minimum standard of living and state of well-being.

Both liberals and conservatives believe tax cuts stimulate the economy by increasing the amount of discretionary income consumers have to spend and invest. However, liberals protest that the Bush Administration's tax cuts are responsible for the current budget deficits that are jeopardizing long-term economic growth. While acknowledging the importance of containing the deficit, conservatives counter that much recent economic growth can be attributed to tax cuts.

TAXATION IMPACT ON INCOME DISTRIBUTION

Much attention has been paid to the fact that compared to other industrialized nations, income in the "land of opportunity" is more unevenly distributed. Analysts attribute much of the problem to the United States' significantly lower taxes, which do little to redistribute income among Americans. According to liberals, conservative tax reforms have worsened inequality by shifting the tax burden to the middle class. Liberals claim that the wealthy no longer pay their share of taxes because the majority of tax cuts go to the rich. Liberals call for repeal of the Bush Administration's tax reform policies, arguing that the tax burden should be at the top of the income ladder.

Generally, conservatives are not fans of tax policy that involves "social engineering." Thus, conservatives do not agree with the liberal conviction that tax policy is an effective vehicle for redistributing income. Several conservative proposals to reform the current tax system aim to abolish the current progressive tax code in favor of a flat tax or a national sales tax. Liberals warn that the highly regressive nature of these taxes could worsen income inequality. In response to conservative proposals, some liberals have called for the adoption of a more progressive tax structure that increases income redistribution. In addition, noting that wealth inequality is even greater than income inequality, liberal advocates have asked Congress to adopt a "wealth tax" of 3 percent.

TRICKLE-DOWN ECONOMICS

Trickle-down theory postulates that prosperity experienced by big business and the upper class increases the overall standard of living for all members of society. According to this theory, the economic status of the middle class and the poor is most readily improved by pursuit of policies that place additional income at the disposal of corporations and wealthy members of society. Theoretically, these resources will be reinvested in the stock market and in capital ventures, ultimately expanding productivity that "trickles down" to those that occupy the lower rungs of the income ladder. Thus, this theory suggests that government efforts to reduce poverty will be most effective if they target tax cuts to the wealthy.

Although conservative policy continues to promote tax cuts for the upper class as a means of achieving overall economic prosperity, liberals consider this policy unsuccessful at stimulating the economy. Liberals argue that over the last half century, tax cuts afforded to the rich have not significantly improved the economic standing of the poor and middle class. In fact, the incomes of upper-class individuals have risen, while the incomes of the lower class have declined in real value. Moreover, liberals maintain that the benefits of the Bush Administration's tax cuts went almost exclusively to those in the highest income tax bracket.

SOCIAL SERVICES SPENDING
AND ITS IMPACT ON THE ECONOMY

Liberals are far more supportive of social services spending and an expanded government role in the provision of social services than their conservative colleagues. Conservatives' emphasis on fiscal conservatism and balanced government budgets arouses suspicion of government spending in general. However, conservatives are particularly reluctant to expend resources on social service programs. They believe that many social programs

are ineffective and do not do what they purport to do. Convinced that social services create dependency and discourage people from accomplishing
activities they could achieve on their own, conservatives worry that funds
spent on social services simply beget more social services spending. Conservatives fear that social services spending has a negative impact on economic growth because tax dollars collected to fund social services are not
available to devote to savings or investment. To this end, conservatives
advance proposals that shift responsibility for social services to the private
sector, contending it is better equipped to handle social services.

Although liberals are also mindful of the need to contain federal spending, liberals question the necessity of having a balanced federal budget. Adherents of Keynesian economics, liberals believe that all forms of government spending strengthen the economy by putting additional money into
circulation. Thus, social services spending sets off a positive economic chain
of events. Social service dollars granted to the poor are immediately spent
in local establishments that then purchase additional goods and services or
hire new workers, activities that stimulate additional economic activity. Finally, liberals believe investment in "human capital" pays off exponentially,
as beneficiaries of these programs are better able to support themselves and
contribute to national productivity.

INFLATION CONTROL

Most economic analysts attribute the economic prosperity of the 1990s to
the anti-inflation policies crafted by Federal Reserve Board chairman Alan
Greenspan and his colleagues. The Federal Reserve Board has become adept
at manipulating interest rates to control inflation. U.S. price stabilization
policy is based on the widely accepted dogma that price stability and full
employment are at odds. Low unemployment is thought to drive up wages
as firms competing for scarce employees are forced to offer higher wages to
attract employees.

While the Federal Reserve Board has been widely lauded for its success
at sustaining economic growth and containing inflation, some analysts
are critical of the Fed's anti-inflation policies. They believe that the Fed's
policies are based on the inaccurate assumption that inflation and
growth cannot coexist. For these observers, it is not necessary to slow
down the economy to slow inflation down. Further, they contend that in
today's global economy, tight labor markets do not have the powerful
impact they once had because corporations needing labor can build
plants elsewhere or outsource jobs to foreign countries. Thus, critics advocate a more balanced approach to monetary policy in which growth

and wage rates receive as much attention as inflation control. On the other hand, most members of Congress are supportive of the Federal Reserve Board's policies and suggest they are on the right track for controlling inflation.

UNEMPLOYMENT INSURANCE

Established in 1935 as part of the Social Security Act of 1935, Unemployment Insurance (UI) provides monetary benefits to persons who are temporarily unemployed through no fault of their own. The injection of unemployment benefits into areas experiencing economic crisis stimulates the local economy and lessens the severity of economic downturn. Unemployment insurance is funded by a combination of state and federal payroll taxes. State payroll taxes finance the weekly jobless benefits and the federal payroll tax helps fund the administration of the program. When state unemployment rates reach a particular level, federal law authorizes thirteen- and twenty-six-week extensions of unemployment benefits.

Liberals and conservatives disagree about the extent the federal government should be involved in UI as well as the level of unemployment that should trigger extensions of benefits. Liberals support proposals to expand the federal government's role in UI, but conservatives support measures that shrink federal involvement in the program. For example, President George W. Bush has proposed significant cutbacks in federal financing of the UI system through the elimination of most of the federal payroll tax. Such a move would transfer almost all responsibility for the daily operation and funding of the program to the states. Conservatives back such measures on the grounds that they return flexibility and control to the states.

Liberals, on the other hand, object to the loss of federal financing that would end joint federal–state funding of emergency extensions. Liberals fear that states experiencing fiscal crises will opt not to fund benefits at current levels. In the event of federal funding cutbacks, states may be forced to cut unemployment benefits or turn to the federal government for loans.

There is also persistent conflict over the level at which Congress authorizes extensions of emergency benefits. Liberals are more favorable toward benefit extensions than are conservatives. Conservatives maintain that added jobless benefits discourage beneficiaries from seeking employment. Liberals respond that unemployment benefits are too low to encourage recipients to loaf. They maintain that people are unemployed because they cannot get a job, not because they don't want to work.

MINIMUM WAGE

Inflation and infrequent raises have left the federal minimum wage of $5.15 per hour at its lowest value in over fifty years. Congressional proposals to raise the minimum wage spark some of the most passionate interchanges observed on the House and Senate floors. The diametrically opposed stances that characterize this debate stem from very different beliefs about the extent that government interference in economic matters benefits the economy.

Liberals contend that the minimum wage is too low for full-time workers to support their families. Liberals support minimum wage hikes on the basis that it is unacceptable for any full-time worker to make sub-poverty wages. Asserting that low-income workers have been shut out of the economic boom, liberals advance minimum wage increases to address poverty and decrease dependence on social service programs.

Conservatives, on the other hand, adamantly oppose minimum wage increases, claiming that they hurt more low-income workers than they help. For conservatives, the minimum wage's lack of "target efficiency" renders it ineffective at reducing poverty. They argue that the majority of minimum wage workers are not poor heads of households, but are single people or second or third workers in nonpoor households. Although they acknowledge that a higher minimum wage reduces poverty for a small segment of the working poor, they believe that it increases employers' labor costs, thereby influencing firms to hire fewer workers or to automate jobs. These job losses are concentrated in low-wage positions so low-wage workers, particularly younger and less skilled workers, are hurt disproportionately by minimum wage increases.

In response, liberals observe that the minimum wage reduced poverty when its value was higher. If high enough, they argue, it helps families lift themselves out of poverty. Liberals counter that 80 percent of beneficiaries are adult workers and more than one-third are the sole breadwinner for their family. Liberals point to research that shows that minimum wage increases do not cause job losses, but actually increase employment rates.

DEFENSE SPENDING

Shortly after taking office, President Bush proposed a sizable increase in defense spending. Committed to defending the United States against attacks from weapons of mass destruction, President Bush requested money to develop a National Missile Defense (NMD) system. Liberals consider the NMD system too costly, and think it places too much emphasis on protecting the United States against missile attacks while ignoring more likely threats from biological, chemical, and nuclear weapons. Thus, liberals call for a more balanced defense strategy that takes a variety of threats into account.

In response to rising defense costs, liberals introduced the Common Sense Budget Act, which would have diverted $60 billion in defense funds to spending on humanitarian programs, social programs, energy conservation, homeland security, and deficit reduction. Liberals object to what they consider wasteful military spending. They point out the hypocrisy inherent in conservatives' attacks on wasteful spending in social service programs while the military spends billions of dollars on unnecessary weapons programs that provide little military value. Liberals also contend that the United States could spend much less on defense and continue to successfully fight the war on terror.

Both liberals and conservatives are concerned that the increases in defense spending following 9/11 were not offset by decreases in "nonessential" spending. They worry that record deficits, partly attributed to defense spending, will have a negative impact on economic growth. Thus, several of Bush's proposals to increase military spending have actually been blocked by members of his own party, who are usually very supportive of defense spending.

CONCLUSIONS

Liberals and conservatives rarely agree on matters related to taxation and the economy. This policy area illustrates that social policy flows from both ideology and political expediency. The divergent ideologies of liberals and conservatives generally result in consistently divergent views about the appropriate level of government involvement in issues such as price stability, farm subsidies, and unemployment insurance. However, the issue of price inflation, which is vitally important to a wide constituency of voters, seems to be accompanied by less ideological dissent, possibly because political futures are at stake.

TAXATION POLICY

Taxation policy has been a point of high contention within American political discourse. Since U.S. citizens pay taxes to three levels of government, many have been calling for an overhaul of the system. The highest point of contention has been the federal government's collection of income tax. Since the income tax is based upon individual income, tax ranges from zero to 35 percent annually.

Sen. Orrin G. Hatch (R-UT) examines the current taxation system. Senator Hatch disputes the notion that the rich are not paying their share of taxes—rather, Sen. Hatch argues that they are overpaying. Sen. Hatch dispels the popular notion of a growing income gap in taxation. Since the majority of taxes are paid by the wealthy, many of those that are earning less money often receive federal assistance in paying taxes.

Rep. Stephanie Tubbs Jones (D-OH) points to the necessity to reform the present tax system. Since the current system is unfair and inefficient, many people are prompted to avoid it. Rep. Jones outlines a five-point program that will allow change to happen. One of the steps points to the fairness of the tax base and the need to reform it.

Conservative Viewpoint

Orrin G. Hatch (R-UT). Now, let's get this straight because I get so tired of hearing the rich are getting richer and the poor are getting poorer. That is a slogan that really is pure folly. The top 1 percent of all earners—the top 1 percent of all earners—receive about 16 percent of all income but pay over 34 percent of all taxes. . . . The top 10 percent of all earners are paying two-thirds of all the taxes paid in this country—the top 10 percent.

Mr. President . . . 97 percent of all income tax revenue comes from the top 50 percent of all wage earners. That doesn't sound to me like the rich are getting richer. What the other side always seems to forget is that, in this great country, the middle class consistently rise to a higher position because of the opportunities in this country if we continue to provide opportunities for economic growth through tax rate reductions and other methodologies.

When you say that the top 50 percent of all earners pay 97 percent of all income tax revenues, this means that the bottom half of income earners in this country are paying only 3 percent of all income taxes collected. Many of them do not pay anything. Many of them get money from the federal government for living. No one can correctly say that the rich are not paying their share of taxes.

· · ·

No one can correctly say that the rich are not paying their share of taxes or that this economy is not a good economy. We all wish it could be even better, but when you have an economy as diverse as ours, as complex as ours, it is hard to say that this is not a good economy. Those who have complained that income growth lagged behind the rest of the economy in the early years of the current economic expansion were absolutely correct. I share their frustration that it takes so long for income growth to permeate throughout all income levels. It is not enough to tell someone who is out of work or has been forced to take a pay cut that once the unemployment rate falls a bit more wages should pick up.

.   .   .

The Congressional Record. September 20, 2006: S9854–S9856.

Liberal Viewpoint

Stephanie Tubbs Jones (D-OH). Mr. Speaker, public distrust. That is the main reason why we urgently need fundamental tax reform.

More and more Americans distrust the current tax system because they perceive it as unfair. Are they wrong? No. Lower and middle class Americans bear a disproportionate tax burden. Small businesses bear a great compliance burden. That is unfair.

Does fairness in our tax system matter? Yes, it matters because tax collection depends on voluntary compliance. And in a democracy like ours, people contribute private resources to provide the public goods and services we deem appropriate as a community, including helping those not able fend for themselves.

In America, paying taxes embodies a civic relationship of mutual responsibility, and people's obligation to pay them is as legitimate as any other public duty. So, I am glad that we are beginning this discussion of comprehensive tax reform—an issue that will only become more important for us in Congress. Let me offer the following five points to consider as we discuss this important issue:

First, fundamental tax reform is a necessity. The current tax system is complicated, inefficient, and unfair. Its unpopularity is warranted, and that is a problem because that breeds distrust.

The tax code must be simplified in order to eliminate wasted time and money spent on compliance. For example, the average taxpayer with a self-employed status has the greatest compliance burden in terms of tax preparation—fifty-nine hours.

Furthermore, the complexity of the tax code is evident by the fact that small businesses overpaid their taxes by $18 billion in 2000 and 2001 because of return errors, according to a GAO report. Small businesses unfairly bear the burden of the tax code's complexity simply because they do not have the financial resources to hire sophisticated tax advisors.

Second, simplification can occur only with fundamental tax reform. This is clear after decades of incrementalism. We know that tax reform cannot be done in a piecemeal fashion. The current tax system is flawed at its root. Hard-working, middle-income class people bear the largest burden in our current tax system.

Third, fundamental tax reform must focus on the tax base. Our tax base is derived from total income. However, this is complicated by the bewildering array of adjustments, deductions, credits, omissions, and mis-measurements. This undermines the fairness of our tax system.

Therefore, fundamental tax reform must focus on the issue of the tax base in order to achieve equity, efficiency, simplicity, and accountability.

Fourth, the tax code must encourage entrepreneurship. Small businesses provide our economy's foundation. They need a tax system that frees re-sources for investment and ensures affordable capital. We must support small businesses, which make up the backbone of our economy.

Fifth, fundamental tax reform is possible. Tax reform is not an easy task. However, the American public demands it. They see our tax system as unfair, and they are right. As it was in the mid-1980s, the time is ripe to begin taking serious steps toward achieving fundamental tax reform. We must listen to our constituents and be up to task to implementing a fair tax system.

The Congressional Record. July 15, 2004: E1389–E1390.

TAXATION IMPACT ON INCOME DISTRIBUTION

There have been many attempts within the United States to reform the tax-ation system. There are three types of taxes: local, state, and federal. The fed-eral government imposes an income tax on all taxable income of individu-als, companies, and estates. Local taxes are based on property value and are the biggest contributors to local school systems. State tax is levied by each state separately and provides the necessary funding to function.

Since taking office, President George W. Bush has been preaching about federal tax cuts. President Bush believes that by cutting taxes, the money is going back to the hard-working family's pocket. Rep. Jerry Weller (R-IL) strongly agrees with the president. Rep. Weller discusses the importance of making the temporary Bush cuts permanent. By allowing the taxation act to continue past 2011, Rep. Weller fully believes in strong economic growth and more spending power for the consumer.

The Democrats have questioned many proposed tax cuts because they are unevenly distributed. As Sen. John Kerry (D-MA) argues, the tax cuts are designed to benefit the richest class in the United States. As Sen. Kerry points out, the rich are not the ones that need the tax breaks. Sen. Kerry also explores the relationship of big firms and taxes. He be-lieves that the taxation system needs to be reformed to ensure that big firms are paying their share of taxes. In addition, the system must ensure that the big corporations are not taking their accounts overseas to avoid paying domestic taxes.

Liberal Viewpoint

John Kerry (D-MA). Mr. President, the recent demise of Enron Corporation has generated national attention and shed light on an alarming trend. A growing number of corporations and individuals are exploiting tax havens in the Caribbean and elsewhere to evade and avoid paying taxes.

Often cloaked in a web of bank secrecy and taxpayer privacy, businesses and individuals operating in offshore financial centers create sham corporations and partnerships. By sheltering tax-dodgers and tax cheats, these overseas tax havens undermine confidence and trust in our federal government. The spread of illegal tax haven activity punishes those who play by the rules. The end result is higher taxes on the little guy—those who comply with the law. They are stuck paying the tab, forced to make up for the lost revenue through unnecessarily high taxes.

The vast majority of American businesses and individuals do not engage in abusive tax schemes. These taxpayers' activities will be unaffected by the Tax Haven and Abusive Tax Shelter Reform Act of 2002. The legislation will not stand in the way of legitimate tax planning and business activity. However, the bill will create real consequences for those individuals who flout the law, and those businesses who engage in transactions with no real business purpose other than generating artificial losses and deductions.

The exact details of Enron's tax avoidance practices are still under investigation by the Senate Finance Committee. What we do know is the energy conglomerate held over eight hundred subsidiaries in tax haven jurisdictions. Enron created six hundred and ninety-two subsidiaries in the Cayman Islands alone. Through the use of sophisticated financial instruments, at least one analyst estimates Enron was able to avoid income taxes in four of the last five years.

Enron is not alone. The use of offshore tax havens by corporations and wealthy individuals is widespread. Through accounting tricks and tax loopholes, large companies not only avoid corporate income taxes, they claim sizable tax refunds. In a typical example, a corporation establishes a foreign subsidiary not subject to American taxes, shifts profits to the subsidiary which then sends them back to the parent corporation in a form that is considered not taxable under U.S. law.

While some corporations use loopholes to skirt the edges of the law, other individuals use tax havens outright illegally. The Internet has simplified the process of launching a corporation or opening an account offshore. While Americans are taxed on their worldwide earnings, individuals operating in offshore financial centers gamble that the IRS will never uncover their overseas income.

· · ·

Clearly, Congress must act to restore public confidence in our federal tax system. We can start by ensuring that honest middle-class Americans are not the only ones left holding the bill. Unfortunately, the Bush Administration has shied away from aggressively attacking tax evasion. Last May, Treasury Secretary Paul O'Neill voiced support for abolishing the corporate income tax. The Treasury Department recently fought to water down an international campaign to reform tax haven practices led by the Organization for Economic Cooperation and Development, OECD. Last fall, the Administration sought to repeal the corporate alternative minimum tax, a tax designed to ensure that large corporations do not entirely escape taxation.

Exempting our nation's largest firms from taxation altogether is not the answer. On the contrary, Congress should take steps to ensure that criminal tax evasion is detected and addressed accordingly. The Tax Haven and Abusive Tax Shelter Reform Act of 2002 would impose strict measures against nations identified as uncooperative tax havens those which use confidentiality rules and practices to undermine tax enforcement and administration or refuse to participate in effective information exchange agreements. The legislation would limit foreign tax credits claimed by taxpayers operating in uncooperative tax havens.

It would require a strict reporting of outbound transfers by U.S. taxpayers. The bill imposes a new civil penalty on U.S. taxpayers who fail to report an interest in an offshore account. Finally, it mandates a comprehensive review of the offshore tax evasion problem, including specific mechanisms used by taxpayers to shelter income and assets. By imposing real consequences for jurisdictions which are identified as uncooperative tax havens, the bill pierces the veil of secrecy which shields tax cheats from scrutiny and provides a strong incentive for otherwise uncooperative tax havens to enter into commitments with the United States to reform their practices.

The peddling of abusive corporate tax shelters also demands attention. Prepackaged, tax-motivated transactions with no real economic risk or business purpose—but which capitalize on technical ambiguities in the tax code—are sold to corporations by creative practitioners to generate artificial losses and deductions. Provisions in the Tax Haven and Abusive Tax Shelter Reform Act of 2002, identical to those introduced in the House by Rep. Lloyd Doggett, D-TX, would disallow tax benefits from transactions that have no real business purpose other than tax savings. In addition, they expand disclosure requirements so that the IRS is fully aware of dubious tax schemes and tighten penalties against gross underpayments resulting from illegal tax shelters.

A tax system which asks working families to pay their fair share but gives large corporations such as Enron a free ride is a national disgrace. And as tax havens and shelters proliferate, confidence in the integrity and fairness of our tax system and government declines. Middle-class families rightly conclude that our own government cannot effectively enforce its laws. The administration, while proposing new disclosure requirements, has offered little in the way of substantive changes to alter the tax treatment of transactions which clearly serve no real business purpose other than tax avoidance. Furthermore, the administration has undermined international efforts to aggressively address sheltering activity in tax havens. The Tax Haven and Abusive Tax Shelter Reform Act of 2002 is the first step in what will surely be a long road to restoring the confidence and faith of the vast majority of hard-working, law-abiding Americans who pay taxes on every dollar they earn.

The Congressional Record. April 26, 2002: S3467–S3479.

Conservative Viewpoint

Gerald C. Weller (R-IL). As President Bush noted this past weekend, the tax cut that the president led, initiated and our Congress passed and was signed into law in June expires in less than ten years, and tonight we felt it was important to talk about the impact of a temporary tax cut because this week, on Thursday morning, the House of Representatives will begin debate on legislation which will make permanent what has become known as the Bush tax cut.

. . .

I was very proud of the president's leadership because he noted in January of last year, and January 2000 when he became president, that the economy was in a downturn. The president inherited a weakening economy and he says we have got this huge surplus, all this extra tax revenue that the federal government is collecting because taxes are too high and we are not spending it all, thanks to the fiscal responsibility of this House. So why do we not take a portion of that surplus, that extra tax revenue, and give it back to working families? Provide an across-the-board tax cut that helps every working family, bring about tax fairness by eliminating the marriage tax penalty, wiping out the death tax, increasing opportunities for retirement savings and saving for a college education?

The president was successful. . . . This House led the effort to lower taxes, and in June of this past year, the president signed into law what has become known as the Bush tax cut. Unfortunately, because of the arcane rules of the Congress, the tax cut was temporary, which meant it had to expire in the year 2011. . . .

When it expires, it is going to mean a big tax increase on millions of working families across this country. That is really what this vote is about on Thursday is whether or not we continue to keep taxes lower for working families, whether or not we continue to have tax fairness or do we bring back an unfair Tax Code that punishes married couples and takes away the family farm and family businesses and makes it harder to save for retirement or a college education, essentially imposing a tax increase on working Americans.

That is what this vote is going to be this week.

. . .

The Bush tax cut did a number of good things to help working families. It provided for marginal rate reductions, reducing the tax rate for every American who pays taxes, creating a whole new tax rate structure. In fact, we created a new lower tax rate for the lowest income Americans, lowering their taxes from 15 percent to 10 percent, helping low-income taxpayers.

We also, of course, repealed the death tax, a tax which has historically taken a majority of the family business away from families who inherit the family business from the founder and that has caused so many businesses to go out of business, and some of my colleagues are going to talk about that.

We doubled the child tax credit from $500 to $1,000 helping families with children better afford their children's needs. We increased retirement savings, increasing the amount one can contribute to their IRA from $2,000 to $5,000, what one can contribute to their 401(k) from $10,500 to $15,000, and for working moms and empty nesters, we allowed those over 50 to make up missed contributions to their IRA and 401(k), essentially what we call catch-up contributions. We helped families save for education, increasing education savings accounts from $500 to $2,000 a year, and allowing families to use that for expenses for elementary and secondary education, as well as for college.

Those are good things. Also, because many families were stepping forward and volunteering to adopt children and give children a loving home, we increased the adoption tax credit to $10,000 for children with special needs, and of course, for those with non-special needs, we have it at $5,000, and we also increased the income level of families that can qualify from $75,000 to $150,000, and we also prevented the alternative minimum tax from interfering or taking away this tax relief for working families.

Of course, part of the debate of who benefits from tax relief is who gets it, and there is always some who say, oh, we cannot cut taxes because those who pay taxes will get it. We should not help those who pay taxes because apparently they are rich. Well, let me note who it is that benefited from the Bush tax cut.

Under the president's tax plan that was signed into law and this Congress supported on and that we are going to make permanent or vote to make permanent this week, over 100 million individuals and families pay lower taxes. Forty-three million married couples see their taxes reduced on average by more than $1,700 a year. Thirty-eight million families with children will receive an average tax cut of almost $1,500. Eleven million single moms with children will be able to keep on average $77 more to care for their children. Thirteen million seniors will see their taxes reduced on average by $920, and 3.9 million taxpayers, including 3 million taxpayers with children, will have their taxpayer liability for the federal tax burden completely eliminated.

Think about that. Almost 4 million taxpayers under the Bush tax cut, those at the lower end of the economic area, pay no more taxes, thanks to the Bush tax cut.

Small business owners and entrepreneurs will receive a big chunk of this tax relief. Whenever my colleagues argue about who is going to get the rate reduction and what that means, they have to recognize that the vast majority of small businesses, almost 80 percent, pay in the top rate, and we lowered their rate to 35 percent.

The Congressional Record. April 16, 2002: H1312–H1318.

TRICKLE-DOWN ECONOMICS

Trickle-down economics has been under heavy criticism in the United States. The theory states that lowering taxes for the wealthy will increase economic growth and produce positive economic results. In turn, the middle and the lower class will indirectly benefit from the tax cuts for the wealthy. The trickle-down economic policy is closely associated with supply-side economics and Reaganomics as well.

Proponents of supply-side economics see the theory as very beneficial. Not only will it deduct taxes from those that own capital, it will also help those in the working sector. By cutting taxes, business owners have more capital to spend on new projects and new opportunities. In turn, more jobs are created and positive economic growth is maintained. Moreover, the standard of living also rises.

Democrats argue that the notion of trickle-down economics is unreasonable. The policy creates tax cuts for the rich, but it does not spread to the middle and lower classes. The tax cuts are only enjoyed by the rich. As Rep.

Peter DeFazio (D-OR) argues, trickle-down economics did not work during the Reagan era and it will not work now. Tax cuts that are made exclusively for the rich do not produce favorable economic growth, nor do they lead to income growth. Furthermore, Democrats argue that the claims of increased wages and jobs are also false.

Conservative Viewpoint

President George W. Bush. As the world's economic powers gather for the G-8, the American economy remains the envy of the world. And this week we received even more positive news about our economy. On Tuesday, my administration's Office of Management and Budget released its annual update on the budget outlook. This year's report is very encouraging. Because our economy continues to enjoy strong growth, federal tax revenues are growing, and we are cutting the federal deficit faster than expected.

This good news is no accident. It is the result of the hard work of the American people and pro-growth economic policies in Washington, D.C. Since 2001, we have cut taxes for everyone who pays income taxes, reduced the marriage penalty, doubled the child tax credit, and put the death tax on the road to extinction. We cut tax rates paid by most small businesses and further encouraged expansion by cutting taxes on dividends and capital gains.

Together, these tax cuts have left nearly $1.1 trillion in the hands of American small-business owners, workers, and families. And you have used this money to help spur an economic resurgence that has produced eighteen straight quarters of growth.

Some in Washington think the choice is between cutting taxes and cutting the deficit. This week's numbers show that this is a false choice. The economic growth fueled by tax relief has helped send tax revenues soaring. When the economy grows, businesses grow with it, people earn more money, and they pay taxes on this new income.

In 2005, tax revenues posted the largest increase in twenty-four years, and they're projected to rise again this year. The increase in tax revenues is much better than we had projected, and it is helping us cut the budget deficit.

Our original projection for this year's budget deficit was $423 billion. This week's report from OMB projects that this year's deficit will actually come in at $296 billion, a reduction of $127 billion. That is a tremendous difference, and 90 percent of it is because our growing economy has produced a lot more tax revenues.

Because of these new revenues, we now project that we'll meet our goal of cutting the federal deficit in half by 2008, a full year ahead of schedule. This is real progress, yet we cannot depend on a growing economy alone to cut the deficit. We must also cut waste and restrain unnecessary Government spending. And my administration is doing its part.

Every year since I took office, we have reduced the growth of discretionary spending that is not related to national security. My last two budgets have actually cut this kind of spending. I am also working with Congress to pass a line-item veto, which will help me and future presidents target wasteful spending that lawmakers tack on to large bills. The House has already passed this measure with significant bipartisan support. Now the Senate needs to act and get a line-item veto to my desk to sign into law.

Finally, I will continue to work with Congress to address the unsustainable growth of entitlement spending so that we can save programs like Social Security, Medicare, and Medicaid for our children and grandchildren.

This week's good news confirms the wisdom of trusting the American people with their own money and being wise with the money they send to Washington. By pursuing pro-growth policies and restraining government spending, we will keep our economy the envy of the world. We will create more jobs and opportunities for all our citizens, and we will deliver results for the American taxpayer.

Public Papers of the President: George W. Bush. July 15, 2006: 1346–1347.

Liberal Viewpoint

Peter A. DeFazio (D-OR). Mr. Speaker, the Republicans have attempted to remake themselves as fiscal conservatives despite the fact that, with George Bush in the White House and the Republicans in charge of the House and the Senate, that the debt of the United States of America has increased by 62 percent, over $8 trillion. They are borrowing $1.4 billion a day to run the government. They are borrowing every penny of the Social Security surplus and spending it on other things, including tax cuts for the wealthy.

Now they want to cut. What do they want to cut? Student loans, Medicare, Medicaid, foster care, and other programs that are important to struggling American families under the guise of fiscal responsibility.

Now they want to do $50 billion of cuts, but they also want to do $70 billion of tax cuts for the wealthiest among us. They want to make permanent the cuts in capital gains taxes. They want to reward wealth, not work; and they want to make permanent the cuts in dividend taxes. In order to facilitate that, they want to cut these other programs.

They want to benefit approximately 1 percent of the society, those who earn over $300,000 a year and have estates worth more than $6 million. But one thing we have got to give them is they are relentless and consistent and they are successful. Last year, the IRS says that 99 percent of the people in America saw their real incomes decline.

Everybody who earned less than $300,000 after inflation saw a decline. Up to $1.3 million, they did okay. Over $1.3 million, they did phenomenally well. Now the president's Tax Commission says that is exactly what the future should be. That is trickle down. We want more for the wealth, not for those who work.

Their proposals are extraordinary. They would say that dividends should be free of tax. So if one is someone who is lucky enough to be born into a wealthy family, they inherit millions of dollars and they invest it in dividend-paying stocks, they would never pay a penny in federal taxes because they are a wealth creator, they are a job generator, they are trickling down on the rest of America. Is that not nice of them? But they would not contribute to the society.

And then we have stocks. Well, on stocks they want to say 75 percent of the gain should be tax-free, again benefiting, for the most part, the same people. But the funny thing they are doing here is they want to talk about wealth creators and entrepreneurs, but they stick it to the small business people.

If one has a small business, they build it up and they sell it for a million bucks, guess what? Their tax rate is 33 percent under the president's new proposal. But if they have been speculating in the stock market, they would only have to pay at 8 percent. If they had been happy enough or lucky enough to inherit money and clip dividend coupons, they would have paid 0 percent. But, no, if they built up their small business, they are going to pay 33 percent; and those suckers who work for a living, they will pay on every penny of income. Somebody who earns $25,000 a year will pay a tax rate at about three times the person who invests in stocks and realizes capital gains.

This is their vision of the world: trickle down economics, trickling on the majority of America and last year trickling on 99 percent of the people in America. It is working well, they say, and we should do more of the same. And, ironically, they want to borrow money to perpetuate this. They are going to take the Social Security surplus and spend it in part to finance these long-term tax cuts for the wealthiest among us.

They should be ashamed, and trickle-down economics does not work.

The Congressional Record. November 2, 2005: H9539–H9540.

SOCIAL SERVICES SPENDING

The debate over whether to increase or decrease social services spending has been prevalent in the United States for a long time. Since many associate social services spending with increased taxes, Americans are reluctant to enter the safety net debate. Social services include saving programs, pensions, Social Security, free or low-cost education as well as financial aid, welfare, and many other government-provided initiatives.

Republicans such as Rep. Marsha Blackburn (R-TN) criticize many liberals for having their priorities switched. She believes that financial focus should be shifted toward the ongoing war and terrorism. If budget concessions were made to incorporate increased social services funding, the budget would have been greatly increased. To pay for such increases, taxes would have had to be raised. Rep. Blackburn does not believe that the American people want to give more money to the government and therefore is advocating for a decrease of social services spending.

Rep. Charles B. Rangel (D-NY) points to Hurricane Katrina as an eye opener. Many of the affected victims of Hurricane Katrina were African Americans. In addition, many of those that were affected were working. Rep. Rangel stresses the importance of social services to supplement working families' income. By allowing social services funding to increase, issues such as poverty will slowly wither away.

Conservative Viewpoint

Marsha Blackburn (R-TN). Madam Speaker, if House liberals had their way, last year we would have spent $7.4 billion more on social programs, and here we are in the middle of a war on terrorism. We are facing new expenses with that war. We are working to rebuild after hurricanes Katrina and Rita, and the Democrats are saying, spend more, spend more.

Madam Speaker, the American people need to know what that means. When they say spend more, it means the American people are going to turn over more of their hard-earned money. Republicans in this House, from our newest members to our leadership, are talking about how to reduce spending. Democrats are either staying quiet and hoping to avoid this subject or simply ignoring the bottom line and calling for increases in their pet projects. Their leadership consistently fails to do anything but complain and is not endorsing spending reductions.

Enough is enough. If the liberals in this body had their way, right now we would be spending $60 billion more.

The Congressional Record. October 19, 2005: H8922.

Liberal Viewpoint

Charles B. Rangel (D-NY). Mr. Speaker, the devastation of Hurricane Katrina exposed what America did not want to see. Beyond the tragedy of this natural disaster, Katrina shined a spotlight on America's poor and disadvantaged. The convenience of disregarding the plight of the poor came to an abrupt halt as a result of Katrina and its aftermath. Katrina pulled the cover off of what prior reports by the U.S. Census Bureau found, which stated for the past four years, the poverty rate has steadily increased; which is a reverse trend from 1993 to 2000.

Katrina also exposed the gross disparities relating to poverty in America. According to the Census Bureau 2004 report, the Black poverty rate of 24.7 percent is almost twice that of the general population. This translates to about 9.4 million African Americans, almost one in-four living below the poverty line. Consequently, those affected by the Katrina devastation were disproportionately Black and poor. Despite the rhetoric of conservative pundits who claim that poverty in the Black community is due to irresponsibility, statistics show that individuals living below the poverty line are hard working citizens who go to work everyday. It should be underscored that poverty is a result of a lack of income. Americans fall into poverty simply because they do not have enough financial resources. So it is plausible that even when people are working in the market place they can still fall into poverty. Statistics show that one-in-ten African Americans above 16 who were poor worked full-time jobs.

Furthermore, 37 million Americans are living in poverty. Statistics in 2004 indicate that 13 million American children lived below the poverty line, translating into 3 in 17. This was an increase of roughly 200,000 from 2003, which means 3,000 children were falling into poverty each week. Moreover, African American children under the age of 18 consist of 43 percent of all poor African Americans. Senior citizens, those 65 and older, have a poverty rate of 23.8 percent. In comparison with other counterparts, statistics show that more African Americans and Hispanics are in poverty at a higher rate than whites and other racial classifications. African American children represent 17 percent of American children, but they make up 31 percent of all poor children in America.

Conservatives attribute poverty to dysfunctional family structures. However, renowned economist such as William Springs suggests that this is a gross over simplification. He contends that poverty is the "result of economy-wide forces and public policy." Mr. Speaker, I share this analysis, hence, it places the onus on policy makers to enact legislation centered on relieving the burden poverty. After the passage of the Civil Rights Act of 1964, the Economic Opportunity Act of 1964 and the Voting Rights Act of 1965 the Black poverty rate decreased to 32.2 percent. During the years of 1993 to 2000, which were marked by strong fiscal policy, the poverty rate for African Americans dropped annually.

Katrina exposed America's weakness, not only in the federal government's delinquent response, but also relative to our inability to address poverty particularly in the minority community. As we consider the 2007 fiscal budget, we must see the opportunity to provide provisions that alleviate poverty in the Gulf Coast and urban communities across the nation. Tax cuts for the wealthy and the slashing of social programs will not suffice.

The Congressional Record. February 15, 2006: E163.

INFLATION CONTROL

Inflation is a devaluation of money caused by rapidly rising income. To control inflation, it is necessary to reduce this rapid growth, which can be done in many ways, including increasing interest rates, reducing the number of people borrowing money, raising taxes, and lowering governmental spending. The U.S. Federal Reserve can affect inflation to a significant extent—and has done so using unemployment and declining production to prevent price increases. Democrats had often preached that a little bit of inflation could create jobs, while Republicans believed in the strong medicine of unemployment to protect investors and retirees on fixed pensions.

Sen. Orrin Hatch (R-UT) begins by examining the positive trends of the U.S. economy under President Bush's leadership. Sen. Hatch underlines the strong economy and positive economic growth by examining revenue increases and tax breaks. Furthermore, Sen. Hatch looks to Dr. Ben Bernanke and Dr. Milton Friedman for inflation advice.

Rep. James McDermott (D-WA) is critical of economic policy. Rep. McDermott points directly to the relationship between tax cuts for the wealthiest class and an increase of national debt. By decreasing taxes for those that can afford to pay them, the future is placed in jeopardy. By further examining the role of the Federal Reserve, Rep. McDermott analyzes the devaluation of money and the process to control inflation through interest rate monitoring.

Conservative Viewpoint

Orrin G. Hatch (R-UT). Mr. President, I have been very interested in the remarks of the distinguished Democratic leader, my friend, and I approach this issue from not just a slightly different perspective but from a very different perspective. I think it is important that we get our facts straight.

The robust health of the U.S. economy becomes more apparent with each passing day. Yet it is something about which we hear precious little except criticism, especially on the Senate floor. I would like to take just a few minutes to remind my colleagues about some of the positive aspects we are seeing about the state of the economy.

As we complete the fifth year of economic expansion, all signs indicate that the economy is as strong as it has ever been, and that we can expect continued economic growth for the foreseeable future. When President Bush became president, we were in the throes of an economic recession at the end of the Clinton years. He inherited that, and the first year of his Presidency was filled with a recession. But in the last five years, we have had an economic expansion. The U.S. economy grew at an annual rate of 4.6 percent in the first half of this year, and that is an impressive clip at any time, but particularly so for a mature economy approaching full employment.

Economic forecasters estimate the gross domestic product in the current quarter will come close to 3 percent. While initially we may not welcome a reduction in the rate of growth, a 3 percent rate is actually very positive news. This is because a growth rate of around 3 percent would put us at a level of growth that many economists believe can be sustained indefinitely without risking inflationary pressures. It is mystifying to me that an economy this strong that has grown steadily for 5 full years now is not being recognized by everyone for what it is; namely, a remarkable jobs-producing machine. We have created 3.5 million jobs in the last three years and have more people employed today than ever before in the history of this country. The unemployment rate is only 4.7 percent, a level that is below any rate seen in the United States between 1970 and 1997. Think about that: a rate below any rate seen in the U.S. between 1970 and 1997.

No matter how one cuts the numbers, the news on the job front of late has been good. The number of long-term unemployed is down, as is the unemployment rate for teenagers, women, African Americans, Hispanics, people without a high school degree, and people with only a high school degree.

While energy prices might have pushed the Consumer Price Index up a bit earlier in the year, I believe there was never a risk of higher inflation, and the financial markets now discount this possibility almost entirely. . . . I think Ben Bernanke has demonstrated his determination to keep the scourge of inflation under control, and for that he deserves commendation. I believe his decision today to leave the short-term discount rate where it is makes perfect sense, given the recent data.

The benefits of sustained economic growth, the likes of which we have seen over the last 5 years, cannot be overstated. We are just now beginning to reap its benefits in the form of higher incomes for American workers. Median household incomes, stagnant since the 2001 recession, went up by 1.1 percent after adjusting for inflation in 2005. Now, that is median household income.

Contrary to the gloom and doom we are hearing from the other side on this floor, it went up by 1.1 percent, after adjusting for inflation in 2005. That is after the adjustment for inflation.

The preliminary data for 2006 suggests that income growth has accelerated strongly, with even the New York Times reporting an estimate that inflation-adjusted wages and salaries have gone up an annual rate of 7 percent thus far this year. This is a pattern that would be entirely consistent with what we witnessed during the expansion of the 1990s, one that ultimately lifted millions of households out of poverty. Yet all we hear is doom and gloom. That is what happens when people want to gain power.

The federal government has also benefited from sustained economic growth. Tax revenues—and this is with the tax cuts that we put in, and because of the tax cuts we put in over the past 5 years—have grown at the fastest rate since the inflationary 1970s. You can't discount that, no matter how much doom and gloom you spread all over this body. Revenue went up by nearly 15 percent last year, and as we approach the end of the current fiscal year, it is likely it will go up 12 percent this year. That is phenomenal.

In 2006, we will collect over a half of a trillion dollars more than we did in 2004—a truly awesome amount. The budget deficit has shrunk rapidly over these same 2 years, from $412 billion in 2004 to roughly $260 billion in 2006. Now, it is still too high, but as a percentage of GDP, it is one of the lowest over the last forty years. That can't be discounted, in spite of the doom and gloom that we hear consistently on this floor.

The Congressional Budget Office was forecasting a budget deficit of $100 billion larger than that as recently as March. Let me repeat, $100 billion larger than the $260 billion it was projected to be as recently as last March. Again, the strong budget growth we have benefited from of late is reminiscent of what occurred in the late 1990s once the economy reached full employment and productivity growth picked up. It is also instructive to look at exactly where the additional tax revenues are coming from.

The Congressional Record. September 20, 2006: S9854–S9856.

Liberal Viewpoint

James A. McDermott (D-WA). Mr. Speaker, today we granted a tax break of nearly $800 billion over the next ten years to the wealthiest among us, and it made me think about a quote from children's literature, which I think is a good place sometimes to learn what we really ought to know.

We all know about the morality tale called the "Lord of the Rings"; and one of them is called "The Return of the King," and the main character is Gandalf, the magician. The children asked Gandalf what they are supposed to do, and he says, "It is not our part to master all the tides of the world, but to do what is in us for the succor of those years wherein we are set, uprooting the evil in the fields that we know, so that those who live after may have clear earth to till. What weather they shall have is not ours to rule."

Now, we stand out here on this floor very frequently and talk about our children and what kind of a world we are leaving to our children, and we are leaving a world of debt to our children. The June 11 issue of the New York Times magazine says, "Debt," and the subtitle is, "America's Scariest Addiction is Getting Even Scarier." Well, we added to the debt today.

Now, the question is, What does it mean when a country goes into debt? It means that we do not tax the people sufficiently for what services they expect, so we have to borrow the money. This year, we are borrowing from the Chinese the entire debt that we are creating in this year, some $300-some-odd billion that we did not raise in taxes, that we gave away this afternoon. We are going to go to the Chinese tomorrow and borrow that money.

Now, what difference does that make? Well, ultimately you have to deal with debt. You all have credit cards. You understand what you have to do with a credit card: you either pay it off, which means we have to raise taxes, or stop giving it away. Or in the case of a country, we can devalue our money.

You say, well, why, what difference does that make? Well, if our money, if the Chinese borrowed a dollar that was worth this amount, and we now drop it down by 50 percent, they have lost 50 percent of what they lent us. How do you think they feel when we do something like that? Well, the next time we come to lend, they say, give us a higher interest rate. Now, lowering the value of the dollar, which happened in 1983, 1985, some people remember when our money went down, and people lost a lot of money. That was a devaluation, and we are heading for another devaluation in this country.

When it happens, we will also have inflation because with the cheaper dollar we can buy more, and it is easier to buy foreign goods. So we will buy more, and they will buy our goods, and they will demand higher interest rates.

Now, the Feds try to control inflation by driving up interest rates. Some may even remember when our interest rates were 22 percent, when buying a house was absolutely impossible. Well, then interest rates came down because we changed our fiscal policy. We paid our debt. We started borrowing. Under Mr. Clinton we actually went into a positive state. We no longer were borrowing. We were actually taking in more and paying down some of that debt. But in the last years since 2000, we have just gone on a wild spree, and we have gotten ourselves deeper and deeper in debt. People like me worry about that because my children are going to pay for it, not me. In fact, it may be my grandchildren that pay for it.

There are two categories of debt that you have to worry about. One, of course, in this country is personal debt. Now, lots of people bought houses in the last year, last years, five, six years, and they have been buying houses because the interest rates were low. They were buying on interest only, or they were buying on ARM, that means adjustable rate mortgages, and all of those had a term, an adjustable rate of four or five years, and those ARMs are coming due now.

Because of what is happening in terms of the dollar and in terms of inflation, the Feds are raising it every month. Since March of 2004, the ARM rate has gone up 59 percent, and it could easily jump 50 percent when these adjustable rates happen. Some people are going to lose their houses. Listen to the children.

The Congressional Record. June 22, 2006: H4499–H4500.

UNEMPLOYMENT INSURANCE

Unemployment insurance is a benefit provided by the federal government to unemployed people. Unemployment insurance often varies state by state and at times is also dependent on the individual's working history. Eligibility criteria have been strengthened to prevent problems from arising. The program is covered under welfare, as it provides for basic needs. Unemployment benefits are given out to those that are registered as unemployed and are contingent upon the person's active search for employment.

Sen. Ted Kennedy (D-MA) begins by acknowledging that the U.S. economy is in trouble. Sen. Kennedy also points out that only a minority of unemployed are receiving unemployment benefits and the historic numbers are only decreasing. As a result, many people are struggling to provide the basic needs to their families. To solve the situation, Sen. Kennedy proposes an economic stimulus to strengthen the U.S. economy. In order to provide relief, more money should be placed in people's possession.

President George W. Bush cites the war as well as the economy as the primary focal points of the upcoming year. President Bush acknowledges that the current state of our economy has placed some people in financial hardships but pledges to do whatever is necessary to help them. President Bush proposes to expand unemployment benefits by thirteen weeks to allow further assistance to be offered. Furthermore, President Bush believes that an improved economy and steady job will allow people to improve their financial well-being.

Liberal Viewpoint

Ted M. Kennedy (D-MA). Mr. President, on Tuesday, we began debate about the economic stimulus package. We know the economy is in trouble, and we know we have to act. Clearly, by any standard, we face an economic emergency that demands responsible action by Congress.

The American people want action by Congress too. They strongly support our Democratic proposals to provide unemployment insurance and health insurance to laid-off workers, and federal assistance to states. They know it's an emergency in the economy and they know it is an emergency for the hundreds of thousands of men and women without unemployment insurance or health insurance.

Yet, some of our colleagues in Congress oppose this action. Instead, they support a bill that would retroactively repeal the corporate minimum tax and give the largest corporations $25 billion in direct payments from the U.S. Treasury. They don't think laid-off workers who can't afford, or don't have, health insurance are an emergency. Instead, they support spending $120 billion to accelerate the reduction of upper income tax rates, 80 percent of which won't go into the economy until after next year.

Our economy is in trouble. There is no denying it. Just ask the men and women who have lost their jobs and have to tell their families every week that they cannot find new employment. They will tell you how hard it is to put food on their families' tables each week. They will tell you how hard it is to watch their bills piling up with no end in sight. If that's not enough, look at the numbers.

Only 38 percent of unemployed workers receive unemployment insurance. This figure is down from 75 percent in 1975. And, the figure is much worse for low-wage workers. According to a new study by the National Campaign for Jobs and Income Support, only 20 percent of unemployed low-wage workers will qualify for benefits during a recession.

These workers are least likely to qualify for unemployment benefits, and they are most likely to be laid off. They are struggling to keep a roof over their families' heads and to afford food for their children. We know that the number of hungry children has grown in recent years.

Unless we do more to help, the number will continue to grow.

Yesterday, America's Second Harvest released the largest, most comprehensive report on the plight of hungry Americans. Last year, 23 million Americans, including 9 million children, sought emergency food relief through America's Second Harvest. The current downturn in the economy means that even more families are facing the difficult choice between feeding their children and paying the rent, a choice no person should have to make.

These findings demonstrate the dramatic rise in hunger and related health problems among children. They demonstrate that current unemployment benefits are not adequate to help working families during the current economic downturn. We need to do more to see that families can afford to put food on their tables. Our Democratic plan provides unemployment benefits to 600,000 more low-wage and part-time workers and increase these benefits by at least $25 a week. The economy needs stimulus now. Workers need assistance now.

The best way to accomplish both of these goals is to get relief to the families who need it the most. Economists across the country agree that providing relief to low- and moderate-income families is one of the most effective ways to stimulate the economy.

The Democratic plan would stimulate the economy right away, by putting money in the hands of the people most likely to spend it—dislocated workers and their families. We do that by strengthening the unemployment insurance system, improving workers' ability to afford health care, and providing a tax rebate for those who did not receive a full rebate earlier this year.

Unemployment insurance is the nation's first line of defense in an economic recession. By putting UI trust fund dollars into the declining economy, we automatically boost consumer spending in communities affected by rising unemployment, while meeting essential needs of households hurt by layoffs.

The Congressional Record. November 15, 2001: S11927–S11932.

Conservative Viewpoint

President George W. Bush. Our highest priorities are clear to all. We must give our military every tool and weapon it needs to prevail in the war against terror. We must strengthen our country's defenses against further attack with a comprehensive program of homeland security. And we must get our country's economy growing and creating jobs once again.

The economy is a concern for all Americans, especially for those out of work. These Americans need extra help. My economic plan proposes an additional thirteen weeks of unemployment insurance benefits for workers who have lost their jobs and direct assistance to protect their health insurance.

My plan is based on the simple truth that people out of work need an unemployment check, but what they need even more is a steady paycheck. So I have joined with Republicans and Democrats in proposing concrete steps to create more jobs and help spur more growth in the economy. The House passed this plan; the Senate needs to act on it.

Difficult economic times bring hardship to many other Americans, as well, single moms or disadvantaged young people trying to get into the workforce. My budget seeks to help them, too, by adding resources to vital programs that have proven their value. One of our government's most effective services is the Women, Infants, and Children program, which counsels mothers on nutrition and health care for their children.

In my budget for the coming fiscal year, I will propose an increase of $364 million for the WIC program. This will be enough to serve nearly 8 million women and children each month.

Another vital program is the Job Corps, which provides employment training to more than 72,000 disadvantaged young Americans. In my budget, I will ask Congress for an additional $73 million to expand the good work of the Job Corps. This will help to pay for new residential training centers. We will also secure high school accreditation for Job Corps training so that more young people can have the advantage of a high school diploma.

These are some of the elements of the budget I will be sending to Congress. My budget focuses on the pressing needs of our country and on the basic needs of our citizens. I am committed to building a strong economy that spreads its benefits to everyone. This goal reaches beyond politics or party, and I'm confident that Congress will join me in the work ahead.

Public Papers of the President: George W. Bush. January 12, 2002: 59.

MINIMUM WAGE

Minimum wage is an hourly, weekly, or monthly wage that must be paid to the employee. In his presidency, William J. Clinton gave states the power to set their own minimum wage laws. Although the current federal minimum is $5.15 per hour, one state is below the federal line. Fifteen states follow the federal minimum as their standard, twenty-nine have set their standard higher than the federal minimum, and five states have no minimum wage law at all.

The supporters of a higher minimum wage argue that the current standards are insufficient in today's society. If the minimum wage were raised, it would not only help people pay their bills and live a more comfortable life, it would also reduce worker exploitation. Furthermore, proponents of the raise argue that by increasing the pay, the employee's work ethic rises and therefore the worker is more productive. From an economic standpoint, raising the minimum wage will stimulate economic growth by putting more money in the hand of the consumers.

The opponents disagree. As Rep. Michael Bradley Enzi (R-WY) argues, raising the minimum wage reduces the demand for workers and it also reduces profit margins for business owners. Furthermore, if employers were forced to pay workers extra money, jobs would be cut and the prices of products would be raised. Moreover, the opposition to the minimum wage increase believes that an increase will lead to outsourcing of jobs and also a higher illegal immigration problem.

Liberal Viewpoint

Steny H. Hoyer (D-MD). Thank you very much. The hour is late and the time is limited. Mr. Speaker, I rise, however, to briefly urge my colleagues to take action on raising the minimum wage. This is an action of fairness. It is the right thing to do. It is an issue of values. The American people believe it is the right thing to do. Eighty-six percent of them have said we ought to raise the minimum wage.

This issue clearly illustrates the different priorities . . . between the Democratic and Republican sides of the aisle. We Democrats have been trying to get this issue on the floor for years now.

Let us look at the facts, Mr. Speaker. Democrats have been fighting to raise the minimum wage from $5.15 to $7.25 an hour over two years. Today, if the minimum wage were at the rate it was in 1968, we would be paying $9.05. We are not getting there, but we ought to do better than we have done.

Unfortunately, Mr. Speaker, the Republican side of the aisle is fighting us tooth and nail while attempting this week to bring up legislation once again that gives the heirs of the wealthiest families in America a break on the estates tax and drive our nation even deeper into debt. That is right, while the working people struggle to make ends meet, doing what we expect them to do, this Congress is rushing an estate tax bill, what I call the "Paris Hilton Tax Relief Act," to the floor.

Of course, as usual, the bill is not paid for and continues the majority's fiscal irresponsibility and will increase our costs of borrowing by $280 billion over the next ten years. We are borrowing because we have no money to give a tax cut, so we are going to have to borrow it from other nations.

Last week, in the Appropriations Committee, I offered an amendment to the fiscal year 2007 labor-health bill. That amendment passed, raising the minimum wage seventy cents on each of the next Januarys, 2007, 2008 and 2009, bringing to $7.25 the minimum wage. Seven Republicans, Mr. Speaker, on the committee voted for that bill, several of whom have tough races. So they were listening very carefully to their people at home; and their people, again by overwhelming majorities, say this is the fair and right thing to do.

We thought we were going to consider that labor-health bill this week. It was announced it would be on the floor this week, but it was pulled. I am not sure exactly of all the reasons, but in part surely it was pulled because there was a question about the rule.

I want to say, Mr. Speaker, when that bill comes to the floor, the rule vote will be a minimum-wage vote. And if you think that the minimum wage ought to be increased, if you think working Americans ought to be given a wage that gets them out of poverty, if you think that somebody who works in America ought to be able to support at least themselves, then you will vote against the rule, unless it gives a waiver for this amendment.

Mr. Speaker, Mr. Miller and I, and the others who will speak on this floor, believe very strongly that in an America that honors work and in an America, the richest nation on the face of the Earth, that is an example for the rest of the world, we ought to make sure that those who work, those who get up in the morning and work hard, play by the rules, as Bill Clinton used to say, ought to get a decent, fair wage.

Mr. Speaker, I hope that when this bill comes forward that every member of this House will vote for a rule that ensures an up-or-down vote on raising the minimum wage in America for all our workers who work at that level. There are 6.6 million people, Mr. Speaker, 6.6 million Americans trying to support themselves and participating in helping to support their children and their families. It is the right thing to do.

Over 86 percent of Americans think it is the right thing to do and the House of Representatives ought to do the right thing.

And, five of those seven Republicans who voted with Democrats last week flip-flopped. The other two failed to vote.

And, the amendment failed.

Mr. Speaker, the failure of this Congress to act on the minimum wage is a national embarrassment.

It has been nine years since we last raised the federal minimum wage—the second longest period without an increase since a minimum wage was first enacted.

Today, the minimum wage is at its lowest level in fifty years, when adjusted for inflation.

Had the minimum wage been indexed for inflation since 1968, it would be $9.05 an hour today—not $5.15.

People who work full-time in the United States of America—the richest nation on earth—should not be poor.

But in 2003 there were 3.7 million workers who worked full-time, year-round, and still lived in poverty.

And, let's disabuse ourselves of this notion that "no one" really makes the minimum wage any more.

Not true.

In fact, a minimum wage increase would directly benefit 6.6 million low-wage workers—most of whom are adults who work to support themselves and their families.

An increase would specifically benefit 760,000 single mothers who toil day in and day out, sometimes at two or three jobs to provide just the basic necessities for themselves and their children.

Let's also dispense with the Republicans' favorite argument—that raising the minimum wage will somehow cost us jobs.

Again, not true.

We know that this argument is false because twenty states and the District of Columbia have raised their minimum wage above the federal rate.

And, a study conducted by the Center for American Progress and Policy Matters Ohio shows the following:

Employment in small businesses grew more (9.4 percent) in states with higher minimum wages than federal minimum wage states (6.6 percent).

And, inflation-adjusted small business payroll growth was stronger in high minimum wage states (19 percent) than in federal minimum wage states (13.6 percent).

Raising the minimum wage is an issue of fairness and an issue of values.

A PEW research poll in December 2005 found that 86 percent of Americans support raising the minimum wage.

The time to increase the minimum wage is long overdue, and Democrats are going to keep fighting for a fair wage for America's working families.

The Congressional Record. June 20, 2006: H4323–H4326.

Conservative Viewpoint

Michael Bradley Enzi (R-WY). I am going to speak now on, I believe, the pending amendment, the Boxer-Kennedy amendment. I will share my thoughts about raising the federal minimum wage. My colleagues on the other side of the aisle keep talking about the loss of American jobs, but their actions don't match up to their words.

If my colleagues are so concerned about unemployment, why would they do something that would eliminate jobs in this country? If my colleagues are so concerned about helping poor families, why would they do something that hurts poor families the most? Their effort to increase the minimum wage, while attacking the president on job creation, is not based on sound policy and economics.

There is an effort underway to put a smokescreen of unrelated amendments that mask election year politics in misleading rhetoric. It is being done on the reauthorization of the welfare bill.

It is time for us to look beyond the smokescreen and see who is really helped and who is really hurt by Senator Kennedy's amendment to raise the federal minimum wage.

Every student who has taken an economics course knows if you increase the price of something—in this case, the minimum wage job—you decrease the demand for those jobs. A survey of members of the American Economic Association revealed that 77 percent of economists believe that a minimum wage hike causes job loss.

For small businesses, where most of the job creation in this country is generated, a minimum wage increase is particularly harmful. Having owned a small business in Wyoming, I can speak from personal experience about how detrimental a minimum wage increase would be for small businesses and job growth.

I need to explain something. Very few people in the shoe business I was in were working at the minimum wage, which my wife and I preferred to call the level of minimum skills. Those are the people who first came in and did not have any capability in the kind of job they were going to be doing and we had a starting wage, a starting skills wage. Anybody who was in that wage more than 3 months was not paying attention, and that is the way with most of the businesses in this country.

The minimum wage is the minimum skills wage, and it is the starting wage. It does have an effect on other wages as well. When we raise the minimum wage, then to keep the proper spread between employees of different skills, other jobs get raises, too. Of course, when that happens, there has to be a way to pay for it, and the way to pay for that almost always comes from raising prices. If you raise prices and wages, there is not much gain.

How do I explain to my constituents, most of whom rely on small business for their livelihood, that Congress wants to do something that would foster job loss instead of job creation?

· · ·

[My constituent] Mr. Harned saw through the phony economics of a minimum wage increase. He reached the same conclusion as two Stanford economists: A minimum wage increase is paid for by higher prices that hurt poor families the most. Some argue that we need to increase the minimum wage to help poor families. However, the 2001 study conducted by Stanford University economists found that only one in four of the poorest 20 percent of families would benefit from an increase in the minimum wage. Three in four of the poorest workers would be hurt by a wage hike because they would shoulder the costs of resulting higher prices. A federal wage hike will hurt the very people the underlying welfare reauthorization bill is designed to help: America's poor families.

I have held on to Mr. Harned's letter as a reminder of the dangers of a "Washington knows best" and a "one size fits all" mentality. An increase in the federal minimum wage is a classic lesson that Washington does not know best and one size does not fit all.

A federal wage mandate does not account for the cost of living that varies across the country. It costs over twice as much to live in New York City than in Cheyenne, Wyoming. However, a federal minimum wage hike that applies coast to coast is like saying a bag of groceries in New York City must cost the same as a bag of groceries in Cheyenne. Local labor market conditions and the cost of living determine pay rates, not federal minimum wage laws dictated from Washington.

I support an increase for all wages, but that increase should be fueled by a strong, free market economy, not by an artificial federal mandate that hurts business and workers alike. Artificial wage hikes drive prices up. We should not trick workers into thinking they are earning more when they still cannot pay the bills at the end of the month. We should not trick the American people into believing that the phony economics of a minimum wage increase will improve the standard of living in this country. Nor should we trick the American people into believing that a minimum wage increase is without cost.

The smoke and mirrors of a minimum wage increase is not the way for American workers to find and keep well-paying jobs. We have to encourage, not discourage, job creation, and we have to equip our workers with the skills needed to compete in the new global economy.

. . .

If we want to take care of jobs in this country, if we want people to be making more and to be making more real money, we ought to get them trained into the skilled positions in the jobs that are vacant in this country right now before we ship them over to another country. We need to have a conference committee. That would provide jobs. That will provide increased wages. That will provide real increased wages, not just inflationary wages that will drive up the price of all of the goods and absorb, as Mr. Harned said, in 1 week the amount of the raise.

. . .

I owe Mr. Harned and all my constituents' sound policy, not election year rhetoric. I owe it to Mr. Harned and all of my constituents to remove the smokescreen around the minimum wage debate and expose its true cost.

The Boxer-Kennedy amendment to raise the federal minimum wage ignores the true cost of a minimum wage increase on America's workers and businessmen.

. . .

The Congressional Record. March 30, 2004: S3347–S3359.

DEFENSE SPENDING

The United States has the largest military force in the world and spends the greatest sum of money to fund it. This year alone, the United States will spend about $440 billion, more than the next six biggest military spenders combined.

President George W. Bush has asked Congress to increase defense spending in order to combat terrorism. In order for that to be accomplished, cuts in health care and other social services would have to be made. President Bush argues that the increase in military spending is necessary to give our troops the necessary resources to accomplish missions. The Republicans also argue that the increase in military spending will yield productive technology expenses that will once again only further America's interests abroad.

Democrats are insistent on capping the defense budget. Many argue that the United States needs to reinvest money in domestic programs. Even though terrorism is an important battle to fight, the already allocated money must be used more efficiently. Furthermore, many Democrats are afraid that raising the Department of Defense's (DOD's) budget even further will lead to a slippery slope and further national debt.

Liberal Viewpoint

Cynthia McKinney (D-GA). Mr. Speaker, on Wednesday, February 6th, Secretary of Defense Donald Rumsfeld testified before the House Armed Services Committee and asked for a record increase in defense spending. He pointed to the brave new world post-September 11th as justification for the largest hike in defense spending in twenty years. Sadly, Secretary Rumsfeld thinks that the brave new world of post-September gives us amnesia about 9/11 and the events before 9/11. He also mistakenly believes that all of his destabilizing proposals can be justified as a reasoned response to 9/11. An incredibly, both the vice president and the president placed calls to Tom Daschle asking that the fog of ignorance around the events prior to and the day of 9/11 not be lifted.

The fact, however, is that September 11 was not a failure of our nation's defenses. Rather, September 11 was a colossal intelligence failure—a failure to act on timely and accurate warnings predicting massive terrorist attacks against our nation. The *L.A. Times* and other leading press agencies have identified some of these missed warnings. And this was not the first time that our intelligence agencies have let us down. The same failure to act on critical warnings happened with respect to the terror attacks against our embassies in Africa.

Even the CIA, the FBI and other senior Capitol Hill figures all now agree that there were serious lapses in the handling of perishable and highly significant warnings preceding the September 11th attacks. But instead of examining what went wrong with respect to these warnings and then trying to prevent it from ever happening again, President Bush and Vice President Cheney now seek to actually prevent the Congress from investigating these and other events surrounding September 11th. Indeed, Senator Richard Shelby, a member of the Senate Intelligence Committee told CNN: "It was a real massive failure . . . In my judgment too many bureaucratic failures, not enough coordination between the Agencies." The active efforts to prevent a Congressional investigation into the events surrounding September 11 not only violate the principles of good government but are an affront to the memories of all those who perished in the September 11 attacks. But sadly, the Administration now chooses to direct us on a path of war while refusing to allow us to know how we got there.

I have been asked by my constituents to explain to them why and how September 11 happened. Indeed, the whole world community continues to search for answers to those exact questions. That cannot be done if the Executive Branch will not cooperative with the Legislative Branch in answering important questions about what was known before, during, and after the tragedies in New York and Pennsylvania and Washington, D.C. Why doesn't the Executive Branch want us to know answers to these questions? Is there something that they don't want the American public to know?

Instead of working with the Congress to search for answers to these questions the Administration has now become obsessed with finding ways to expand the U.S. military budget. The White House is now using our new War Against Terror as a means of siphoning public attention away from the events surrounding September 11th in order to generate widespread support for the largest increase in defense spending in a generation. The Administration has even identified a dubious "axis of evil" to further justify this increased spending.

The president has requested an increase of $48.1 billion in defense spending. Sadly, many commentators have already pointed out that his father stands to personally gain immense profits from the president's proposals because of the former president's relationship with The Carlyle Group, a leading defense conglomerate. One particular defense contract, for the development and purchase of a mobile howitzer, the Crusader, exists with the Carlyle Group. Though the company has received millions for this, the Crusader is too hefty to transport, has not yet reached its production phase despite years of engineering and re-engineering, and is far from fulfilling its purpose or need.

In his testimony before the Congress Wednesday, Secretary of Defense Donald Rumsfeld said that America can afford this increase just fine. This comes after defense spending snared a whopping 62 percent of all new spending for the year 2002. This accounting is specious, as Rumsfeld himself noted on the eve of September 11th, that "according to some estimates we cannot track $2.3 trillion in transactions." Increased spending should occur under no circumstances without increased financial accountability. Does Arthur Anderson keep the Pentagon's books?

Rumsfeld's trick of throwing bones to would-be critics in the form of pay raises for the troops should not obscure the fact that the bulk of this budget hike goes not for pay raises, but for expensive gadgets such as missile

defense, three new, separate fighter planes and space-based lasers. Of the
$48.1 billion requested in more funding, less than 5 percent of that increase
is for soldier pay raises. And let us not forget that the president's first act in
this war on terrorism was to waive the high-deployment overtime pay for
our troops who are on the front line of this war.

I might remind Mr. President that we still have veterans from the Vietnam
war suffering from the ill effects of Agent Orange, we still have Vietnam veterans impoverished and sleeping on the streets of our nation's capital, we
still have veterans from the Gulf War suffering the ill effects of Gulf War syndrome and we still have service men and women in our armed forces living
on food stamps and residing in poor housing. How in good conscience can
the Secretary of Defense come before this committee and ask for yet more
money for aircraft, ships and missiles and not adequately address these critical issues concerning the personal welfare of our veterans and serving men
and women?

Sadly, however, at the same time that the president proposes the largest
defense spending hike in 20 years, his budget also proposes to cut funds for
programs that bridge the digital divide, reducing funds for highway construction and urban development and cutting funding for the EPA by $300
million. And despite the down-turned economic situation, the president
has also proposed to cut back on job training, assistance for low income
home heating, and rural housing and utility improvements. Moreover,
funds to cleanup the Savannah River Site nuclear weapons complex are
sliced, and abroad, international food aid and peacekeeping funds are also
shrunk.

At $379.3 billion, the president's proposal will not tell us how just a
few months ago during the trial of suspects charged with initially bomb-
ing the World Trade Center in 1993, a suspect told U.S. officials that bin
Laden's group was trying to make war on the United States and in particular would bomb an embassy, yet we did nothing and lost hundreds
of lives in Nairobi and Dar Es Salaam. Nor will this budget explain the
Mossad warning of a major terrorist force of 200 individuals entering the
U.S., which apparently again fell on deaf ears. What of the supposed
warning to German police by an Iranian in Hamburg of an impending
attack on the U.S. using hijacked planes? And nor will this budget illu-
minate for us who performed the unusual stock trades on the Friday and
Monday before September 11th, but has since decided not to pick up the
tidy profit that was made. The U.S. Government is now being sued by
survivors of the African embassy blasts because it has become clear that
the United States had ample warning but chose to do nothing rather
than prevent the loss of life. Given the prior warnings, insider stock
trades, and convoluted financial interrelationships, September 11th represents yet another wasted chance to save innocent lives.

The most shocking aspect of the president's request involves the New Defense Strategy to be implemented now. Secretary Rumsfeld testified that a major role now for the U.S. military will be to occupy an opponent's capital and replace his regime. In as much as the Secretary has identified some 60 countries, including our own, that host terror cells, and publicly stated his intention to "drain the swamp," we can only surmise that the U.S. military is now in the business of taking over capitals around the world and replacing regimes . . . starting with Washington, D.C.

The Congressional Record. February 26, 2002: E189–E190.

Conservative Viewpoint

James Bunning (R-KY). Mr. President, I was proud to support the recent passage of S. 2514, the National Defense Authorization Act for fiscal year 2003. This bill continues to strengthen our military and is vital to the war on terrorism.

This is the most important bill we have debated in the Senate all year. The threats against us are real and I am pleased the Senate acted swiftly in passing this strong defense package. This bill authorizes $393.4 billion for national defense. That is $43 billion above the 2002 level, and the largest defense spending increase in over 20 years.

We are in this war against terrorism for the long haul and our increased military funding is justified. We now have troops on the ground in Afghanistan, the Philippines, and many other places we could not have foreseen before September 11. Depending on what happens as we fight this war, we may have to deploy our troops elsewhere to contain and battle threats against our nation and freedoms.

This bill focuses on five objectives for our national defense.

First, it improves the compensation and quality of life for our soldiers, retirees and their families. For the fourth year in a row this bill includes a 4.1 percent across the board pay raise for all military personnel, with a targeted pay raise between 5.5 and 6.5 percent for mid-career personnel. A new assignment incentive pay of up to $1,500 per month is authorized to encourage personnel to volunteer for hard-to-fill positions and assignments.

The bill rewards our retirees and disabled veterans. The bill authorizes concurrent receipt of retired military pay and veterans' disability compensation for all disabled military retirees eligible for non-disability retirement.

For our troops with families, this bill increases the housing allowance, with the goal of eliminating average out-of-pocket housing expenses by 2005. And on our installations, $640 million is being added above the budget request to improve and replace facilities. This will help improve the housing, dining and recreation facilities for our trainees and troops.

These quality of life issues boost the morale of our troops, and send a strong signal that we in Congress and across the nation appreciate their defense of America and her freedoms.

Secondly, this bill also contains those necessary readiness funds to allow the services to conduct the full range of their assigned missions. We have added $126 million for firing range enhancements so that we can properly and effectively train our troops to fight and win.

And to show that defense is a top priority for our nation, this bill authorizes the administration's $10 billion request to cover the operating costs of the ongoing war on terrorism for next year. After speaking with various military leaders and hearing their testimony before the Senate Armed Services Committee, we heard how important the issue of readiness is for every branch of the military today. This bill addresses this important issue by funding the most pressing shortfalls.

Third, in this bill we also address the goal of improving efficiency and increasing savings with DOD programs and operations. These savings will allow us to redirect and focus on high-priority programs within the DOD.

Some of these provisions include $400 million in anticipated savings by deferring spending on financial systems that would not be consistent with those financial management systems available and used by non-government entities. Soon we will have a system to better keep track of valuable DOD and service funds. This brings not only savings, but accountability to the DOD and the services. Although the DOD's mission is more unique than any other federal department, it is not immune to wasteful and duplicative spending which we often see in other federal departments.

Furthermore, this bill holds a provision requiring the DOD to establish new internal controls to address repeat problems with the abuse of credit cards we have seen for the purchase of non-essential and questionable travel spending by military and civilian personnel. And with the $393.4 billion we are authorizing in this bill, it is imperative now more than ever that we have a real sense of accountability for oversight reasons and for the sake of making sure we are giving the taxpayers the biggest bang for the buck. After all, this bill spends more than $1 billion a day on national defense activities. For that price, the taxpayers should get their money's worth.

Fourth, this bill also helps our military meet more non-traditional threats. We increased funding for fighting these threats to help secure our nuclear weapons and materials at Department of Energy facilities, and defend against chemical and biological weapons and other weapons of mass destruction.

Finally, our Senate Armed Services Committee wanted to be sure that our military always stay on the cutting edge of new technologies and strategies to meet the threats of the 21st century. Promoting and embracing transformation of our forces is not easy. But it is essential. This bill helps us to promote a new mind set for the future. I know it is tough to wean ourselves off of some of the legacy systems and structures in place in our armed forces. And I know that some in our armed forces are skeptical about change. But we have to begin to think differently. The world is changing, and not necessarily for the better. Our military has to keep up with that change.

While I did vote for this bill in the Senate Armed Services Committee, I did not agree with the fact that it originally slashed missile defense spending by just over $800 million. This drastically altered President Bush's national security strategy and made our nation and allies more vulnerable to a possible missile attack.

But thankfully we found a way on the Senate floor during the bill's consideration to move just over $800 million back to President Bush's missile defense priorities to protect America. I was proud to cosponsor an amendment which fulfilled this obligation by using expected DOD inflationary savings and adjustments. This offset was responsible because it did not cut any other valuable DOD programs needed to strengthen our military. And I was pleased that this was a bipartisan effort by the Senate with the amendment's unanimous acceptance.

But, thankfully this amendment was accepted. Without it, this vital bill was jeopardized. After all, Secretary Rumsfeld, in a letter to the Senate Armed Services Committee wrote, "if the missile defense provisions in the Senate Armed Services Committee's version of the bill were to be adopted by Congress, I would recommend to the president that he veto the Fiscal Year 2003 National Defense Authorization Act." So, its inclusion helped pave the way to an optimistic path to President Bush's desk.

Finally, we have had a very intense debate about the Crusader Artillery System. I would like to note that while I supported the compromise Levin amendment last week over the Crusader program, I remain concerned about our ability to effectively support our troops with adequate fire support. Right now we are vastly under-gunned in artillery by some nations. Our own artillery systems could not even meet our needs during the Gulf war more than a decade ago. And those systems have not significantly changed since then.

The possibility of shifting funds from Crusader to other indirect fire weapons concerns me in that we are again delaying when we will actually deploy sufficient fire support to protect our armed forces. The DOD hopes to speed up the deployment of these new technologies so they would be available around the same time Crusader will be. I am concerned about our ability to meet this time line.

Throwing money at a program does not necessarily mean you can magically speed up its development. Some things just take time, and Crusader is a lot farther along in the development process than many of these other technologies. I will be watching this process closely to ensure that effective indirect fire support capability reaches our troops quickly.

Overall, this is a solid bill. The sooner we get this bill to President Bush, then the better chance we have at providing our military with the essential training and strength resources to fight terrorism or anything else that seeks to destroy America, our people and our freedoms.

The Congressional Record. June 27, 2002: S6203–S6225.

SELECTED READING

Taxation Policy

"A Tax System That Gives to the Rich and Takes From the Poor." People for the American Way. 2006. www.pfaw.org/pfaw/general/default.aspx?oid=15554.

Burns, Scott. "Some Call Flat Tax Unfair." *Dallas Morning News.* October 20, 2006. www.dallasnews.com/sharedcontent/dws/bus/scottburns/columns/2006/stories/101906dnbusburnstoo.50f89926.html.

"Fact Sheets: Taxes." United States Treasury. 2006. www.ustreas.gov/education/fact-sheets/taxes/ustax.html.

"Testimony of Chairman Alan Greenspan: The Tax System." March 3, 2005. www.federalreserve.gov/BOARDDOCS/TESTIMONY/2005/20050303/default.htm.

"The Case for Flat Taxes." *The Economist.* April 14, 2005. www.economist.com/displaystory.cfm?story_id=3860731.

Taxation Impact on Income Distribution

Bush, George W. "President's Agenda for Tax Relief." The White House. www.whitehouse.gov/news/reports/taxplan.html.

Folsom, Burton W. "What's Wrong with the Progressive Income Tax?" Mackinac Center for Public Policy. May 3, 1999. www.educationreport.org/article.aspx?ID=1706.

"SOI Tax Stats—Individual Income Tax Rates and Tax Shares." Internal Revenue Service. 2006. www.irs.gov/taxstats/indtaxstats/article/0,,id=129270,00.html.

Zodrow, George R., and Peter Mieszkowski, eds. *United States Tax Reform in the 21st Century.* New York: Cambridge University Press, 2002.

Trickle-Down Economics

Blair, Jim. "Trickle-Down Economics and Ronald Reagan." 2006. users.ox.ac.uk/~mert2049/politics/blair-trickledownreagan.shtml.

Etebari, Mehrun. "Trickle-Down Economics: Four Reasons Why It Just Doesn't Work." United for a Fair Economy. July 17, 2003. www.faireconomy.org/research/TrickleDown.html.

Farah, Joseph. "The Real Trickle Down Economics." November 21, 2002. www.worldnetdaily.com/news/article.asp?ARTICLE_ID=29739.

Sowell, Thomas. "Trickle Down Ignorance." *Capitalism Magazine*. April 2, 2005. capmag
.com/articlePrint.asp?ID=4183.

Social Services Spending

De Rugy, Veronique. "'Conservative' Bush Spends More Than 'Liberal' Presidents Clin-
ton, Carter." CATO Institute. July 31, 2003. www.cato.org/dailys/07-31-03.html.
Kagan, Robert. "Don't Cut Defense." *The Weekly Standard*. 2006. Carnegie Endow-
ment for International Peace. www.ceip.org/people/kagstan4.htm.
Lakoff, George, Sam Ferguson, and Marc Ettlinger. "Bush Is Not Incompetent." *Rock-
ridge Institute*. 2006. www.rockridgeinstitute.org/research/lakoff/incompetent.
Riedl, Brian M. "Still Spending: Senate Set to Bust Budget Caps by $32 Billion." The
Heritage Foundation. September 25, 2006. www.heritage.org/Research/Budget/
wm1222.cfm.
Sinai, Ruthie. "Study: Rate of Government Spending on Social Services Continues to
Fall." October 30, 2006. www.haaretz.com/hasen/spages/781360.html.

Inflation Control

"Consumer Price Indexes." United States Department of Labor. 2006. www.bls.gov/
cpi.
Mishkin, Frederic S. *The Economics of Money, Banking, and Financial Markets*. New
York: HarperCollins, 1995.
Spencer, Roger W., and Denis S. Karnosky. "Curbing Price Expectations: The Key to
Inflation Control." 2006. research.stlouisfed.org/publications/review/72/05/
Curbing_May1972.pdf.
"United States Federal Reserve System." 2006. www.federalreserve.gov.
Vasudevan, Ramaa. "Inflation." *Dollars & Sense*. 2006. www.dollarsandsense.org/
archives/2006/0906drdollar.html.

Unemployment Insurance

"About Unemployment Insurance." Department of Labor. September 12, 2005.
www.workforcesecurity.doleta.gov/unemploy/aboutui.asp.
Atkinson, Robert D. "How to Modernize Unemployment Insurance." January 11, 2002.
www.ppionline.org/ppi_ci.cfm?knlgAreaID=107&subsecID=175&contentID=
250002.
Bousey, Heather. "Coming Up Short." 2006. www.epinet.org/content.cfm/issuebriefs_
ib169.
Kopecki, Dawn, and Roger Thompson. "Jobless Benefits Cost Firms More—
Unemployment Insurance Taxes." *Nation's Business*. August 1994. findarticles
.com/p/articles/mi_m1154/is_n8_v82/ai_15637942.
"Unemployment Insurance." *Economic Policy Institute*. 2006. www.epinet.org/content
.cfm/issueguides_unemployment_index.

Minimum Wage

Blake, Aaron. "Few GOP Hopefuls Commit to Raising Minimum Wage." *The Hill.* 2006. www.hillnews.com/thehill/export/TheHill/News/Campaign/072006.html.

Cauchon, Dennis. "States Say $5.15 an Hour Too Little." *USA Today.* May 30, 2005. www.usatoday.com/news/washington/2005-05-30-minimum-wage_x.htm.

Deere, Donald, Kevin M. Murphy, and Finis Welch. "Sense and Nonsense on the Minimum Wage." *The Cato Review of Business & Government.* 2006. www.cato.org/pubs/regulation/reg18n1c.html.

Saxton, James. "The Case against a Higher Minimum Wage." Joint Economic Committee Report. May 1996. www.house.gov/jec/cost-gov/regs/minimum/against/against.htm.

"Six States Consider Raising Minimum Wage." *Washington Post.* October 2, 2006. www.washingtonpost.com/wp-dyn/content/video/2006/09/29/VI2006092900773.html.

Defense Spending

"Department of Defense." Office of Management and Budget. 2006. www.whitehouse.gov/omb/budget/fy2005/defense.html.

De Rugy, Veronique. "Bush the Budget Buster: When It Comes to Spending, George W. Bush Is No Reagan." October 19, 2005. www.reason.com/news/show/34112.html.

"Implications of Additional Reductions in Defense Spending." October 1991. www.cbo.gov/showdoc.cfm?index=6281&sequence=0.

Rosenberg, Eric. "Bush Pushes to Increase Defense Spending." *San Francisco Chronicle.* February 12, 2006. www.sfgate.com/cgi-bin/article.cgi?f=/c/a/2006/02/12/MNG41H78RK1.DTL.

Spring, Baker. "Defense Spending." The Heritage Foundation. 2006. www.heritage.org/Research/features/issues/issuearea/Defense.cfm.

3

Health

Health policy is one of the most debated areas of government policy in state and federal government today. From a practical standpoint, this is explained by the nature of health policy, in that virtually every person is affected by this policy and its subsequent changes. The way that people are affected varies depending on the stance legislators take on health policy and the myriad issues this genre encompasses. As such, it is informative to analyze the views of both liberals and conservatives in reference to health policy in current times.

Before analyzing specific issues, it is vital to remember that views on these issues do not directly correspond to a complete conservative or liberal stance on health policy in general. With health policy, specific cases of interest dictate that rational stances for either side may give way to more emotionally based interests within the conservative or liberal ranks. Keeping this in mind, the following issues will be examined: national health insurance, individual savings accounts, HIV prevention, stem cell research, abortion/the morning-after pill, and the Terri Schiavo case, in reference to the greater issue of euthanasia.

NATIONAL HEALTH INSURANCE

The issue of national health insurance illustrates the significant differences between classic liberal and conservative stances. A national health insurance policy may come in various forms, including (1) partial coverage for major operations, with optional/superfluous procedures left to the patient; (2) complete coverage for all major or minor operations; or (3) a combination of the above.

Typically, a classic liberal position would argue in favor of any of the three options, while conservatives have been known for advocating private insurance options. This stance is partially due to two major factors: fiscal management and/or favoring privatization as a more efficient alternative to publicly funded health insurance.

This stance by conservatives against publicly funded health insurance has been slightly eroded over time, given the difficulties of individuals and small businesses in meeting premiums for insurance coverage. As such, many conservatives are starting to become more interested in at least partial coverage for major operations in the case of individuals or small businesses in dire financial straits. This change also comes as conservatives within the United States are noticing policies in the European Union (EU) that show promise. In the EU options for health coverage are possible along with aggressive job training programs to enable people to return to the workforce more quickly.

However, before judging this situation, it is informative to know other alternatives that are present. One example is the option of government support for specialized insurance plans from private firms at discount rates for needy families and small businesses. This is not the only alternative option, but it does illustrate a union of both liberal and conservative ideals, as a kind of universal health insurance can be offered, while potentially maintaining the private sector affiliation preferred by most conservatives.

INDIVIDUAL SAVINGS ACCOUNTS

This issue already combines certain stances by conservatives and liberals, embracing both government protection of individuals and potential private sector benefits for people investing in this program. Under a basic interpretation of this issue, an individual is allowed to invest a set amount per year in a private fund protected by the government from both capital gains taxes and income taxes on money paid into these accounts. Depending on the account or the nation implementing this system, these accounts can be managed by public officials or by the private sector with varying amounts of government oversight. These accounts function similarly to typical Social Security accounts, except the money invested is substantially larger, under more control by investors, and can potentially be used by private companies, rather than publicly accountable officials and bureaucrats.

A liberal stance envisions this issue as having potential, but serious possible flaws. While the potential profits of this savings plan appear promising to citizens, malfeasance by investing firms is also possible. Therefore, a classic liberal stance takes issue with a government-protected account (no taxes, etc.) under the direction of private sector firms, without adequate government oversight. It is necessary, then, for bipartisan support for this issue, that sufficient government oversight be utilized in this program. This concern for potential private sector illegalities demonstrates a deeper conflict between conservatives and liberals, that is, the reservations on the part of liberals toward private sector involvement in public sector arenas.

Conservatives, on the other hand, have high hopes for this issue, but reservations about too much public control over these accounts. In an almost diametrically opposed setting, conservatives have voiced reservations about the potential for public sector meddling in private sector affairs, to the detriment of people who have invested in these accounts.

HIV PREVENTION

HIV prevention is an area of health policy where the standpoints of both liberals and conservatives are largely consistent. Both groups view HIV and AIDS as serious problems, and both have pledged to work to stop the spread of HIV/AIDS. However, the methods by which they are attempting to fight HIV are significantly different.

First, the issue of funding comes into play. While liberals have advocated government funding to various "trouble spots" around the world for HIV education and preventive measures, conservatives have expressed concern about this practice. This concern is derived from various sources, primarily the fact that many of the nations most affected by HIV also have serious charges of corruption against their governments. This corruption has led to concerns that funding for HIV awareness could be instead funneled away to private bank accounts for the corrupt leadership of these nations.

Second, the question of "to whom does funding go" is also important. In this area of concern, a separation is typically made between public policy funding on the part of HIV-affected nations and funding to private sector companies working on a preventive HIV vaccine. Conservatives have been typically more in favor of funding toward a cure, as opposed to only funding social measures. However, in this context, it is important to recognize President Bush's recent advocacy of increased funding to African nations affected by HIV/AIDS as a continuing effort to support both measures of HIV control and prevention.

An important aspect of this issue relates to the methods by which HIV prevention is advocated. A classic cause of concern in this case is the advocacy by liberal groups of sex education—specifically, the advocacy of safe-sex methods: condoms and the like. Many conservatives have traditionally viewed this option as encouraging a culture of sex that could potentially spread HIV even more. In addition, significant concerns have been raised by various religious groups as to the morality of encouraging sexual relations, which is anathema to many religious interpretations of various canonical texts (the Bible, the Koran, etc.). This concern is partly based on the economic conditions favoring increased sex in a society that would face a lower possibility of STD transfer due to increased usage of safe-sex items (contraceptives, such as condoms).

STEM CELL RESEARCH

Stem cell research has garnered support recently from various individuals on both the liberal and conservative sides of the political spectrum. Stem cells are cells found in both human embryos and adults, in various places, which can be used in areas composed of dead/dying cells in the human body. When applied to these areas, stem cells take on the characteristics of the dead/damaged cells, providing a return to normalcy for patients of stem cell therapy. Where significant disagreement occurs is primarily in the area of harvesting stem cells and the rights of embryos used in these harvesting procedures. On this specific point, liberals and conservatives have expressed very different opinions.

A liberal perspective views this issue as a pressing need to develop stem cell research, especially on the embryonic level, to develop potential curative therapies for various diseases. While the use of embryonic tissue is unfortunate, it is for the greater good of humanity to reduce or eliminate major diseases that stem cell therapy has been shown to be effective against. As such, liberal groups have actively lobbied for increased federal funding and endorsement of the study of all possible stem cell lines of research, which would allow increased use of embryonic stem cells.

The conservative perspective typically finds fault with the views expressed above. First, concern is noted toward the endorsement of embryonic stem cell use, as the human embryos used are potentially available for artificial insemination and a new life. The use of human embryos in this research is seen as ultimately destructive toward society, as potential productive members of human society are used up to attempt development of possible cures for diseases.

In addition, concerns about eugenics have been made. The eugenics issue is based on the late-nineteenth- to mid-twentieth-century belief that human life could be manipulated and ordered to the betterment of mankind. This belief led to many instances of inhuman research on people to develop treatments and cures for other people. This system culminated in the Holocaust of World War II, as researchers (including Dr. Joseph Mengele—the Auschwitz Angel of Death) treated concentration-camp inmates as guinea pigs for their ghastly experiments. While very few people see a return to this extreme, the use of stem cells is a step on a possible slippery slope leading to people picking and choosing what traits they wish to keep in their children, and what traits they want to change (blue eyes instead of green eyes, blond hair instead of red hair).

A final concern that has been raised by some on both sides of the issue of stem cell research is the near silence in the argument for usage of adult stem cells. These cells are cultured from the menstrual fluids of women, among other sources. In addition, adult stem cells have been used to beneficial effect in a number of tests and trials so far. While the possibilities may be increased for the usefulness of embryonic stem cell research, the current effectiveness of adult stem cell use is very promising.

ABORTION AND THE MORNING-AFTER PILL

The debate over the morning-after pill and abortion in general is a defining debate between conservatives and liberals in our modern age. This debate places individual rights against the (potential) rights of the unborn. At the heart of this debate between liberals and conservatives is the support for the rights of mothers versus the perceived rights of their unborn children.

A conservative perspective places this issue as an attack on the rights of unborn American citizens. The current policy of open abortion with limits on the abortive period available to pregnant mothers is seen as a cavalier treatment of human life that totally abridges the rights of future citizens. While the child/fetus is in the mother's body, the child itself has significant rights that must be defended.

The liberal perspective, on the other hand, views the mother's rights as sacrosanct. In this argument, there is no reason to call the fetus a baby, as it has not been born yet. This issue is seen as politicized by conservatives who invoke emotional wording in support of an issue that is seen as potentially encroaching on the individual rights of American citizens.

The morning-after pill is another debate within the issue of individual reproductive rights. At the heart of the issue is the debate over the rights of a potential child/fetus at conception over the rights of the potential mother. A typical conservative concern in this issue is that the usage of this pill will lead to an increase in the sexual activity of individuals, broadening the possibility of increased STD transference and more potential abortions if the pill does not work, or is not taken regularly.

THE TERRI SCHIAVO CASE

This debate centers on the rights of individuals to "die with dignity" at the time of their choosing (typically, but not encompassing the liberal/libertarian perspective) and the obligations of doctors to preserve and sustain the lives of their patients (again, typically, but not encompassing the conservative perspective). This debate places liberals in the perspective of encouraging the rights of individuals to control their own life and their ability to live it or end it as they choose. In contrast to this, conservatives view this as an affront to the responsibility of doctors to sustain the lives of patients under their watch. In addition, conservatives (typically religious) have argued that the possibility of a miraculous recovery always exists, so that individuals choosing to take their own lives, with or without the assistance of certain doctors such as the infamous Dr. Kevorkian, is not only wrong by laws against suicide, but also an affront to God who is viewed as the decider of the extent of people's lives.

This issue has seen new light due to the recent Terri Schiavo case, in which her husband sought to take her off life support during her vegetative state while her parents sought to keep her on life support. This is a curious example as her state was such that if she regained consciousness, she would still be unable to perform most basic tasks of movement and even speech. Therefore, it brings up the question of whether it is right to have the option to end one's life if it is very likely to be not at all productive. There is no easy answer to this question, which has been brought up in Europe and will likely resurface in America in the coming years.

CONCLUSIONS

Health policy continues to be one of the most disputed policy realms in politics today, with conservatives and liberals taking significant stances in opposition to each other on a variety of issues. While conservatives have typically taken a promarket individual approach to problems, seeking to curtail government involvement, liberals have been much more inclusive and open to government interaction in this area, viewing government as having the obligation to offer vital health coverage to people unable to afford it any other way. Significant research has been done and continues to be done in limiting and eliminating the effects of diseases, but issues of funding and morality must be decided before a coordinated health policy can be implemented. The coming years will see debate and hopefully conclusions about various stances as liberals and conservatives seek to implement their separate ideas for the betterment of the population at large.

NATIONAL HEALTH INSURANCE

The idea of universal health care has been strongly debated in the United States. According to the U.S. Census Bureau, the number of uninsured people in the United States is 45 million people, or 15.6 percent. The number is continuously on the rise as many employers are eliminating health insurance due to high costs. The United States continues to be the sole developed country without a universal health care policy.

Supporters of universal health care argue that everyone should be entitled to receive health care benefits regardless of their health status. By allowing everyone to be covered, the whole nation would benefit. Since many people in the United States are uninsured and often wait to use the health care system until it is too late, they drive up the costs of care. By allowing everyone to be insured, the profit-driven medical field would be more efficient and the health care professionals could concentrate on curing patients instead of their administrative tasks.

Those who oppose universal health care argue that the government is overstepping its boundaries. Not only would universal health care increase waiting times but it would also decrease the quality of care. Critics often cite the example of Canada, where the patients often wait months for necessary treatment. Furthermore, universal health care would increase taxes, which would most likely cut spending in other important areas of the government. Finally, critics of universal health care are often worried that health care professionals would leave their profession due to their dramatically decreased salary.

Conservative Viewpoint

President George W. Bush. Fortunately, the positive news is that we've got the best health care system in the world. And we need to keep it that way. We need to keep it that way by keeping the private market strong, by resisting efforts that are happening in Washington, D.C., to say the federal government should be running health care. See, we don't believe that. I don't believe it. I believe the best health care system is that health care system generated in the private markets.

And the best way to keep the private markets strong is to make sure we've got the best research and development, is to make sure the doctor–patient relationship is strong, is to empower consumers to make more choices, is to give them more opportunities to make choices in the private sector.

We're making progress in terms of the modernization of the health care system, starting with the Medicare bill that was passed. The Medicare bill said we have an obligation to our seniors in our country, and we need to fulfill that obligation. And for the first time since Medicare was founded, I had the honor of signing a bill that modernizes the system, which essentially says there needs to be prescription drug coverage for seniors; there needs to be preventive care available for seniors; and seniors need to be given options to choose from, to tailor a program that best meets their needs. The Medicare bill is a vital part of a vibrant health care system. I was proud to sign it, and any attempt by Congress to weaken it will meet my veto.

One of the ways to help make sure health care functions better is to help people who can't afford health care to have access to health care, access other than emergency rooms and hospitals. And so I'm a big proponent of what's called community health centers that operate primary care services in rural and underserved urban areas. When I showed up here in Washington, there was about three thousand of them. I vowed that we would expand and/or open twelve hundred more. We've done six hundred—we've met six hundred—we've fulfilled half our obligation, as far as I'm concerned. And in the budget I'm submitting, we will finish the additional six hundred in years 2005 and 2006. This is a smart way to make sure that people get health care. It's more cost-effective that people are able to go to these centers and not go to an emergency room, which is by far the most expensive way for somebody to get health care.

Congress needs to pass refundable tax credits to help the working uninsured. It's an approach that says we trust low-income Americans to be able to make the rational decision for their health care.

Another thing we need to do here in Washington is to promote the—make sure health care technology is widespread, that the—even though medicine is modern in the sense that we're making great new discoveries, it's kind of ancient when you think about how the records are kept. When you're still writing records down by hand and sharing information through files, it's not exactly a modern system. And we believe a lot of medical errors can be saved as a result of the use of proper technology, and there will be cost savings to be had as well.

Another way to save costs, to stop the rise of the cost of health care, is there for to be rational laws in dealing with doctors. Our legal system is out of control right now. There's just too much litigation. There are frivolous and junk lawsuits all over the country. It's like there's a giant lottery, and the lawyers are the only winners. And we're driving good docs out of business. Make no mistake about it, a lot of good docs are stopping to practice medicine because their premiums are going up because of the junk and frivolous lawsuits. And so these lawsuits, which are—people will settle just to get them out of the way—raises costs. Doctors, for fear of being sued, practice what's called defensive medicine. That raises the cost. As a matter of fact, the cost of premium increases and the cost of defensive medicine—in other words, prescribing too much to cover yourself so if you get sued, you can say, "Well, wait a minute. I did everything I could"—costs the federal government about $28 billion a year. Think about that—$28 billion. That means it's costly to the taxpayer.

I view this as a national issue that requires a national solution. And so I proposed medical liability reform. The House passed a good bill that recognizes that if—by the way, if you get hurt, you ought to recover full economic damages. In other words, if a bad doc practices bad medicine, there ought to be a consequence. But there ought to be a cap on non-economic damages.

. . .

The Medicare bill I signed in December created an additional tool that will help workers lower their health care costs, and they're called health savings accounts. They became available on January 1st. Health savings accounts address a growing need in our health care system. These accounts will help working Americans afford health insurance that is growing out of their reach. They will help restrain the health care costs that are affecting us all.

Right now, many insurance plans will cover virtually all of your health care costs in exchange for a high premium payment, which is paid by employers and their employees in various percentages, in different percentages. Under America's system of private medical care, families will continue to have this option, of course. We just want to provide additional options for families from which to choose, and the health savings account is one such option.

Under the system that currently exists, consumers really don't know how far their health care dollars are going. You pay the premium, and then you just show up and collect the benefits. You have no idea what you're spending money on. They pay a flat rate for insurance, but they really don't know the true costs of medical services they receive. There's no demand for better prices. There's no selectivity in the marketplace. There's no pressure on the price structure of health care.

. . .

And we need a consumer-driven health care system, and we need better information about health care prices. And a consumer-driven health care system with better information will help control the cost of health care. That's the rationale of the health savings accounts.

The best way to empower citizens is to let them save and spend their health care dollars as they see fit—in other words, start to empower people to make the right decisions with their health care dollars; give them control over routine costs so that people see the doctor when they need to, spend their dollars wisely, and still be able to have coverage for major medical bills.

. . .

Imagine the combination of health savings accounts and association health care plans together. I mean, you're talking about providing interesting opportunity for the small-business sector in America. And remember, we're interested in job creation, and we need to make sure the small-business sector is as strong as possible. Tax relief is one way to invigorate the small-business sector. Congress needs to make all that tax relief permanent, by the way. And another way is to address the high cost of health care by rational policy. And today I described a series of steps of rational policy. The Congress must act on it. If they're truly interested in health care costs in America, I've just laid out a way, a strategy for them to address the costs, address the costs in a way that does not undermine the private sector, undermine that part of our health care philosophy that has made us the greatest in the world.

We don't want the federal government running health care. We don't want the federal government making decisions. Private medicine needs to be invigorated and strengthened, and the way to do that is give people more options, empower consumers, protect the doctor-patient relationship, and allow small businesses to pool their risk so they can provide good insurance for their employees.

. . .

Public Papers of the President: George W. Bush. January 28, 2004: 152–157.

Liberal Viewpoint

Edolphus Towns (D-NY). Mr. Speaker, over $1.6 trillion is spent on health care annually in the U.S., which is over 13 percent of the GDP. According to the National Coalition on Health Care, U.S. health care spending increased to $1.7 trillion in 2003 and was projected to reach $1.8 trillion in 2004. Furthermore, our country spent 15.3 percent of the GDP on health care in 2003 and a projected increase of 18.7 percent is expected within the next 10 years.

Even though the U.S. spends more on health care than any other industrialized nation, and those countries provide universal health coverage to all of their citizens, approximately 45 million Americans are uninsured. Nevertheless, the U.S. remains the only industrialized nation that does not guarantee health care for all of its citizens.

Clearly, universal health care is needed for all American citizens and a universal health care plan is certainly in the best economic interest of our country.

When one considers that health care spending accounted for only 9.7 percent of the GDP in our sister nation Canada, it becomes apparent that we are not best managing our resources and serving the interest of our nation as a whole.

As members of Congress we are entrusted with the responsibility of protecting and advancing the nation's health. It is a given that health care costs are rising for all American citizens. Let us not deceive ourselves. We are all interconnected as human beings and the health status of one impacts the health status of all regardless of one's ability to pay for health services or not.

Disease, especially communicable and infectious, has no boundaries. The current health disparities and unnecessary suffering experienced by vulnerable populations such as the poor, elderly, uninsured, women and children and racial and ethnic minorities is outright immoral. It is a national disgrace and international embarrassment that America, a country with astounding wealth and means, chooses not to provide universal health care to her citizens while her sister country Canada does so for her citizens, as does the country of Cuba whose wealth is not even comparable to that of the U.S. and other industrialized nations.

I urge Congress today to fully assume its responsibility as the defender of our nation's health, and exercise its political will and sincerely work towards the implementation of a universal health care system and guarantee universal health care as a right for all American citizens.

The Congressional Record. October 20, 2005: E2136.

INDIVIDUAL SAVINGS ACCOUNTS

In his 2005 State of the Union address, President George W. Bush highlighted the intricate situation of Social Security. His solution to the ever-growing problem lay in privatization, more specifically individual savings accounts. President Bush argued that individual choice would allow for greater return of savings as people would have the option of investing part of their Social Security benefits in the private sector, which includes mutual funds and bonds.

President George W. Bush and Sen. Rick Santorum (R-PA) look toward individual savings accounts to fix Social Security. Sen. Santorum argues that the problem of Social Security lies in the demographics. As more people are living longer, Social Security is unable to keep up with the aging population. Since the birthrate has declined in the United States within the past decades, there are fewer workers in the workforce that contribute to the Social Security's pay-as-you-go system. Both President Bush and Sen. Santorum argue that individual savings accounts will increase the return of benefits.

Democrats such as Sen. Richard J. Durbin (D-IL) strongly oppose President Bush's plan of individual savings accounts. Sen. Durbin argues that privatization will not strengthen Social Security but it will weaken it. By privatizing Social Security, the program will go bankrupt even faster than originally expected. In addition, the individual savings accounts will cut benefits for those involved in Social Security and the savings accounts will contribute to the rise of the national deficit. Moreover, many Democrats have criticized the Bush administration for their focus on tax cuts instead of improving Social Security. Democrats claim that the proposed tax cuts will only benefit the wealthy class and they will not save Social Security.

Conservative Viewpoint

Richard J. Santorum (R-PA). The problem with Social Security is it is driven by demographics. Social Security is a pay-as-you-go system. That means the people working pay into the system for those who are retired. The system worked well when you had a lot of people working and only a few people retiring. But that has fundamentally changed over the years. As a result of that change, what you see in the red line is a dramatic increase in taxes—from 2 percent, which is what the tax was on Social Security in 1936, now up to 12.4 percent. It was 2 percent on the first $3,000 you made. That is the green bar. Now it is up to 12.4 percent of the first $90,000 you make. If you are working in the system now, that is when you start, high based; in other words, almost every dollar most people make is going be taxed at a very high rate.

This is a big tax burden on future generations of America as we stand to-day. But this tax right now doesn't pay for the benefits that are going to be provided for future generations. Why? Demographics are changing.

The first thing to happen is the fact that we are not having as many children. There are some exceptions to that. But we are not having as many children as we had in previous years. You see the baby boom generation, 6.3 children of women of childbearing age. We are now going to be below a sustainable birth rate. But for immigration, we would be losing population in America.

We see a gradual decline in the number of workers going into the system. That is number one. Number two, we have a problem—a good problem. People are living longer. Life expectancy at the time Social Security started was age sixty-one. Truly, at the time, Social Security was an old-age program. What does that mean? It was for people who could no longer work. People didn't live to age sixty-five back in 1936. Now we are seeing seniors living to age seventy-seven, and increasing one month every two years. What we are going to be asking future generations of Americans to do—these workers, fewer of them—is to support seniors up to almost one-third of their lifespan in "retirement" on Social Security.

People are living longer, fewer people paying benefits, and the final big blow to the demographic perfect storm is the number of people turning sixty-five.

If you look back over the last forty years, back and beyond 1982, the average number of people turning sixty-five in America was two million. When boomers start to retire, as you can see in the year 2011, the average going out over the next forty years is going to be four million people. We are going to double the number of people retiring, and they are going to be living longer, and fewer people are coming into the workplace to pay for those benefits. As a result of this combination of three factors, we see this very important distinction. This is what is driving the personal accounts. That is what is driving the need for changes in the Social Security system. It worked fine when you had a lot of people paying 42 to 1.

Now we have a system where almost one person is paying for one person in retirement; it is two to one. Franklin Roosevelt would never design a system where workers were paying for retirees if you only had two workers paying for one retiree. No one designing a system today would design a system with demographics looking like this. In a sense you are almost paying for one person's retirement.

If you do that, anyway, why not have a personal account? Why not have the money paid to you and accrue that money over time, earn interest, have the miracle of compound interest being used to benefit from the taxes you are paying, instead of simply paying it to someone who is getting a transfer payment from you as you work today.

Franklin Roosevelt was right; members never thought a Republican would say that. He was right to design a system such as this because it made sense. There was a very small burden on taxpayers. But we have changed. America has changed. And as a result of that change we need to look at the system differently.

Here is what happens now because of this demographic. Huge deficits in the future. Why? Fewer people paying and more people retired live longer. We have a short window of ten or twelve years when we are paying more into the system than we need to pay benefits.

Why don't we lockbox that? How do you lockbox it? You can't lockbox it. Every senator I have ever talked to says the money goes to pay for other government programs. The answer is right. How do we lockbox it? Put it into personal savings accounts for their benefits in later years. That is how you lockbox Social Security today. That surplus that is there right now, put it into personal accounts. If we don't do that, we will have a cash flow problem in our ability to pay benefits. We cannot pay benefits with IOUs. The president showed that today in Parkersburg, West Virginia. You have to pay benefits with cash. That is the cash deficits we will be running in the Social Security program alone: $63 billion in ten years, $250 billion cashflow. What does that mean? Someone will have to pay more in taxes in ten or fifteen years, someone will get less benefits, or we will have huge borrowing to pay current benefits—not doing anything about saving money, not doing anything about having a better benefit, just to pay the current benefits being promised and that we cannot deliver on.

The Congressional Record. April 5, 2005: S3227–S3235.

Liberal Viewpoint

Richard J. Durbin (D-IL). The first question the American people ought to ask is a very basic question: Congress, if you did nothing, if you didn't change one word in the Social Security law, how long would the Social Security system make payments to every retiree with a cost-of-living adjustment every single year? To listen to my colleague from Pennsylvania, it sounds as though doomsday for Social Security is right around the corner. But the professionals tell us it is thirty-five to forty-five years away; thirty-five to forty-five years if we do nothing.

President Bush and Senator Santorum and others have said, but what about beyond that date? That is a legitimate challenge to all of us. When I came to Congress in 1983, I faced that challenge on a bipartisan basis. We met that challenge. We extended the life of Social Security for fifty-nine years with commonsense changes. That is what we should do again.

Yet the president comes to us and proposes privatization. Now I have said it. I said the word which drives the Republicans into a rage. They don't want to use "privatization." It is as Senator Bumpers said, they hate privatization like the devil hates holy water. But the fact is when the Cato Institute dreamed up this scheme, that is exactly what they called it.

So now the Republicans have a softer side of privatization; they call it personal accounts. But it comes down to the same thing. If you are going to take money out of the Social Security trust fund to invest it in the stock market, the first and obvious question you have to ask is, does this strengthen Social Security? The president has already answered that question: It doesn't. It weakens Social Security. It means the Social Security trust fund will run out of money sooner. That is obvious. You are taking money out of the trust fund.

What else does it do? It forces you to cut benefits for Social Security retirees. There is less money in the trust fund. You cannot pay out as much in a pay-as-you-go system. That is fairly obvious.

How would they achieve that? The White House memo that was released said they would move to this new price index. Wage index to price index does not mean much to the average person until you sit down and ask, what does that mean in realistic terms? So we ask, what does that mean for today's retirees? What if we had dealt with a price index instead of a wage index?

· · ·

So there we have the perfect storm. All three have come together: A privatization plan that doesn't strengthen Social Security but weakens it; a privatization plan that is going to cut benefits dramatically in the out years; and a privatization plan that is going to create a deficit of $2 trillion to $5 trillion.

If we moved to the president's plan immediately, the Social Security system would go bankrupt even sooner, be insolvent even sooner. How can that be the right approach?

Now, let's get down to the politics of this situation. This is all about choices. We have made some choices. We had a vote as to whether we were going to cut taxes in America or save Social Security. Look at these Bush tax cut votes where we asked our Republican friends who wanted to join us in saving Social Security, are you willing to sacrifice a penny in tax cuts to make Social Security stronger. Time after time after time, to amendments offered by Senator Byrd, Senator Harkin, Senator Conrad, Senator Reid, Senator Hollings, they have said no, we would prefer tax cuts even for the wealthiest people in this country rather than to strengthen the Social Security trust fund. The reason the Social Security trust fund may be in peril in the out-years is we have taken so much out of it to finance tax cuts.

I have a chart which shows what the tax cuts mean, the Social Security shortfall and the cost of other administration politics over the next seventy-five years. The Social Security shortfall is about the same as the president's tax cuts for the top 1 percent of Americans. If we took the money we are giving in tax cuts to the wealthiest people in America and put it back into the Social Security system, we would not be having this debate. We would be talking about other issues that are equally if not more important.

The Congressional Record. April 5, 2005: S3227–S3235.

HIV PREVENTION

The needle exchange program is a controversial program that was started by President William J. Clinton. The needle exchange program was aimed to give hypodermic needles and syringes to people for little or no cost. The primary function of the needle exchange program was to ensure that blood-borne diseases are not spread through the sharing of dirty needles by drug users.

Many supporters, including Rep. Sheila Jackson-Lee (D-TX) argue that needle exchange programs are an effective way to reduce the usage of contaminated needles and in turn decrease the rates of HIV/AIDS and Hepatitis C. Reports show that at least a third of diagnosed HIV cases within the United States can be traced to unsafe needle sharing. HIV/AIDS infections from dirty needles are a nationwide problem. If the users had access to clean needles, it would decrease the chance of contracting HIV/AIDS and more importantly, the chance of spreading it.

Opposition to the needle exchange program is immense. Rep. James A. Gibbons (R-NV) argues that the needle exchange programs give drug users free access to needles. As a result, the "War on Drugs" weakens. Instead of preaching education and solvency for HIV/AIDS and the war on drugs, the opposition argues that this program is a federal way of increasing the drug problem in the United States. The program was introduced during the Clinton Administration but due to the massive public outrage was shortly dismantled.

Conservative Viewpoint

James A. Gibbons (R-NV). Mr. Speaker, the scourge of illegal drug use in this country has reached epidemic proportions. Countless hours and lives have been lost fighting to free our communities from the grasp of these drugs.

Given the severity of the situation, how does the Clinton Administration plan to continue the fight? They want to give out free needles to drug addicts.

Shoot me up, Mr. Speaker. What next? Free drugs?

This cannot be his brilliant battle plan to win the war on drugs. If it is, Mr. Speaker, I shudder to think of the president's plan for the rest of society's ills. Are we going to give out free pornography to sex offenders? Heaven forbid the United States should in any way inconvenience those who are breaking the law.

It is discouraging to see the White House embrace such a defeatist policy. It goes against the values upon which this great country was founded.

I urge my colleagues to join me in opposing this free needle policy.

The Congressional Record. April 29, 1998: H2442.

Liberal Viewpoint

Sheila Jackson-Lee (D-TX). Mr. Speaker, I hope this morning we can start afresh and not play politics with illegal drug use. My Republican friends know full well that both Democrats and Republicans have been strong against the illegal use of drugs. We understand that along with talking about being against illegal use of drugs comes prevention and intervention.

The needle exchange program has nothing to do with supporting the illegal use of drugs. It is plain common sense, folks. People who use drugs are addicted, they are sick, they need intervention, they need prevention, and they need treatment.

The use of clean needles saves lives, it prevents the spread of HIV, it keeps from killing our children, wives, husbands, family members, Americans, and we need to get off this politics on the illegal use of drugs and comparing that to clean needle exchange.

The Congressional Record. April 29, 1998: H2595.

STEM CELL RESEARCH

In September 2006, President George W. Bush used his first presidential veto since taking office to oppose stem cell research. President Bush heavily opposes any restriction on embryonic stem cell research due to moral and ethical reasons. The medical procedure is highly controversial because it involves the destruction of a human embryo for medical research. Furthermore, many studies have shown that the majority of American people strongly support using federal funds for stem cell research.

President Bush has made it clear that he opposes using any federal funds to aid the destruction of a human life. Despite possible medical breakthroughs, President Bush has labeled embryonic stem cell research as murder that he simply cannot condone. He argues that embryonic stem cell research will lead researchers on a very slippery slope that will include cloning. President Bush's policy is simply a continuation of his 2001 speech when he pledged to limit federal funding for embryonic stem cell research to the stem cell lines that had already been created by that time.

Many Democrats as well as Republicans strongly disagree with President Bush's policy on embryonic stem cell research. Supporters of stem cell research argue that it is necessary to continue if there is any hope of significant progress. Through stem cell research, cures for Parkinson's disease, Alzheimer's disease, and others may be possible. Many Democrats criticize President Bush for his restrictive policy and have lobbied hard to overturn the veto in both houses of Congress. Unfortunately, not enough support was gained to overturn the veto. Even though federal funding for stem cell research has been opposed, many states including California have passed state legislation allowing federal funds to be used.

Conservative Viewpoint

President George W. Bush. I am returning herewith without my approval H.R. 810, the "Stem Cell Research Enhancement Act of 2005."

Like all Americans, I believe our nation must vigorously pursue the tremendous possibilities that science offers to cure disease and improve the lives of millions. Yet, as science brings us ever closer to unlocking the secrets of human biology, it also offers temptations to manipulate human life and violate human dignity. Our conscience and history as a nation demand that we resist this temptation. With the right scientific techniques and the right policies, we can achieve scientific progress while living up to our ethical responsibilities.

In 2001, I set forth a new policy on stem cell research that struck a balance between the needs of science and the demands of conscience. When I took office, there was no federal funding for human embryonic stem cell research. Under the policy I announced five years ago, my Administration became the first to make federal funds available for this research, but only on embryonic stem cell lines derived from embryos that had already been destroyed. My Administration has made available more than $90 million for research of these lines. This policy has allowed important research to go forward and has allowed America to continue to lead the world in embryonic stem cell research without encouraging the further destruction of living human embryos.

H.R. 810 would overturn my Administration's balanced policy on embryonic stem cell research. If this bill were to become law, American taxpayers for the first time in our history would be compelled to fund the deliberate destruction of human embryos. Crossing this line would be a grave mistake and would needlessly encourage a conflict between science and ethics that can only do damage to both and harm our nation as a whole.

Advances in research show that stem cell science can progress in an ethical way. Since I announced my policy in 2001, my Administration has expanded funding of research into stem cells that can be drawn from children, adults, and the blood in umbilical cords with no harm to the donor, and these stem cells are currently being used in medical treatments. Science also offers the hope that we may one day enjoy the potential benefits of embryonic stem cells without destroying human life. Researchers are investigating new techniques that might allow doctors and scientists to produce stem cells just as versatile as those derived from human embryos without harming life. We must continue to explore these hopeful alternatives, so we can advance the cause of scientific research while staying true to the ideals of a decent and humane society.

I hold to the principle that we can harness the promise of technology without becoming slaves to technology and ensure that science serves the cause of humanity. If we are to find the right ways to advance ethical medical research, we must also be willing when necessary to reject the wrong ways. For that reason, I must veto this bill.

The Congressional Record. July 19, 2006: H5435–H5451.

Liberal Viewpoint

Diana DeGette (D-CO). Mr. Speaker, today the president of the United States has snuffed out the candle of hope for 110 million Americans who suffer from debilitating diseases like diabetes, Parkinson's, Alzheimer's, nerve damage and many, many more. He snuffed out this candle of hope because he used the first veto of his six-year Presidency to veto H.R. 810, the embryonic stem cell legislation.

Mr. Speaker, this is the president's first veto in over 1,100 bills. The president issued veto warnings in nearly 150 bills, but he signed all of those bills. The president has signed bills to increase the national debt. He has signed bills to increase tax cuts for wealthy corporations and oil companies. He signed hundreds of post office naming bills, but he decided he would veto this one bill. This is not some minor legislation. This is legislation that would foster the only research that has shown hope for millions of Americans. He said in his veto message that he was vetoing this legislation because "American taxpayers would be compelled to fund the deliberate destruction of human embryos." One might think that the president would read this bill, his first veto, before he said that, because if he had read that bill, he would know that H.R. 810 specifically does not allow federal funds to be used for the destruction of embryos. Rather, H.R. 810 says that federal dollars can be used for the research on embryonic stem cell lines which have already been created with private dollars.

This policy is the same as the policy President Bush looked at in 2001 when he issued an executive order restricting the number of stem cell lines used. What he said at that time was embryonic stem cell research was okay, but he limited it to embryonic stem cell lines in existence as of that day.

So I ask the president, why is it wrong to simply expend federal money for stem cell lines that have been created by private researchers since that date? It seems wrong, and it is certainly not what this bill is intended to do.

The president wants it both ways. He wants to say that he supports embryonic stem cell research, but he doesn't want to do it in a way that will actually effect cures.

Mr. Speaker, it seems to me that the president is confused about his role as chief executive of this country. We don't live in a theocracy. We live in a constitutional democracy in this country where we form a consensus about ethics and medical research. There is a widespread consensus. The public supports this almost three-quarters. Pro-life, pro-choice, Democrat, Republican, Independent, all of them share the same concern that we protect lives, but that we expand research in a way that will benefit millions and millions of Americans.

I urge this House to take this very seriously. Don't make a political vote. Think about the lives that could be saved. Think about what H.R. 810 actually does, and vote "yes" to override this veto.

The Congressional Record. July 19, 2006: H5435–H5451.

ABORTION AND THE MORNING-AFTER PILL

Abortion has been one of the most polarizing issues in the past forty years. Through the use of the media, pro-choice advocates and pro-life advocates have battled for supremacy. Though the debate has been over-simplified, it contains many loaded terms such as "pro-life" and "pro-choice." Within the abortion debate itself, there are other significant issues raised as well: when is the beginning of life, how is an embryo distinguished from a fetus, do the circumstances of conception matter, what are the viable alternatives to abortion, and many more. In 1973, in a landmark decision, *Roe v. Wade*, the Supreme Court overturned all state and federal laws dealing with abortion restrictions because the laws violated a woman's right to privacy.

President Bush and the "pro-life" advocates believe that human life begins at conception and therefore the embryo is immediately entitled to governmental protection. Furthermore, the pro-life advocates believe that the termination of a fetus at any stage is murder. In addition to pro-life beliefs, the advocates also emphasize strong family values and abstinence from premarital sex. As an alternative to abortion, the pro-life advocates promote adoption.

The "pro-choice" argument supported by Rep. Sheila Jackson-Lee (D-TX) argues that it is the woman's right to control her pregnancy. According to Rep. Jackson-Lee, government does not have the right to interfere in private matters. Furthermore, Rep. Jackson-Lee worries about the repercussions of banning abortion. The safety of the girl would be endangered as she would seek other far more dangerous ways to terminate her pregnancy.

The debate on abortion continues to rage despite the Supreme Court ruling. In February 2006, South Dakota became the first state to outlaw abortion within its borders.

Pro-Life Viewpoint

President George W. Bush. You believe, as I do, that every human life has value, that the strong have a duty to protect the weak, and that the self-evident truths of the Declaration of Independence apply to everyone, not just to those considered healthy or wanted or convenient. These principles call us to defend the sick and the dying, persons with disabilities and birth defects, all who are weak and vulnerable, especially unborn children.

We're making good progress in defending these principles . . . and . . . are working together, along with others, to build . . . a culture of life. One of my first acts as the president was to ban the use of taxpayer money on programs that promote abortion overseas. I want to thank you all for getting that ban on partial-birth abortion to my desk, a bill I was proud to sign and a law which we are going to defend—and are defending vigorously in our courts.

Because we acted, infants who are born despite an attempted abortion are now protected by law. Thanks to "Laci and Conner's Law," prosecutors can now charge those who harm or kill a pregnant woman with harming or killing her unborn child as well.

We're vigorously promoting parental notification laws, adoption, teen abstinence, crisis pregnancy programs, and the vital work of our faith-based groups. We're sending a clear message to any woman facing a crisis pregnancy: We love you; we love your child; and we're here to help you.

There's more work to be done. The House has passed a bill to ensure that state parental involvement laws are not circumvented by those who take minors across state lines to have abortions. And the United States Senate needs to pass this bill so I can sign it into law.

We also must respect human life and dignity when advancing medical science, and we're making progress here as well. Last month, I signed a pro-life bill supporting ethical treatment and research using stem cells from umbilical cord blood. I also renew my call for Congress to ban all forms of human cloning. Because human life is a gift from our Creator and should never be used as a means to an end, we will not sanction the creation of life only to destroy it.

By changing laws, we can change our culture. And your persistence and prayers . . . are making a real difference. We, of course, seek common ground where possible. We're working to persuade more of our fellow Americans of the rightness of our cause. And this is a cause that appeals to the conscience of our citizens and is rooted in America's deepest principles, and history tells us that with such a cause, we will prevail.

· · ·

Public Papers of the President: George W. Bush. January 23, 2006: 101.

Pro-Choice Viewpoint

Sheila Jackson-Lee (D-TX). Right now, there are a myriad of anti choice legal efforts designed to undermine the basic tenets of *Roe v. Wade*. Never in my time in Congress have I seen so much misleading legislation geared towards women, court cases that refuse to vindicate our right to privacy, and so many blatant anti choice judicial nominees.

Americans have the right to live their lives and make decisions that are the best for them and their children. We are falling down a slippery slope of having the government dictate our moral, ethical, and private decisions. There is a small, fundamentalist, religious group which is overexerting their influence on the way our government is being run, and we must immediately put a stop to it.

· · ·

I am proud to be at the forefront of this battle, and I want to share some of my insight and strategy aimed at protecting a woman's right to choose. I joined over a million people who believe that it is time to stand up for women's rights and demand a change in our administration on April 25, 2004 at the March for Women's Lives.

We marched because there is an attempt by our administration to undermine our fundamental rights. Women's health care includes reproductive services, access to contraception, and informed decisions made by individuals about their body, not their government.

My predecessor and longtime role model, Barbara Jordan, once said, "We want to be in control of our lives. Whether we are jungle fighters, craftsmen, company men, gamesmen, we want to be in control. And when the government erodes that control, we are not comfortable."

The government is trying to erode that control, and this is something we must come together to prevent.

Right now we have an Administration that actively seeks to undermine a woman's right to choose. They falsely claim to be doing this in the interest of women and children, citing both the mother and child's well being as justifications for their actions. This same Administration has frozen the Title X family-planning program in each budget for the last three years. They have also cut domestic-violence prevention programs and frozen important programs for women and children, including the Maternal and Child Health Block Grant, Head Start, and child-nutrition services.

By contrast, they have proposed more than doubling funding for unproven, dangerous "abstinence-only" programs that censor health information from young people—and instead of supporting programs that help women who face violence, they have resorted instead to exploiting the issue for an anti-abortion political base. President Bush signed the so-called "Unborn Victims of Violence Act" with a false claim of being in a woman's best interest. This legislation would, for the first time in federal law, recognize an embryo or fetus as a separate "person" with rights separate from, and equal to, a pregnant woman.

·   ·   ·

Raising awareness must be a high priority, younger and older generations in America must begin to take this threat very seriously. Our right to choose is at its most precarious point since over thirty-one years ago, when *Roe vs. Wade* was decided. Our message will be clear: we will not tolerate the persistent government attacks on women's health and reproductive rights.

I am pleased that for the first time in its ninety-five-year history, the National Association for the Advancement of Colored People (NAACP) board of directors unanimously endorsed a pro-choice march. The Black Women's Health Imperative has also signed on. These organizations are part of a growing majority that believe contraceptive education and abortion rights for black and minority women must be a priority. Unintended pregnancy rates for African American women is almost three times the rate of Caucasian women, maternal mortality is four times higher for African American women than Caucasians. One out of four African American women had less involvement than they would like in decisions effecting their health care, with only 73 percent of African American women receiving first trimester prenatal care.

By making abortion illegal, we are going to harm those who turn to back alleys and home remedies to "fix" their situation, a scenario faced disproportionately by minorities and the underprivileged. We cannot make abortion inaccessible, illegal, or shameful. We must stand up for women's rights and let them make informed choices.

After the March for Women's Lives, I thought we had begun to get our message across. It seems to have fallen on deaf ears. Last month, the Food and Drug Administration denied the application to make Plan B (emergency contraception) available for sale over-the-counter. This is an unprecedented intrusion of politics into science. Never has an administration so politicized an over the counter application, nor set aside the overwhelming recommendation of its panel of experts. Our administration would rather appeal to the far right than work to reduce the number of abortions. If over-the-counter availability of EC could prevent even ten percent of unintended pregnancies annually, it would result in 150,000 fewer abortions per year.

This decision stands in direct opposition to the administration's stated goal of reducing the number of abortions. Emergency Contraception is not an abortion. It is simply concentrated doses of the regular birth-control pill, taken soon after sex in order to prevent pregnancy. Emergency Contraception is not the same as RU 486, which terminates an already-established pregnancy. EC is safe and effective, and is not harmful if taken after a pregnancy has been established.

Over-the-counter sales would be particularly beneficial for sexual assault victims. According to scientific studies, approximately 25,000 women per year in the United States become pregnant as a result of rape. An estimated 22,000 of these pregnancies—or 88 percent—could be prevented if sexual assault victims had timely access to emergency contraception.

I hope that all of you are willing to take the step and be the voice to fight against this slippery slope. The battle for reproductive freedom is far from over. I want to close with a quote from one of our truly great female leaders, Susan B. Anthony, "Men, their rights, and nothing more; women, their rights, and nothing less."

The Congressional Record. June 22, 2004: Page E1213.

THE TERRI SCHIAVO CASE

When Theresa Schiavo's case reached the national headlines in March of 2004, it sparked an ethical and political debate that engaged the entire country. In 1990, Theresa "Terri" Schiavo suffered severe brain damage that resulted in a ten-week coma and subsequently a "permanent vegetative state" (PVS) for the next fifteen years. Her husband, Michael Schiavo, who was also her legal guardian, petitioned the court in 1998 to remove Terri's feeding tube. Despite the lack of a living will, Mr. Schiavo insisted that his wife would not have wanted to live in a vegetative state. Mrs. Schiavo's parents, Bob and Mary Schindler, maintained that their daughter was not in a permanent vegetative state and had a videotape of her movements. They insisted that it was Terri's wish to be alive and keep fighting.

After the feeding tube was removed on March 18, 2005, Congress rushed to pass new legislation that would keep Terri Schiavo alive. As a result, a federal judge in Florida considered the Schindlers' plea to reinstate the tube due to violation of Terri's civil rights. The court once again ruled against the parents and their appeal was denied as well. The U.S. Supreme Court refused to hear the case six times.

Despite the lack of intervention by the Supreme Court, President George W. Bush as well as many congressmen came to the support of the parents of Terri Schiavo. President Bush argued that it is our responsibility to protect American citizens, even those who have disabilities. President Bush acknowledged that every life should be valued and the feeding tube should be reinstated. The Schindlers also found support from the Vatican as the Catholic Church condemned euthanasia practices, especially since no living will was present.

The supporters of Michael Schiavo argued in favor of euthanasia and the right to die with dignity. They believed that Terri's state was permanent and change in her status was highly unlikely. Furthermore, the case drew criticisms of government interference. Rep. Debbie Wassermann-Schultz (D-FL) argued that it was not the job of the U.S. Congress to regulate private decisions. In addition, Wassermann-Schultz questioned President Bush's stance as he came to the opposite conclusion in a similar case when he was the governor of Texas. Terri Schiavo died on March 31, 2005, 13 days after her feeding tube was removed. As a result, many states have adopted legislation dealing with the end of life. The debate still rages on whether Schiavo's death was merciful or merciless.

Conservative Viewpoint

F. James Sensenbrenner (R-WI). Mr. Speaker, I rise in support of S. 686, For the relief of the parents of Theresa Marie Schiavo. As the House convenes this Palm Sunday, the Florida courts are enforcing a merciless directive to deprive Terri Schiavo of her right to life.

Terri Schiavo, a person whose humanity is as undeniable as her emotional responses to her family's tender care-giving, has committed no crime and has done nothing wrong. Yet the Florida courts have brought Terri and the nation to an ugly crossroads by commanding medical professionals sworn to protect life to end Terri's life. This Congress must reinforce the law's commitment to justice and compassion for all Americans, particularly the most vulnerable.

On March 16, the House passed legislation to avert the tragedy now unfolding in Florida. The House bill, H.R. 1332, The Protection of Incapacitated Persons Act of 2005, passed the House by voice vote. Earlier today, I introduced H.R. 1452, For the Relief of the Parents of Theresa Marie Schiavo. The Senate-passed legislation now before us is identical to that bill.

Mr. Speaker, while our federalist structure reserves broad authority to the states, America's federal courts have played a historic role in defending the constitutional rights of all Americans, including the disadvantaged, disabled, and dispossessed. Among the God-given rights protected by the Constitution, no right is more sacred than the right to life.

The legislation we will consider today will ensure that Terri Schiavo's constitutional right to life will be given the federal court review that her situation demands. Unlike legislation passed by the Senate a day after House passage of H.R. 1332, the legislation received from the Senate today is not a private bill. Also, and of critical importance, S. 686 does not contain a provision that might have authorized the federal court to deny desperately needed nutritional support to Terri Schiavo during the duration of her claim.

Unlike earlier Senate legislation, S. 686 also contains a bicameral and bipartisan commitment that Congress will examine the legal rights of incapacitated individuals who are unable to make decisions concerning the provision or withdrawal of life-sustaining treatment. Broad consideration of this issue is necessary to ensure that similarly situated individuals are accorded the equal protection under law that is both a fundamental constitutional right and an indispensable ingredient of justice.

It is important to note that this legislation does not create a new cause of action. Rather, it merely provides de novo federal court review of alleged violations of Terri Schiavo's rights under the Constitution or laws of the United States. Furthermore, Senate 686 makes it clear that "nothing in this act shall be construed to create substantive rights not otherwise secured by the Constitution and laws of the United States or of several States."

In addition, the legislation does not reopen or direct the reopening of a final judgment; it merely ensures that opportunity for the review of any violation of Terri Schiavo's federal and constitutional rights in a federal court. As a result, the legislation is clearly consistent with both the separation of powers envisioned by our Founders and the weight of judicial precedent on point. As the Supreme Court held in *Plaut v. Spendthrift Farms*, "While legislatures usually act through laws of general applicability, that is by no means their only legitimate mode of action."

Finally, S. 686 presents no problems regarding retrospective application. As the Supreme Court held in *Landgraf v. USI Film Products*, "A statute does not operate `retrospectively' merely because it is applied in a case arising from conduct antedating the statute's enactment." Rather, the court must ask whether the new provision attaches new legal consequences to events completed before its enactment. S. 686 does not attach any new legal consequences to events completed before its enactment; it merely changes the tribunal to hear the case by providing federal court jurisdiction to review alleged violations of Terri Schiavo's federal and constitutional rights.

Mr. Speaker, the measure of a nation's commitment to the sanctity of life is reflected in its laws to the extent those laws honor and defend its most vulnerable citizens. When a person's intentions regarding whether to receive lifesaving treatment are unclear, the responsibility of a compassionate nation is to affirm that person's right to life. In our deeds and in our public actions, we must build a culture of life that welcomes and defends all human life. The compassionate traditions and highest values of our country command us to action.

The Congressional Record. March 20, 2005: H1700–1728.

Liberal Viewpoint

Debbie Wassermann- Schultz (D-FL). I just wanted to correct some of those facts for the record, Mr. Speaker. The circumstances that bring us here today are horribly tragic. No matter where you may fall on this issue, the details of Terri's case are heart-wrenching. No one in this Chamber questions the pain, heartache, and personal struggles that every member of Ms. Schiavo's family has had to deal with over the last fifteen years. But heartbreaking decisions like this are deeply intimate, personal, and private matters; and the federal government and this body, in particular, should not inject itself into the middle of this private family matter.

This very personal matter should not be politicized as it is being here today. Do we really want to set the precedent of this great body, the United States Congress, to insert ourselves in the middle of families' private matters all across America? If we do this, we will end up throwing end-of-life decisions into utter and complete chaos; and we cannot and should not do that. We are members of Congress. We are not doctors. We are not medical experts. We are not bio-ethicists. We are members of Congress.

When I ran for Congress, I did not ask my constituents for the right to insert myself in their private, personal families decisions; and they do not want me to make those for them. They do not want you to make those for them either. That is the bottom line. I cannot get into the kind of questions that we are getting into being asked here because we do not know. I have never met Michael Schiavo or Terri Schiavo or the Schindlers and the vast majority of people in this body have not either.

We do not have the expertise or the facts in enough detail to get into these kinds of decisions and make decisions on these kinds of cases. We are not God and we are not Terri Schiavo's husband, sister, brother, uncle or relation. We are members of Congress. We make laws and we uphold the law and we swore to uphold and protect the Constitution and we are thumbing our noses at the Constitution if we do this here tonight.

Now, I have heard a lot of things said about this legislation and about the very proceeding that we are engaging in this evening. I have heard accusations that because this body is debating this legislation, we are threatening somehow the life of Ms. Schiavo. I think it is really important to note that this is a legislative body created by our forefathers for the express purpose of deliberations and representation.

The accusation that because we have three hours of debate on an unprecedented piece of legislation that seeks to insert the federal government in between a family while overruling state courts and circumventing the Constitution, that is an outrageous accusation and not worthy of a representative elected to craft and debate legislation.

I notice today that President Bush has returned from Crawford hoping to sign this legislation if it is passed by Congress. I think it is important to note that President Bush when he was Governor of Texas in 1999 signed a Texas law that is on the books today that was just used a few days ago to allow a hospital to withdraw, over the parents' objections, the life support of a 6-month-old boy, over the parents' objections.

President Bush signed a law called the Texas Advanced Directives Act, when he was Governor of Texas. This law, that has been used several times and as recently as a few days ago, liberalized the situations under which a person in Texas can avoid artificial life support. Under it, life support can be withheld or withdrawn if you have an irreversible condition in Texas from which you are expected to eventually pass away.

Indeed, this law, signed by then Governor Bush, allows doctors to remove a patient from life support if the hospital's ethics committee agrees, even over the objections of a family member, only allowing the family ten days to find another facility that might accept the patient, barring any state judicial intervention.

It appears that President Bush felt, as governor, that there was a point at which, when doctors felt there was no further hope for the patient, that it is appropriate for an end-of-life decision to be made, even over the objections of family members. That was a law that President Bush did not just allow to become law without his signature, he came back from a campaign trip to sign it.

There is an obvious conflict here between the president's feelings on this matter now as compared to when he was governor of Texas, so I thought that was an important conflict that should be raised here this evening in our discussion.

Let me just close my remarks by reiterating there is no room for the federal government in this most personal of private angst-ridden family matters, in which a family has to make the most personal of decisions when dealing with the course of care of a loved one. We should not politicize this very personal family matter.

Ms. Schiavo made it clear, as opposed to what the gentleman from Wisconsin said, that she would not have wished to remain in a persistent vegetative state, and the guardian ad litem report well documents that. In fact, it documents it to such a degree that it cites the specific conversations referenced by her family members when she attended funerals of loved ones who were in similar situations when they had life support removed; and she had stated that if, God forbid, she was ever in this situation, that she would not have wished to remain on life support.

The Congressional Record. March 20, 2005: H1700–1728.

· · ·

SELECTED READING

National Health Insurance

Cowen, Tyler. "Universal Health Care." *New York Times.* September 26, 2006. www.nytimes.com/2006/10/05/business/05scene.html?_r=1&oref=slogin.

Cutler, David M. "The Cost and Financing of Health Care." *The American Economic Review* 85 (2), 1995.

Gratzer, David. "A Prescription for Health." December 21, 2004. www.nationalreview.com/comment/gratzer200412210900.asp

Mayer, David N. "Clinton Health Plan: Wrong Prescription." *On Principle* 2 (1): January 1994. www.ashbrook.org/publicat/onprin/v2n1/mayer.html.

Ralston, Richard E. "Clinton vs. Your Health." The Ayn Rand Institute. July 28, 1998. www.aynrand.org/site/News2?page=NewsArticle&id=5261&news_iv_ctrl=1021.

Individual Savings Accounts

Buckner, Gail. "A Primer on Bush's New Savings Accounts." *Fox News.* February 7, 2004. www.foxnews.com/story/0,2933,110695,00.html.

Ginsburg, Paul. "Tax Free but of Little Account." *Modern Healthcare* 34 (2004): 21.

Jacobius, Arleen. "Huge Implications." *Pensions and Investments* 31 (2003): 38–39.

Skorburg, John. "Bush to Support Lifetime Savings Accounts." *Budget & Tax News.* September 1, 2004. ww.heartland.org/Article.cfm?artId=15630.

Wasow, Bernard. "Promoting Retirement Savings: The Bush Plan vs. a Better Way." The Century Foundation. February 6, 2004. www.tcf.org/Publications/RetirementSecurity/retirement_savings.pdf.

HIV Prevention

Hurley, Susan F., Damien J. Jolley, and John M. Kaldor. "Effectiveness of Needle-Exchange Programmes for Prevention of HIV Infection." *The Lancet.* June 21, 1997, 349: 1797–1800.

Murphy, Jenny. "Are Needle Exchange Programs a Good Idea?" Speak Out. June 15, 2000. www.speakout.com/activism/issue_briefs/1352b-1.html.

National Institutes of Health Consensus Panel. "Interventions to Prevent HIV Risk Behaviors" (Kensington, MD: NIH Consensus Program Information Center, February 1997), 6.

"Update: Syringe Exchange Programs—United States, 2002." *Morbidity and Mortality Weekly Report* 54 (27): July 15, 2005 (Atlanta, GA: Centers for Disease Control), 673.

Vlahov, David, and Benjamin Junge. "The Role of Needle Exchange Programs in HIV Prevention." *Public Health Reports* 113 (Supplement 1): June 1998, 75–80.

Stem Cell Research

"Bush to Allow Limited Stem Cell Funding." *CNN.com.* August 10, 2001. www.cnn.com/2001/ALLPOLITICS/08/09/stem.cell.bush/index.html.

California Institute for Regenerative Medicine. "Homepage." 2006. The State of California. www.cirm.ca.gov.

Lacayo, Richard. "The Stem Cell Debate." *Time.com.* 2001. www.time.com/time/2001/stemcells.

"Policy Brief, Stem Cell Research." American Association for the Advancement of Science. October 30, 2006. www.aaas.org/spp/cstc/issues/stemcells.htm.

Yang, Carter M. "Stem-Cell Dilemma: Bush 'Conflicted' over Controversial Research." *ABCNews.* June 26, 2001. abcnews.go.com/sections/ politics/DailyNews/Stem_Cells010626.html.

Abortion and the Morning-After Pill

Bauer, Patricia E. "The Abortion Debate That No One Wants to Have." *Washington Post.* October 18, 2005. www.washingtonpost.com/wp-dyn/content/article/2005/10/17/AR2005101701311.html.

Brant, Martha. "The New Abortion Debate." *MSNBC.* March 2006. www.msnbc.msn.com/id/11569379/site/newsweek.

Cuthbertson, Peter. "10 Fallacies in the Abortion Debate." *Conservative Commentary.* November 8, 2002. www.freerepublic.com/focus/news/785378/posts.

Frost, Martin. "Reality vs. Rhetoric in the Abortion Debate." *Fox News*. October 24, 2005. www.foxnews.com/story/0,2933,173332,00.html.

Lewis, Andrew. "Abortion: When Do Rights Begin?" *Capitalism Magazine*. February 14, 2000. capmag.com/article.asp?ID=273.

Sollisch, Jim. "How Abortion Bans Might Help the Debate." *Christian Science Monitor*. March 27, 2006. www.csmonitor.com/2006/0327/p09s02-coop.html.

The Terri Schiavo Case

Babbington, Charles. "Congress Passes Schiavo Measure." *Washington Post*. March 21, 2005. www.washingtonpost.com/wp-dyn/articles/A51402-2005Mar20.html.

Bhattacharya, Shaoni. "Terri Schiavo Dies as Politics and Medicine Collide." *New Scientist*. April 1, 2005. www.newscientist.com/article.ns?id=dn7222.

Feldmann, Linda. "The Terri Schiavo Legacy." *Christian Science Monitor*. April 1, 2005. www.csmonitor.com/2005/0401/p01s01-ussc.html.

Quill, Timothy E. "Terri Schiavo—A Tragedy Compounded." *New England Journal of Medicine* 352 (2005): 1630–33.

Smith, Wessley J. "Saving Terri Schiavo." *Weekly Standard*. www.weeklystandard.com/Content/Public/Articles/000/000/003/276fpkqk.asp.

"Terri Schiavo Dies, but Battle Continues." *MSNBC*. March 31, 2005. www.msnbc.msn.com/id/7293186.

4

Criminal Justice

Since the early 1990s, crime has dropped steadily in the United States. This decline has spanned all major areas of violent crime, including murder, assault, and rape, as well as property crimes like burglary and theft. The drop has been especially pronounced in the Northeast. Possibly the most celebrated decline was in New York City. Once considered a prime example of urban decay and the violence related to this phenomenon, it has evolved into a much safer city. By 2002, crime rates in the city were lower than at any point since the mid-1960s.

Despite this significant drop, and to some degree because of it, criminal justice remains a hotly debated issue in American politics. Generally speaking, conservatives support a tougher stand on crime. They are more likely to argue that when someone is found guilty of a crime, he or she should be incarcerated for an extended period. They are more likely to support mandatory sentences for particular felonies, and they also believe in spending a higher percentage of state and federal budgets on prison construction. Liberals see great failings in this approach. They argue that prisons generally make people more violent, and they also argue that the justice system is hardly fair. The poor and minorities are far more likely to be incarcerated for the same crimes than the middle class and whites, for example.

Liberals and conservatives also generally disagree on the causes of criminal behavior. Liberals see crime as a primarily a product of poverty or of general social despair. For this reason, they believe that the best method for reducing crime is to redistribute wealth, to make sure that most people have a reasonable standard of living. Conservatives mostly argue that the primary cause of crime is family disintegration. For this reason, they often argue that the key to reducing crime is to promote stable families, such as by promoting marriage and discouraging divorce.

PUNISHMENT VERSUS REHABILITATION

Much of the debate between liberals and conservatives on criminal justice relates to whether the primary strategy for dealing with convicted criminals should focus on punishment or rehabilitation. Conservatives generally argue for punishment on three grounds. The first, they argue, is that the primary role of the criminal justice system is to deter behavior that hurts others. When people know that they might live for an extended period in horrendous conditions, they will be less likely to commit those crimes. The more severe the punishment, the argument continues, the greater the deterrence. Second, giving criminals longer prison sentences reduces the time they spend in society, thereby eliminating the possibility of their committing more crimes during that period. Third, the victims of crimes or their families deserve to have some form of retribution taken against those who committed those crimes.

Liberals generally believe that the criminal justice system should focus more on rehabilitating those who commit crimes. They generally believe that criminal behavior is a response to some form of despair, and they therefore believe that rehabilitation is simply a more pragmatic approach to reducing crime. For example, one cause of criminal behavior, they believe, is poverty. Therefore, if an inmate gains training so that he or she can acquire a stable job after leaving prison, that person will have less need or time to commit crimes. Similarly, if there is a psychological reason for the criminal behavior, counseling might help reduce the emotional attraction of destructive behavior. Also, if someone commits crimes in order to pay for a drug addiction, drug rehabilitation eliminates the need for those robberies or assaults. In this way, liberals hope that they can reduce recidivism rates, and they believe that they can deal with inmates in a more enlightened and ethical manner.

For these reasons, conservatives are more likely to support long incarcerations while liberals would often prefer that the state use this as a last resort. So, while both would agree that people who commit violent crimes must be sent to prison, liberals are more likely to support alternative punishments for lesser crimes, since they consider it more effective, more humane, and more likely to save money that could be better spent on other state needs like education. Conservatives have generally thought that liberals are soft on crime and that rehabilitation of a hardened criminal is extremely unlikely and therefore deterrence is the best strategy. Since the best deterrent available to the American government in most cases is prison, they generally support incarceration for a higher percentage of crimes than liberals.

Since around 1980, conservatives have been winning this debate at least in terms of government policy. Over the past few decades, the United States has dramatically increased the number of people who are incarcerated, and in the process the federal government and the states have dramatically increased the number of prisons. The United States now has the highest incarceration rate (that is, the percentage of adults behind bars) in the world, with several states from the former Soviet Union, like Russia and Belarus, being the next group. Between 2 and 3 percent of the American public has spent time in prison, and by some estimates one of every fifteen Americans will be incarcerated during their lifetimes. Some conservatives argue that these "get-tough" policies have been a primary reason for the drop in violent crime, but others counter that internationally there is no relationship between crime rates and incarceration rates. For example, the United States has twenty times the incarceration rate of Japan *and* five times the rate of violent crime. Conservatives counter by arguing that cultural differences among countries, like the divorce rate, make these statistical comparisons spurious.

MINORITIES IN PRISON

One of the primary debates on this get-tough policy is whether our criminal justice system is more likely to incarcerate minorities for the same crime. Throughout the nation, approximately 1 percent of white men are incarcerated as compared to 8 percent of black men and 2.5 percent of Hispanic men. In some states, like West Virginia and Wisconsin, the difference is even more stark: incarceration rates for whites match the national rate of 1 percent, but 13 percent to 15 percent of the black male population is in prison. The racial disparity is especially pronounced when one focuses on drug-related arrests. Even though there are five times as many whites estimated to use illegal drugs as blacks, African-Americans make up two-thirds of the drug offenders in prison. Indeed, when arrested for drug-related crimes, blacks are eight times more likely to be incarcerated than whites.

These dramatic differences in incarceration rates by race are not disputed. But, the reasons for the differences are hotly debated. Liberals argue that the criminal justice system works against minorities, even when this occurs unintentionally. In the first place, there could be more of an implicit and even subconscious presumption of guilt by police and juries when a black man is accused of a crime. Second, since a higher percentage of minorities are poor, they are less able to afford proper legal representation.

Conservatives generally see other reasons for the difference. Minorities are more likely to be poor, and they point out that poor people are more likely to commit crimes. Moreover, minority children and especially black children are much more likely to be raised in a single-parent family. The lack of a stable, traditional family unit increases the likelihood of committing crimes, they argue.

DEATH PENALTY

One of the most contentious criminal justice issues is whether the death penalty should be outlawed. It has been banned in many democracies, and it was temporarily deemed unconstitutional in the United States, from 1973 to 1976. However, the Supreme Court banned this punishment for a specific reason. In the 1972 *Furman v. Georgia* case, the court found capital punishment to be cruel and unusual punishment because the jury was making the decision of whether the accused was guilty and whether he or she should be executed in a single step. Once states separated the process by first having the jury determine guilt or innocence and then having a separate hearing on whether the penalty should be death, the court upheld the use of capital punishment.

Most conservatives support capital punishment, arguing that it is the ultimate form of deterrence, since it makes the price of a crime like murder extremely high. They add that once someone is executed, the issue of recidivism disappears; there is no chance of repeating the crime. Many liberals disagree with this line of thinking on several grounds. First, they consider capital punishment to be inhumane, especially since there is no possibility for someone to be proven innocent and released once the execution is carried out. They argue further that capital punishment is very unlikely to deter murderers any more than the threat of life in prison, particularly once one considers the low percentage of murderers who are actually executed. Finally, they argue that the employment of this punishment is heavily influenced by race; minorities convicted of potential capital offenses are more likely to be sent to death row than whites convicted of the same crime.

WAR ON DRUGS

The War on Drugs is one of the key reasons for the exponential increase in the number of people incarcerated. This war was declared by the Nixon Administration in 1971 in response to the rising use of recreational drugs over the previous decade as well as the rising crime rate. Nixon also signed into law the Comprehensive Drug Abuse Prevention and Control Act of 1970, which included the Controlled Substance Act, which produced the general structure of the drug laws since. For example, it categorized drugs in five schedules, or levels, based on their potential for abuse, medical usefulness, and safety, thereby creating the framework for determining punishments for possession or sale. However, after Nixon resigned, the Ford and Carter Administrations supported a policy of distinguishing between what they considered more dangerous drugs, like heroin, and more innocuous drugs, like marijuana. Carter even proposed decriminalizing marijuana during his 1976 campaign.

This situation changed dramatically in the 1980s, partially because the conservative Reagan Administration took office and partially because a relationship between drugs and violence became clearer. In particular, the use of crack, a potent form of cocaine that is smoked, rose to epidemic proportions in some parts of the country, and with it violence escalated in urban areas. President Reagan signed the Anti-Drug Abuse Act of 1986 into law, which included significant amounts of money for drug education and treatment but also for the construction of new prisons. It also created mandatory minimum penalties for people found guilty of possessing or using particular drugs. At this point, the United States criminal justice system became very tough on drug-related crimes.

Generally speaking, liberals oppose this shift in policy. They support softer penalties or treatment for nonviolent drug users, and some argue for the decriminalization of certain drugs, like marijuana. They tend to see drug addiction as more of a disease than a crime, like alcoholism, and therefore believe that the appropriate response in many cases is treatment. Liberals are also more likely to disagree with the ranking system used by the federal government, arguing that marijuana does not pose nearly the same threat as heroin or LSD. Many liberals also believe that marijuana should be made legal if used for medical purposes, as California voters supported in 1996 when they passed Proposition 215.

Conservatives, especially social conservatives, generally disagree with these points. They argue that all the drugs identified by the federal government as dangerous are exactly that. While treatment can be an option in some situations, the government needs the threat of incarceration to deter people from using these drugs. They also disagree with legalizing marijuana for medical use, even if it requires a doctor's prescription, arguing that this simply produces another avenue for people to acquire it for recreational use.

One area where liberals have been more successful has been with the development of drug courts. In some cases, and mostly when the accused is a first-time offender, was not also selling drugs, and had not committed a violent crime as well, the case can be passed to a separate drug court. In order to avoid incarceration, the accused will generally plead guilty and take steps required by the drug court judge to overcome his or her addiction to narcotics. They often include treatment but also could include education and other positive benefits. The court generally also tests this person for drug use on a regular basis, and if he or she fails the test, the judge can send him or her to prison or impose other penalties.

Drug courts have been largely supported by both liberals and conservatives. They have reported low recidivism rates, and they appear to be much cheaper than incarceration. The Bush Administration even put out a National Report Card on this policy in 2004, praising its many successes. Nonetheless, these specialized courts do contain elements of both the liberal and conservative approaches to fighting crime: While the emphasis is on rehabilitation and education, the actions of drug courts are backed by a very real threat of incarceration.

CONCLUSIONS

Incarceration is costly. It takes significant money out of state treasuries, reducing funds for other programs, including education. While liberals are much more likely to oppose capital punishment than conservatives, the American public generally seems to support the death penalty. Indeed, despite the intensity of the debates over criminal justice, there does not appear to be a significant public outcry for changing course. For that reason, it appears that the American prison population will continue to grow for the foreseeable future. However, public opinion can shift, and so can the desires of particular states. While the get-tough approach has dominated the criminal justice system since the mid-1980s, it could be reversed in the coming decades.

PUNISHMENT VERSUS REHABILITATION

Incarceration is the main form of punishment for crimes in the United States. Prisons are operated by the federal government as well as state governments. They range from minimum security prisons, which house nonviolent offenders, to maximum security prisons, which house violent offenders. The terms of incarceration depend on the severity of the crime. The United States has the highest per capita incarceration rate in the world.

Many Republicans believe that to deter crime, tougher crime sentences need to be enforced. Rep. Ira William "Bill" McCollum (R-FL) specifically points to the juvenile system that is in severe need of reform. He believes that crime offenders receive lenient sentences for their crimes, if a sentence is even given out. Rep. McCollum wants to address the lack of accountability within the juvenile judicial system. In order for that goal to be achieved, an increase of funding needs to be appropriated towards the prison system. Punishing juveniles for their crimes is the only way to decrease crime.

Since the repeat offender rate is very high, alternatives to imprisonment have gotten more attention. Many Democrats look at rehabilitation as a possible solution to crime. Rehabilitation would allow the person to be integrated into the society, making him or her less likely to return to prison. Many people believe that incarceration alone is going to correct the behavior of the offender. But statistics have shown that upon release, many prison inmates do not know how to deal with life outside of prison and they fall into the same traps that got them incarcerated in the first place. Rehabilitation includes community service, probation, and some sort of guidance in the aftermath. Rehabilitation, along with a lesser sentence, will help the offender to integrate into the society and become a productive member of society.

Conservative Viewpoint

Ira William McCollum Jr. (R-FL). Mr. Speaker, this bill, as has been stated previously, contains the elements of two major youth crime bills and an effort to improve our juvenile justice system very dramatically as the work product of two different committees of this House.

· · ·

First of all, it is extremely important for us to recognize that we have a crisis in juvenile crime today in this nation. Our juvenile justice system is truly broken because juvenile judges, juvenile prosecutors, juvenile probation officers, are overwhelmed by the caseload that is out there.

We find in the streets of America today young people committing crimes, oftentimes the traditional crimes we think of as going to juvenile court of doing something like spray painting graffiti on a warehouse wall or running over a parking meter, and not even seeing the police officer taking them into the juvenile authorities because the juvenile authorities are so overworked, they have to spend their time on the violent crime that we hear so much about in society today, that they are not focused and cannot take the time to focus on these lesser crimes.

Then when they are taken in, they may or may not receive any punishment at all. We have a lot of reports in some of our major urban areas where they do not receive any punishment, which is the reason why law enforcement hesitates to carry these young people in that commit misdemeanor crimes and wait for the really serious stuff, which may be many, many crimes down the road. Then those who do get some punishment frequently cannot be supervised, because there is no probation officer who has the time to do that and so on down the line.

As a net consequence, what I have learned as chairman of the Subcommittee on Crime in this House over the last 3 or 4 years is that we have a lot of young people who believe that there is no consequence to their juvenile acts when they go out and commit these relatively petty crimes. The experts say in that case, since they may commit all kinds of these crimes and never get any punishment, never even be taken into the juvenile authorities, is it any wonder that when they are a little older and rob a 7-Eleven store with a gun that they do not hesitate to pull the trigger because they do not think that there is going to be any consequences.

So, what is in this bill that was in H.R. 3, which is the gist of that bill on juvenile justice reform, is an effort to hold these young people accountable, knowing and recognizing that the vast majority of juvenile justice problems are in the States, not at the federal level. This is not a federal bill in that sense. It is, instead, a bill that would provide for some effort to put some accountability in there by a grant program to the States and local communities for the purposes of promoting this accountability.

The funds that would be authorized in this bill are $500 million a year over three years for State and local communities to be able to spend for the purposes of increasing accountability in their juvenile justice systems for anything they want to. More judges, more probation officers, more prosecutors, more juvenile detention facilities if that is what they need, but within the framework of juvenile justice for anything they want.

There are only a couple of provisions that they have to assure the Attorney General of the United States in order to get the grant money, the first and foremost of which is that the State would have to ensure that there is a sanction, some kind of punishment, for every delinquent or criminal act of a juvenile and that there will be an escalating greater sanction for every subsequent delinquent act that is more serious.

That is very critical. It does not exist today, unfortunately, in most communities and it needs to exist. That is the real reason for this part of the legislation, why H.R. 3 was passed, and why it is in this bill today. It is a grant program to provide those additional resources so that these overworked juvenile justice systems can be given a jump start, knowing that the States will have to pump even more money into the system, but at least saying we are out there to offer a helping hand of $500 million a year, which is a lot of money, to the States which comply with that.

They also would have to establish a system of records for juveniles adjudicated delinquent for a second offense that would be a felony if committed by an adult, which is a system equivalent to that maintained for adults that commit felonies.

They have to assure that State law does not prevent a juvenile court judge from issuing an order against a parent or guardian of a juvenile offender and from imposing sanctions for violation of that order, which most States already do.

The last one that is often talked about, but that is far milder than has been represented even here today, they have to assure the Attorney General that when juveniles commit an act after attaining the age of fifteen years of age that would be a serious violent crime on only one of those four, murder, aggravated, sexual assault, and armed robbery with a firearm if committed by an adult, may be prosecuted as an adult within the discretion of the prosecutor, which is, of course, the law in almost all States today.

The heart of this is that we want money to go to the States to improve their juvenile justice systems. This is a grant program to do that. It is primarily attached to the principal string that they will start punishing and assure us that they are punishing juveniles for their first delinquent acts and then increase that punishment thereafter with the misdemeanor crimes to put consequences back into the law and stop a lot of these kids from committing the violent crimes that they do later. It is a very important bill and I urge its adoption.

The Congressional Record. September 15, 1998: H7726–H7745.

Liberal Viewpoint

Jesse Francis "Jeff" Bingaman Jr. (D-NM). Mr. President, I rise today, along with Senators Biden, Specter, and Landrieu, to introduce the Enhanced Second Chance Act of 2004.

I believe this is an important bill that will significantly improve public safety by providing $130 million a year for a competitive grant program to State, local, and tribal governments to reduce recidivism rates and improve the transition of offenders back into society. In addition to the adult and juvenile demonstration projects, the bill would create a federal reentry task force, reauthorize funding for drug treatment programs in state and federal correctional facilities, establish a program within the Bureau of Prisons to promote family reunification, bring additional literacy funds to correctional institutions, and establish a mentoring grant program for community-based organizations to assist inmates with their reentry back into the community.

We as a society have an interest in ensuring that when prisoners are released that they be reintegrated back into the community in a manner that reduces the likelihood of them committing additional crimes. Providing assistance to these individuals is not a charity, it is a matter of good public policy. Without employment, without housing, without basic life skills, without help in treating drug addiction or mental illness, offenders are likely to relapse into criminal behavior. It is insufficient to just punish offenders; we also need to look for ways that we can rehabilitate offenders and create an environment that fosters their ability to make a positive contribution to society.

There are programs in state and federal detention facilities that are beginning to address some of these issues, but frankly, I believe we need to be doing more—especially with regard to jails across the country. By neglecting to focus on inmates in local jails we are also losing out on targeting the largest population of offenders that is returning to the community—it is estimated that jails return ten to twenty times the number of people into the community as do federal and state prisons, approximately ten million releases a year. I am very pleased that my suggestions regarding recognizing the role of local jails in the reentry process were incorporated into this bill.

I also believe we need to pay more attention to the issue of illiteracy among inmates. According to the National Institute of Literacy, 70 percent of all prisoners function at the two lowest literacy levels. Considering that studies have consistently demonstrated that correctional educational programs reduce recidivism rates by up to 30 percent, I strongly believe this is an area that deserves attention, and I am happy that this bill will bring additional resources for literacy programs.

If we are going to reduce the recidivism rate, we can't overlook the importance of getting these offenders the tools necessary to succeed in the community without recourse to crime. With over 2 million people incarcerated in the United States, if punishment is all we do, without any effort to rehabilitate and reintegrate offenders into the community, society will bear a heavy burden. Over 650,000 offenders are released from state and federal facilities each year, in addition to 100,000 juveniles and the numerous individuals coming in and out of local jails that I previously mentioned. It makes sense to do all we can to ensure that these people are rehabilitated and have the skills necessary to successfully change course.

In recent years, many States and localities have begun to improve ways to transition offenders back into communities, and I believe that this bill provides the resources necessary to continue this effort.

The Congressional Record. October 7, 2004: S10704–S10747.

MINORITIES IN PRISON

Among all developed nations, the United States continues to have the largest percentage of its population behind prison bars. Statistics show that the current prison population in the United States is around 2.2 million people. The majority of the prisoners come from minority groups. Minority groups, particularly African Americans, are more likely to be sentenced to jail, given longer jail sentences, or sentenced to death than white Americans. This fact has some critics looking at the different rates of incarceration between whites and minority groups.

Many Republicans such as Sen. Orrin Hatch (R-UT) are also concerned about disproportionate minority confinement; however, they point out that crimes are still being committed by people. Sen. Hatch argues that offenders are sentenced to jail because they commit crimes, not because they represent a certain group of people. He does not believe that some offenders should be given a break solely because they are from a minority. In fact, Sen. Hatch questions the constitutionality of such law. Sen. Hatch maintains that crimes should be punished harshly regardless of race.

Critics of the judicial system continue to point out the blatant discrimination against minorities within the judicial system. Statistics show that minorities receive harsher sentences for the same crimes than whites do. As Sen. Russ Feingold (D-WI) points out, the practice is referred to as disproportionate minority confinement. Even though many states have begun to examine the problem, the discriminatory practice still exists.

Liberal Viewpoint

Russell D. Feingold (D-WI). This bill also deeply troubles me because it will put a halt to efforts to reduce discrimination in our juvenile justice system. The bill ignores reality: we are throwing African American kids into jails at a higher rate than white kids who commit the exact same offense. This phenomenon is called disproportionate minority confinement.

Our nation has come a long way toward achieving racial harmony and equality, but we still have a long way to go. In nearly every state, children of minority racial and ethnic backgrounds are over-represented at every stage of the juvenile justice system and receive harsher treatment by the system. A California study has shown that black youths consistently receive harsher punishment and are more likely to receive jail time than white youths convicted of the same offenses. Current law requires states to identify disproportionate minority confinement in their states, to analyze why it exists and to develop strategies to address the causes of disproportionate minority confinement. The law does not require and has never resulted in the release of juveniles. Nor does the law provide for quotas. And no state's funding under the Juvenile Justice and Delinquency Prevention Act has ever been reduced as a result of noncompliance.

In fact, the current law has been very effective. Forty states are implementing or developing intervention plans to address disproportionate minority confinement. This bill will bring to a halt this good work conducted by the states. These states have just begun to address the disturbing reality of disproportionate minority confinement. But under this Juvenile Justice bill, the law enforcement community will no longer be required to address the problem of discriminatory treatment of minority juvenile offenders. This is outrageous.

I am outraged, and this body should be outraged, that we are punishing black kids more harshly than white kids for the exact same offenses. The debate on this issue illustrated how much more work we still need to do on civil rights. Many of my colleagues would have you believe that there is no longer a race problem in this country. I beg to differ. To those colleagues, I ask you to look around this chamber and identify for me the senator of African descent. You cannot because there is not one. I am troubled that on this and other important civil rights issues, we do not have a member of the African-American community as one of our colleagues. I cannot help but think that our debate would have been better informed if we had the voice of an African-American senator speaking at one of our podiums. I cannot help but think that the vote on the Wellstone–Kennedy amendment would have had a different outcome if we had the vote of an African American senator cast on this floor.

We have come a long way toward ridding our nation of discrimination against African Americans and other minorities. But we need to keep forging ahead for the good of our children and the future of our country. Let us not turn back the clock.

The Congressional Record. May 20, 1999: S5683–S5732.

Conservative Viewpoint

Orrin G. Hatch (R-UT). As usual, I have to commend the senator from Minnesota for his heart and for his desire to try to resolve problems that are difficult in our society. I have to say that I am concerned about the disproportionate confinement of minority youth, especially young African Americans and Hispanics, in our society—especially African Americans because it is disproportionate. If you really stop and think about it, the issue is who is committing the crimes.

· · ·

This is probably the first bill in history that has 45 percent of the money in the bill for law enforcement and accountability purposes and 55 percent of the money for prevention purposes. But, you know, you still can't ignore the fact that these kids are committing crimes. Just because you would like the statistics to be relatively proportionate, if that isn't the case, because more young people commit crimes from one minority classification than another, it doesn't solve the problem by saying states should find a way of letting these kids out.

Now, if there is another problem, if there is literally a civil rights violation or a discrimination against minority youth, then that is a problem I think would need fixing. But I don't think that is a case that has been made so far.

The Democrats' amendment requires states to address efforts to reduce the proportion of juveniles who have contact with the juvenile justice system who are members of minority groups, if such proportion exceeds the proportion such groups represent in the general population. It fails to take into consideration who is committing these crimes. If a higher proportion of young African Americans are committing the crimes, do we just ignore that because we don't like the fact that it is disproportionate compared to Hispanic Americans or Anglo Americans? I don't see how you get around the fact that the ones who are committing the crimes are the ones who are arrested or incarcerated.

This amendment is not only ill-advised as a matter of policy and principle, but it is also unconstitutional. The amendment makes an overt racial classification. Juveniles must be classified according to race in order for this amendment to be followed.

. . .

Now, such a classification could be upheld if there is an extraordinary justification, but that is not evident here. I just hear that there are more young African American kids who go to jail than white kids; therefore, there must be something wrong with the system.

I don't agree with that. If there are more young African American kids committing crimes, and especially vicious crimes and violent crimes, you don't help the problem by saying they should not be punished and they should not be incarcerated somehow or other be sent to—unless there is a justification for that.

. . .

This amendment does not pass strict scrutiny. The only "compelling interest" the Supreme Court has recognized in this context is the remediation of past discrimination. Moreover, the Court requires a particularized showing of past discrimination. I don't think anybody would disagree with that.

Here there is no such proof of discrimination, and the current law, which this amendment replicates—and, I might add, expands—is not narrowly tailored to remedy past discrimination. In fact, the Justice Department regulations under current law require states to intervene regardless of the cause of disproportionate confinement. Instead of remedying past discrimination, much of the current law is aimed at prevention programs. This amendment, and the current law it replicates, cannot pass strict scrutiny.

I wish I could support this amendment, but its constitutional flaws prevent that. And, frankly, I believe that this amendment is bad social policy, because basically this amendment just says that these young people who have been engaged in criminal activity, somehow or other, should be proportionately given a break because there are more—in this case—young African Americans than young whites who are convicted. Now, that is unconstitutional in the light of Adarand and the Feeney case, and, frankly, under any principle of race neutrality in the justice system.

The proponents of this amendment are motivated, in my opinion, by the best of intentions. I share their concern. That is one reason I want this juvenile justice bill to pass, so we can get serious about violent juvenile crime and so we can use the tools of this bill to help to prevent that in the future. And we have significant prevention moneys in this bill to help get these kids away from ever committing crime again.

Like I say, the proponents are sincere. They want to help minority children avoid detention. However, I believe the best way to prevent the detention of juveniles is to prevent juveniles—of all races—from committing crime. I am proud that S. 254 provides $547.5 million in new funds for prevention programs. I have had to fight to get that. That is on top of and in addition to the $4.4 billion that we already have on the books every year for prevention programs.

It is unhealthy for the Government to focus only on reducing the detention of minority juveniles. We should focus on preventing crime committed by juveniles of all races and recognize that detention of juvenile offenders is sometimes necessary. As this current debate illustrates, it is inherently divisive when the Government makes racial classifications.

Look, if there is discrimination against minority kids, then you can count on me. I will fight alongside of my Democrat colleagues to end that discrimination. But to just say it is disproportionate without consideration to what crimes were committed, it seems to me, is not only unconstitutional, it is wrong.

S. 254 has a better provision. It requires that prevention resources be directed to "segments of the juvenile population" that are disproportionately detained. Such "segments of the population" could include, for example, certain socioeconomic groups that are more likely to be at risk. S. 254 directs prevention resources to such groups who need these resources the most.

Finally, not only is this amendment unconstitutional, it sets a terrible precedent. The premise of this amendment—requiring states to provide racial groups special attention if members of those groups are disproportionately likely to be detained—could be used to justify racial profiles. In my opinion, racial profiling is also unconstitutional, and I believe a significant number of constitutional authorities would agree with my analysis on that.

The government simply cannot use race as a classification or a factor in the criminal justice system, because our system of justice should be color blind. If it is not, then I will work to correct that. But I don't have any evidence that it is not at this particular point, other than the visceral feeling of some that because more young African Americans than whites are convicted and sentenced to detention, there must be something wrong with the system.

Mr. President, I strongly urge the Senate to oppose this amendment.

I also understand that in our society a lot of young African American kids, a lot of young Hispanic kids, a lot of young Native Americans—and you can just go down almost every minority; there are literally dozens of minorities in this country—a lot of them don't have the best chance in this life. They are born in poverty. They are born into situations where there is no father, or they have a father who takes off on them, or they have a father who won't accept responsibility. They start off with a couple of strikes against them. I acknowledge that. We have to do something about that. But that doesn't mean we have to start racial profiling or that we have to start racial classifications to get there, unless we can show that there is prejudice, unless we can show that there is a reason to have this amendment.

If I might add a final note, I have bent over backwards to craft language which addresses the concerns raised by my colleagues. I think my language is constitutional and it has bipartisan support. Senator Biden supports the underlying amendment, and with good reason, because it is constitutional.

Having said all of that, again I will reiterate that I respect my colleagues. I respect their desire to right wrongs in our society. They know that I work on that too. I respect their desire to make sure that everybody is treated equally and in a decent manner. I respect their approach to try to end discrimination in our society. I join with them in those matters. But this particular amendment, it seems to me, is unconstitutional, and I certainly hope our colleagues will vote against it when I move to table it.

The Congressional Record. May 19, 1999: S5507–S5583.

DEATH PENALTY

In the recent past, a few death row inmates have been exonerated of their crimes thanks to technological advances and the use of DNA testing. As a result, debates over capital punishment have once again come to the forefront of American politics. Capital punishment, also commonly referred to as the death penalty, is the most severe form of punishment used for capital offenses. These capital offenses include murder, treason, espionage and other crimes. Although both sides believe that the judicial system is in great need of reform, the similarities end there. Even though capital punishment laws vary by state, the United States continues to be the only developed country that still uses capital punishment within its judicial system.

Proponents of capital punishment believe that it is a just sentence for those that have committed the most heinous crimes. By executing the perpetrators through lethal injection, the sentence brings retributive justice to the victims and their families. Additionally, many proponents of capital punishment argue that it serves as a deterrent for future crimes. Capital punishment also affirms the right to life by punishing those that have violated the sanctity of life.

Opponents of the death penalty address the fallibility of the judicial system. Throughout history, people have been executed and then later cleared of the crime. Death penalty opponents believe that lesser punishments such as life imprisonment are better suited for perpetrators. Many look toward the overfilled jails as proof that the death penalty does not serve as a deterrent to crime. Many religious figures have also joined in opposition to the death penalty as it perpetuates the circle of violence, only this time by the state. In addition, many opponents argue that the death penalty is torture and constitutes cruel and unusual punishment.

Conservative Viewpoint

Lloyd Ted Poe (R-TX). Mr. Speaker, Kenneth Lee Boyd committed a violent and vicious crime on the evening of March 4, 1988, in North Carolina. On that night, Boyd armed himself with a .357 Magnum pistol and committed cold-blooded murder against members of his very own family.

On that evening, Boyd picked up his children from his father-in-law's home and told the boys they were going for pizza. But that was a lie. With the pistol sitting in the seat of the car between Boyd and his children, he went back to his father-in-law's home, a place where his estranged wife was staying.

His thirteen-year-old son, Christopher, sensing something was up, tried to hide that pistol. And when Boyd pulled up to his father-in-law's driveway, Christopher, frightened, jumped from the car and ran to warn his grandparents and his mother.

Boyd then approached the house and began his shocking shooting spree. He first shot and killed his father-in-law, Thomas Curry, through the door. He then found his estranged wife in the doorway of her bedroom. He shot her several times and then went outside and reloaded his murder weapon, came back and shot her some more. In the end, it was decided Julie Boyd was shot a total of eight times.

Boyd went back outside, shot some more, and this time at his brother-in-law, Craig Curry, who was moving Boyd's children and a nephew to a wooded area to safety. The bullet missed Craig, who was trying to hide in the woods.

Boyd then returned to the home, called 911, informed the operator he had just killed his wife and father-in-law and told them to come get him. When the police arrived, he surrendered.

Last week, finally, Kenneth Boyd became the 1,000th execution to take place in the United States since the Supreme Court allowed the death penalty to resume in 1976. Last week, Kenneth Boyd was finally punished for his sins and crimes that he committed over seventeen years ago.

Last week, when justice was served, the weak-kneed do-gooders and media had a heyday. Headlines surfaced and everyone focused on the number 1,000. Boyd was portrayed as a martyr. If the media was so gung ho keeping score, why did very few of them also report the number 558,000?

Mr. Speaker, this higher number is the total number of murder victims since the ruling in 1976. That is 558,000 people murdered by killers here in the United States. And who is carrying the torch for their cause? We continuously hear about the murderers, but we hear very little about the victims of crime.

Mr. Speaker, as a former judge and prosecutor, I have witnessed firsthand how victims are being treated in the justice system. Being a victim is a terrifying and unforgettable nightmare; then to become a victim at the hands of the criminal justice system is shameful, especially in a system that claims to have justice for all. The first duty of government must be to protect its citizens and victims, and victims should never be ignored to the benefit of criminals.

A federal judge in Houston is now playing his role in overlooking the victims of crime as well. In June 1994, Charles Raby was sentenced to death for the 1992 slaying of seventy-two-year-old Edna Franklin. Her throat was slit twice, her ribs were broken, and her body was stabbed numerous times with a knife. Charles Raby is currently on death row waiting to be executed, but he has filed another lawsuit challenging the constitutionality of lethal injection on the grounds it is cruel and unusual punishment.

U.S. District Judge Lynn Hughes recently denied a motion by the State Attorney General to dismiss Raby's ridiculous claim, and now he will be given access to state documents and employees to try to prove this worthless claim. This man brutally killed a seventy-two-year-old woman with a knife and Judge Hughes is concerned his execution may be painful. Where was this federal judge when Edna Franklin was brutally executed? This ought not to be.

Mr. Speaker, victims deserve to be treated better than this. We as a culture must not stand by and do nothing while those 558,000 were murdered and others hurt in our country. We must support victims of crime, and we must make sure the criminals who commit crimes against them pay for those acts of violence.

There are too many victims who cannot stand up for their own rights, and so it is up to us as concerned citizens, justice officials, public policy-makers, and members of this Congress to stand up for the rights of every homicide victim in this nation to honor their memories through action. By continuing our commitment to helping the families and friends of murdered victims, and promoting a crime policy that ensures a place at the table of justice for them, we honor those lives that were stolen by senseless violence.

The theme of the 2005 National Crime Victims Week put it best: Justice is not served until crime victims are. That is just the way it is.

The Congressional Record. December 7, 2005: H11183–H11184.

Liberal Viewpoint

Russell D. Feingold (D-WI). Mr. President, we recently passed a disturbing milestone in this country. One morning just a few weeks ago in North Carolina, Kenneth Lee Boyd was put to death by lethal injection. Mr. Boyd's was the one thousandth execution since the death penalty was reinstated in 1976. While a jury decided that his guilt was not in doubt, confidence in the extraordinary punishment he received increasingly is.

Across the nation, people are reconsidering capital punishment. Recent polls, jury verdicts, and actions taken by all three branches of government in states across the country reflect the changing attitudes about the death penalty in this country. Americans are increasingly concerned about the use of this very final punishment.

With advances in DNA technology, numerous exonerations of people on death row, and new revelations that innocent people have actually been put to death, more and more people are questioning the accuracy and fairness of the administration of the death penalty. In addition, more and more people have qualms about the very concept of state-sponsored executions. This trend is a hopeful sign, as I believe there continue to be numerous moral, ethical and legal problems with the death penalty.

According to a series of Gallup polls, opposition to the death penalty has grown from 13 percent of Americans in 1995 to 30 percent in October of this year. Think about that. In just ten years, we went from a vast majority of Americans supporting the death penalty, to nearly one-third now opposing it. That is the highest level of opposition since its reinstatement almost thirty years ago. And a CBS News poll from April indicates that when people were asked whether they prefer the death penalty or life without parole for individuals convicted of murder, only 39 percent supported the death penalty.

. . .

This issue can no longer be used as a political grenade. A majority of Americans may not yet oppose the death penalty, but the electorate understands what a serious issue this is, and it will not stand for capital punishment to be exploited for political purposes.

. . .

Much more is happening at the state level that has not received nearly as much attention. North Carolina and California recently created commissions to study the administration of the death penalty in their respective states, joining many other states that have already done so. Moratoriums on executions remain in place in Illinois and New Jersey, and are under consideration in other states. Many state legislatures have worked to address flaws in their systems or even rejected efforts to reinstate the death penalty. State courts have limited or banned the death penalty, including the Kansas Supreme Court, which in 2001 ruled that state's death penalty law unconstitutional. That case, *Kansas v. Marsh*, was heard in the U.S. Supreme Court just last week. Even in Texas, the state that executes by far the most people every year, a life-without-parole sentence was recently enacted, giving juries a strong alternative to the death penalty. And Texas Governor Perry also established a Criminal Justice Advisory Council to review the state's capital punishment procedures.

These signs of progress have coincided with critical new restraints imposed by the Supreme Court, which in recent years has issued two key rulings that limited the application of the death penalty. In 2002, the Court held in *Atkins v. Virginia* that applying the death penalty to mentally retarded defendants was excessive and constituted cruel and unusual punishment in violation of the Eighth Amendment. And just this year, in *Roper v. Simmons*, the Court made the same decision with regard to individuals who commit crimes before their eighteenth birthday. Capital punishment for mentally retarded defendants and juveniles is now unconstitutional in the United States.

. . .

Mr. President, as I mentioned before, there are many reasons people are questioning the death penalty in ever-increasing numbers. A common concern is that innocent people end up on death row, and we cannot tolerate errors when the state is imposing such a final penalty. More than 120 people on death row have been exonerated and released. Think about that. Just over one thousand people have been executed in the era of the modern death penalty, while a number equaling 12 percent of those executed have been exonerated. Those are not good odds, Mr. President.

Even more horrific is the prospect that we have already executed individuals who were, in fact, innocent. It saddens me greatly to report that information has come to light strongly demonstrating that two men put to death in this country in the 1990s may well have been innocent. That sends chills down my spine, as I'm sure it must for my colleagues.

. . .

Mr. President, I know that many people in this country say that it doesn't matter what other countries do or say, that we should not look abroad for ideas. But the fact is that attitudes are changing around the world about capital punishment, and the United States is in poor company internationally on this issue. We are the only Western democracy ranked in the top ten countries in executions in 2004. And increasingly, other countries are rejecting capital punishment. Over the past 10 years, according to Amnesty International, an average of three countries per year has abolished the death penalty.

In closing, I urge my colleagues to take a long, hard look at capital punishment. Years of study have shown that the death penalty does little to deter crime, and that defendants' likelihood of being sentenced to death depends heavily on whether they are rich or poor, and what race their victims were. We have experienced again and again the risks, and realities, of innocent people being sentenced to death. I believe that is it wrong for the state to put people to death, especially when we can achieve our public safety goals by sentencing them to life without parole. It is heartening to see so many people reconsidering the death penalty, and it is my hope that in time we will end it in the United States.

The Congressional Record. December 21, 2005: S14301–S14302.

WAR ON DRUGS

The War on Drugs is an initiative started by the United States to combat the production, distribution, and consumption of certain illegal drugs. Soon after President Richard Nixon coined the term "War on Drugs," he also created the Drug Enforcement Administration (DEA) in 1973 to combat drugs within the United States. Through prohibitive policy, the United States focuses on interference with production of drugs, thus increasing the cost of the product. By increasing the cost of the drug, many hope that it exceeds the value and the demand decreases.

The War on Drugs has produced many solutions and inventive policies of enforcement. Unfortunately none of them seem to be working. The debates between Republicans and Democrats continue to shift blame to the other side, yet neither party has been able to create a comprehensive resolution. Such blame can be seen in Sen. Orrin Hatch's (R-UT) rhetoric. Sen. Hatch believes that America is at a crossroads with its illegal drug policy and must proceed with caution. He blames the Clinton Administration, particularly the president himself, for being too lenient with drug policy initiatives. As a result, drug consumption has increased dramatically especially within the teenager age bracket.

Former president William J. Clinton clearly outlines his drug strategy within his speech. He argues that cooperation is necessary among everyone to ensure that drugs do not penetrate our society. First, President Clinton pledged to increase the budget to combat drugs. Increased funding will partially go toward an educational campaign against drugs. Furthermore, President Clinton acknowledged the prevalence of drugs in criminal behavior and has pledged to increase sentences for drug offenders but at the same time, he has offered help to those that want to change. The use of illegal drugs, particularly marijuana, for medicinal purposes has broadened the debate on illegal drugs.

Conservative Viewpoint

Orrin G. Hatch (R-UT). Mr. President, our federal drug policy is at a crossroads. Unfortunately for Americans, drug control is not a national priority for the Clinton administration. For some time now I have been saying that President Clinton has been AWOL—absent without leadership—in the war on drugs. Put another way, the Clinton White House has been MIA in the drug war—mired in arrogance. Ineffectual leadership and failed federal policies have combined with ambiguous cultural messages to generate changing attitudes among our young people and sharp, serious increases in youthful drug use.

This is painfully evidenced by this chart on my right, which shows that after a 12-year steady decline in drug use by high school seniors, from 1980 to 1992, there has been a sharp increase in such drug use during the last 3 years. As you can see, the decline came from 1980 downhill in every one of these categories, and in every one of the categories since 1992 drug use has started to go up sharply.

Even more troubling is that this increase has been uniform as to those who have used drugs in the past month, in the past year, and those children trying drugs for the first time.

No one is more responsible for our current dilemma than President Clinton. For more than three years, I have taken to the floor of the Senate to warn my colleagues and the nation about the threat we face due to President Clinton's abdication of leadership in the war on drugs. What also troubles me is that a defeatist outlook in the drug war appears now to be supplemented by a softer attitude tolerating or excusing drug use.

The Clinton Administration has caused serious damage to this country as a direct result of failed policies and absent leadership in the war on drugs. Indeed, as one more manifestation of the administration's arrogance of power, we now know that the White House strong-armed the Secret Service into granting security passes for at least a dozen persons who had engaged in the recent use of, among other illegal drugs, crack cocaine and hallucinogens. In responding to questions concerning this matter, White House spokesman Mike McCurry disdainfully suggested that prior drug use was no big deal. What a terrible message to send to the country, especially to our young people. Where was President Clinton during this episode? Why didn't he admonish his spokesman? When will someone at the White House acknowledge that drug use is a big deal.

The Congressional Record. July 29, 1996: S9016–S9027.

Liberal Viewpoint

President William J. Clinton. Good morning. Today I want to talk about what we must do to strengthen our effort to keep drugs away from our neighborhoods and out of our children's lives. First, we must fight drugs before they reach our borders and keep them out of America. This is a battle we must fight together with other nations.

Every year the president is legally required to certify whether other nations are doing their part. Yesterday, I accepted Secretary of State Madeleine Albright's recommendation to certify Mexico, to certify that Mexico is cooperating with us in this fight.

. . .

Stopping drugs at their source is a critical part of the antidrug strategy I announced earlier this week. My balanced budget pays for the largest antidrug effort ever. Under the leadership of our national drug czar, General Barry McCaffrey, who is here with me at the radio address this morning, this plan will crack down on drug dealers and help parents teach their children just how dangerous drugs are. We must give our children the straight facts. They need to hear a constant drumbeat from all of us: Drugs are wrong; drugs are illegal; drugs can kill you. The more children know about how dangerous drugs are, the less likely they are to use them.

Our drug strategy includes an unprecedented national advertising campaign to get out the facts and shape the attitudes of young people about drugs. And we must do more to sever the dangerous connection between illegal drugs and violent crime.

Illegal drugs are involved with the vast majority of violent crimes in America—drug dealers carrying guns, violent criminals on drugs and out of control, gang wars over drug-trafficking turf. One million Americans are arrested every year for breaking the drug laws. Two thirds of all the men in state prisons have abused drugs regularly.

Unfortunately, most of the people who enter jail as drug addicts leave jail still addicted or about to become addicts again. When criminals on parole or ex-convicts out of jail go back on drugs, the chances are enormously high they will commit new crimes. According to some experts, 60 percent of all the heroin and cocaine sold in America is sold to people on bail, parole, or probation. Two-thirds of prisoners with a history of heroin or cocaine use who are released without treatment are back on drugs within just three months. We must break this cycle of crime and drugs once and for all.

Last fall, Congress passed my proposal to require drug testing and treatment for prison inmates and convicts on parole. Our prisons must not be illegal drug markets, and anyone given a chance to go straight and live a better life must be absolutely drug-free. The bill I signed said to the states, we want to continue helping you build prisons, but if you want the money to do that, you must start drug testing prisoners and parolees.

In December, I announced Justice Department guidelines to help states meet this requirement. The guidelines are straightforward. By March 1, 1998, one year from today, every state must submit to the Attorney General a clearly defined, comprehensive plan to test prisoners and parolees, to treat those who need it and punish those who go back on drugs.

Today I'm announcing that I am sending all fifty governors a letter to make it clear that General McCaffrey and Attorney General Reno are prepared to help every state get this job done. We'll provide guidance and resources, experts, technical assistance, access to new technology. We'll give that to every state that needs help in developing its plans. At the same time, this, too, should be perfectly clear: Any state without a prisoner and parolee drug testing plan one year from today will lose federal prison assistance until a plan is submitted. We want to help states build the prison space they need, but we will not help to build prisons that tolerate drugs by turning a blind eye.

The federal government and state governments must work together as partners to get this done. It's time to say to inmates, if you stay on drugs, you'll stay in jail; if you want out of jail, you have to get off drugs. It's time to say to parolees, if you go back on drugs, you'll go back to jail; if you want to stay out of jail, stay off drugs.

We must fight drugs on every front, on our streets and in our schools, at our borders and in our homes. Every American must accept this responsibility. There is no more insidious threat to a good future than illegal drugs. I'm counting on all of you to help us win the fight against them.

Public Papers of the President: William J. Clinton. March 1, 1997: 271–272.

SELECTED READING

Punishment versus Rehabilitation

DiIulio, J. J. *No Escape: The Future of American Corrections.* New York: Basic Books, 1990.

"Does Punishment Deter?" *NCPA Policy Backgrounder* no. 148. August 17, 1998. National Center for Policy Analysis. Dallas, TX.

Hogan, Charles H., and Gerald G. Gales. "Meta-Analsysis and the Rehabilitation of Punishment." *Justice Quarterly* 10 (1993).

"Justice Canada Monitor." *Keeping Canadians Informed.* 2006. www.justicemonitor .ca/correctionalissues.htm.

Miller, J. "Is Rehabilitation a Waste of Time?" *Washington Post.* April 23, 1989.

The Sentencing Project. 2006. www.sentencingproject.org/pubs_06.cfm.

Minorities in Prison

Bullock, Henry A. "Significance of the Racial Factor in the Length of Prison Sentences." *Journal of Criminal Law, Criminology and Political Science* 52 (1961): 411–17.

Lieb, R. "Juvenile Offenders: What Works? A Summary of Research Findings." Olympia: Washington State Institute for Public Policy, 1994.

Rosenthal, Alan. "Racial Disparities in the Local Criminal Justice System." Center for Community Alternatives. March 2001. www.communityalternatives.org/articles/ racial_disparities.html.

"United States: Punishment and Prejudice." *Human Rights Watch.* 2000. www .hrw.org/reports/2000/usa/Rcedrg00.htm.

Death Penalty

"Bush Voices Death Penalty Support." *BBC News.* December 3, 2005. news.bbc.co .uk/1/hi/world/americas/4493978.stm.

"Death Penalty." American Civil Liberties Union. 2006. www.aclu.org/capital/ index.html.

"Death Penalty Information Center." 2006. www.deathpenaltyinfo.org.

Porter, Phil. "The Economics of Capital Punishment." MindSpring. 1998. www .mindspring.com/~phporter/econ.html.

"The Death Penalty." Amnesty International. 2006. web.amnesty.org/pages/ deathpenalty-index-eng.

War on Drugs

"Bush Denies Using Any Illegal Drug during the Past 25 Years." *CNN.com.* August 19, 1999. www.cnn.com/ALLPOLITICS/stories/1999/08/19/president.2000/bush .drug.

Bush, George W. "President Bush Announces Drug Control Strategy." The White House. February 12, 2002. www.whitehouse.gov/news/releases/2002/02/20020212-8.html.

"Illegal Drugs Archive." *Time*. www.time.com/time/archive/collections/0,21428,c_illegal_drugs,00.shtml.

"Illegal Drug Use." National Center for Health Statistics. 2006. www.cdc.gov/nchs/fastats/druguse.htm.

"Report: Illegal Drug Use Up for Boomers." *MSNBC News*. September 7, 2006. www.msnbc.msn.com/id/14712630.

5

Child Welfare

Child abuse and neglect emerged as a social problem in the 1960s. Its recognition coincided with technical developments in radiology that permitted the identification of previously unrecognizable fractures and brain injuries indicative of child abuse. Prior to the 1970s, the responsibility for intervening in child abuse and neglect was left entirely to the states. However, since the enactment of the Child Abuse Prevention and Treatment Act (CAPTA) in 1976, the federal government has assumed a leadership role in crafting legislation, establishing minimum federal standards, and funding child welfare services. Historically, federal funding for child welfare services consisted primarily of matching grants to states. However, conservative dominance in Washington has resulted in greater reliance on block grants. Block grants provide states with flexible funding, but cap funding levels. These funding limits effectively rescind the entitlement to child welfare services because funding levels do not automatically increase when caseloads grow.

Child welfare services comprise a broad continuum of social services concerned with promoting the well-being of children and their families. Such services include child protection services (CPS), day care, early childhood education, foster care, and adoption services. Congressional failure to enact balanced funding incentives has often resulted in overuse of some services as states attempt to draw down maximum federal dollars. Thus, some analysts maintain that the 1970s are characterized by an overemphasis on investigation and reporting and a neglect of prevention and treatment. In the 1980s, congressional adjustments in funding incentives resulted in an overemphasis on family treatment at the expense of child safety. The most recent major child welfare legislation, the Adoption and Safe Families Act

(ASFA) of 1996, emphasizes child safety and permanence, especially adoption. The powerful incentives for adoption included in this legislation have tripled adoptions in many states, illustrating the power of incentives.

CHILDCARE FUNDING

The Personal Responsibility and Work Opportunity Reconciliation Act (PRWORA) of 1996 altered the federal government's method for providing childcare funding to the states. It established the Child Care Development Fund (CCDF) by combining childcare funds under the former Aid to Families with Dependent Children (AFDC) program and discretionary Child Care Development Block Grant (CCDBG), making the CCDF the primary source of federal funding for child care. In addition, states can elect to access additional childcare funds by transferring up to 30 percent of their federal Temporary Assistance to Needy Families (TANF) block grant to the CCDF or by spending these funds directly on child care. Federal childcare funding is now comprised of mandatory childcare funds that do not require a state match, childcare funds that require a state match, and discretionary CCDBG funds that do not require a state match. Thus, states are guaranteed an annual amount of child carefunds and may also draw down additional funds if they provide matching state funds.

Although the CCDF received strong bipartisan support, liberals and conservatives support the measure for drastically different reasons. In actuality, liberals hope to expand federal funding for child care and early intervention programs, but conservatives hope to limit the federal government's role by reducing funding and regulation to decrease the deficit. Liberals argue that more stringent work requirements have increased the need for childcare subsidies, and that small increases in funding since implementation of PRWORA are insufficient to offset increased demands. They also maintain that cuts to other social programs have left the poor with even fewer resources to devote to child care. As a result, liberals claim that only one in seven eligible families receives childcare assistance. In addition, liberals allege that many families do not apply for childcare assistance due to lack of knowledge. According to liberals, states have responded to federal funding cuts and rising childcare costs by cutting programs, tightening eligibility standards, passing on costs to families, and lowering subsidy rates. Liberals contend that low subsidy rates often place high-quality child care out of the reach of the poor. They cite anecdotal evidence that since subsidies often do not cover the full cost of providing day care, many childcare providers will not accept them out of fear they will lose money. Therefore, liberals advocate substantial increases in childcare appropriations. They have introduced proposals to reinstate the entitlement feature and aim to double the number of children served. They also want to improve outreach efforts to reach more eligible families.

On the other hand, conservatives dispute the existence of a "childcare crisis." They charge that liberals overestimate the number of children needing care. They argue that liberal estimates include some children who do not need assistance, such as those who attend school, have a stay-at-home parent, receive care from relatives and friends, and are middle-class. Further, conservatives counter that federal spending on child care has increased more than 200 percent since passage of PRWORA and assert that approximately 90 percent of the eligible applicants receive assistance. Conservatives maintain that the average family pays less than $15 a week for child care, making it very affordable. Finally, conservatives challenge liberals' assumptions that congressional appropriations are the only sources of funding increases. Instead, they maintain that much of the increase in childcare funding has come from savings in the TANF program that have been redirected to child care.

Conservatives champion the use of block grants as a means of streamlining funding and program requirements while allowing states to maximize flexibility. Staunch believers in parents' right to raise their children as they please, conservatives endorse childcare subsidies in the form of vouchers because they allow parents to purchase any type of day care they prefer. The paramount importance placed on parents' right to shape their children's moral and religious development extends to parents' right to purchase day care from religious providers that endorse religious activity. Conservatives believe that policies prohibiting the use of federal subsidies for childcare programs that include religious activity unfairly penalize religious institutions. They further object to the fact that unfair competition from taxpayer-subsidized institutions drives some religious daycare providers out of business. On the other hand, liberals, strong proponents of the separation of church and state, support measures to restrict the use of government funding for childcare programs that include religious activity. Instead, liberals insist that such religious activities be funded only from private dollars.

ADOPTION AND SAFE FAMILIES ACT

The Adoption and Safe Families Act (ASFA) (P.L. 105-89) was enacted to ensure children's safety and to expedite permanency for children in the child welfare system. To achieve this goal, ASFA mandates that each child in out-of-home placement have a "concurrent" case plan that simultaneously focuses casework on reunification with the family and also on the development of an alternative permanent living arrangement such as adoption or subsidized guardianship. Since the passage of ASFA in 1997, the number of children who have been adopted has increased by over 50 percent.

The debate surrounding ASFA was characterized by strong bipartisan consensus that children should not languish in foster care. There was also bipartisan recognition that 50 to 80 percent of parents of children in the child welfare system are substance abusers and that insufficient resources have been directed toward addressing this problem.

Both liberals and conservatives advocate a more efficient use of taxpayers' money, but they favor different solutions. Conservatives call for block grants to increase state flexibility. In contrast, liberals shun block grants, believing they do not keep up with inflation and frequently require states to spend more of their own limited fiscal resources. Liberals hope to preserve federal funding as an entitlement and grant states more flexibility through measures that do not tie flexibility to block grants. Liberals advocate increased federal expenditures on child abuse prevention services, early intervention services, and family reunification services, believing this will reduce the subsequent need for more cost-intensive services. In contrast, conservatives charge that program costs have risen without evidence they are working. They are convinced that child welfare spending can be reduced through more judicious use of child welfare resources. Conservatives endeavor to reduce the size of the child welfare system by promoting adoption and limiting services.

Conservatives maintain that ASFA has been a positive step in reforming a flawed child welfare system. In their view, ASFA addresses many of the shortcomings of the child welfare system by beginning to eradicate the culture of dependency, increasing state flexibility, reducing the taxpayer burden through strategic expenditures, and encouraging citizen involvement and volunteerism. Conservatives' strong belief in the right of children to be raised by a mother and father are at the foundation of their support of time limits on family reunification services. Such limitations, they believe, will improve children's chances of being adopted.

Liberal commentary stresses that reducing child abuse and neglect depends on more aggressive intervention into its antecedent causes such as poverty, the lack of affordable housing, and widespread use of corporal punishment. Further, liberals strongly object to the current structure of the child welfare system, which relies too extensively on out-of-home care and does not devote enough attention toward ensuring child safety and family reunification. Although liberals support time limits on the provision of family reunification services and recognize the importance of encouraging adoption, they stress society's obligation to provide timely substance abuse treatment, family counseling, parent skills training, and other social services to maximize children's chances of returning home. Liberals acknowledge the Bush Administration's support of child welfare programs, but strongly object to their cuts in programs that promote family stability, suggesting that these funds have been used to finance ASFA.

INTERRACIAL ADOPTION

Historically, child welfare services sought to preserve racial heritage by matching children with same-race foster and adoptive parents. In evaluating the best fit between children and prospective families, race and ethnicity were considered along with other factors such as religious affiliation and geographic proximity. Shortages in the number of African American foster and adoptive homes meant that numerous children of color were waiting for adoption. This problem was compounded by the custom of preventing Caucasian parents from adopting children of color they had fostered.

The Multiethnic Placement Act (MEPA) of 1994 prohibits the use of a child's or prospective parent's race, color, or national origin in determining eligibility for foster care or the appropriateness of foster care or adoptive parenthood. However, race and ethnicity could still be a consideration in placement decisions if it was in the child's "best interests." Passage of MEPA failed to significantly increase the number of transracial adoptions since child welfare agencies often felt that race matching was in many children's best interests. Intent on strengthening MEPA, Congress passed the Interethnic Placement Act (IEPA) of 1996. IEPA repealed the clause that allowed race to be considered if it was in the "best interests" of the child, affirming that discrimination against children waiting for suitable homes or discrimination against prospective adoptive parents was illegal. IEPA also strengthens compliance and enforcement procedures by permitting the withholding of federal funds and the initiation of court action against states or counties accused of violating MEPA.

Much of the controversy surrounding passage of MEPA and IEPA centers on the issue of race matching. Opponents of MEPA and IEPA believe it discounts the enormous impact that race and culture have in our society. They believe that African American children will inevitably encounter unique obstacles and challenges that Caucasian families cannot understand. Therefore, African American children must establish intimate connections with other African Americans to help them develop a strong cultural identity and the ability to cope with discrimination. Detractors of this legislation worry that the lack of a racially similar reference group could negatively impact children's social and psychological well-being. Finally, others object to race matching on the grounds that it perpetuates race consciousness and separatism. They accuse proponents of race matching of putting the interests of the ethnic community before the best interests of individual children.

According to this perspective, it is essential for child welfare practice to take race into account.

In contrast, proponents of the legislation believe same-race matching unnecessarily limits the opportunities for children of color to be placed in a home-like environment. Liberal advocacy organizations such as the National Association of Black Social Workers (NASBW) are virulent in their opposition to transracial foster care and adoption. The NASBW issued a well-known resolution that states unequivocally that African American children raised in Caucasian homes could not develop a healthy sense of themselves as African Americans.

Liberals attribute the majority of child abuse and neglect to environmental factors such as parental stress, frustration, and poverty. Liberals in Washington have called for vigorous efforts to address social injustices that lead to the disproportionate removal of African American children from their homes, and regularly advocate comprehensive government interventions to allow African American families more equality in society. Liberals like Sen. Howard Metzenbaum, the Democratic force behind MEPA-IEPA, think that same-race adoptions facilitate adjustment to new families, but they also realize this option is unavailable to the majority of African American children. Liberals believe that the recruitment of African American parents is inadequate, and that the child welfare system imposes unrealistic standards on prospective African American foster and adoptive parents who often have fewer resources to comply with state regulations. They maintain that these regulations create unnecessary barriers that render many otherwise capable African Americans ineligible to be foster or adoptive parents on the basis of age, marital status, income, and home environment. In contrast to conservatives, liberals downplay the notion of "individual responsibility" for raising children, preferring to concentrate on the collective obligation of the state to ensure the welfare of all children.

Conservatives' strong conviction that every child should grow up in a household headed by a mother and father underlies their commitment to overturning barriers to transracial adoption. Convinced that abused and neglected children do better in foster and adoptive homes than their own dysfunctional homes, conservatives refer to studies that show that African American children adopted by Caucasian parents are generally well adjusted and happy. This research also shows that children who are raised in two-parent adoptive homes display superior educational, emotional, behavioral, and health outcomes compared to children living in female-headed families.

Conservatives contend that although government is capable of enacting more effective policies, it is less equipped to nurture children than are families, schools, and churches. Conservatives hope to encourage adoption through tax credits that defray the initial costs of adoption.

They assert that $5,000 tax credits provided to adoptive families for a few years following adoption would save taxpayers a significant amount of money since each foster child costs more than $10,000 per year. Believing that government subsidies increase dependency, conservatives are intent on reducing the size of the child welfare bureaucracy and empowering private charities, religious and civic organizations, and private individuals to accept the primary responsibility for caring for children in need.

CONCLUSIONS

In need of assistance through no fault of their own, children are categorized as "deserving welfare recipients." Therefore, liberals and conservatives generally support government interventions to enhance children's development. However, strong budgetary pressures from the Iraq war, tax cuts, and costly new social programs like the Medicare drug prescription program have lessened this long-standing commitment to taking care of children. Analysts attribute the continued support for child care to Congress's realization that past welfare reform efforts have failed due to lack of child care, thus its provision is integral to the success of PRWROA. Budgetary pressures and fear of big government appear to be the biggest obstacles to establishing a more comprehensive family policy that provides preventive services. Such services could forestall problems that subsequently place children in the child welfare system. Societal values that stress individual responsibility and a limited government have left the U.S. with limited family support systems compared to most other industrialized countries, which consider support for children and families a federal obligation.

CHILDCARE FUNDING

Childcare funding has been a polarizing issue in the United States. There are no mandatory public preschools in the United States. The federal government funds Head Start, a preschool program for children from low-income families, but most families are on their own in regards to finding a preschool or child care. Since the workforce has expanded in recent years, many parents are faced with dramatically increasing childcare costs.

Republicans such as Sen. Jefferson Sessions (R-AL) are concerned about the effect of child care on American taxpayers. Sen. Sessions argues that Congress is already committed to child care and the budget does not need to be expanded. Furthermore, taxes do not need to be raised to pay for the proposed increase. Sen. Sessions outlines programs that have already raised taxes to accommodate welfare programs, but he believes that the list needs to stop.

Sen. John Kerry (D-MA) also outlines the childcare funding problem, but believes that childcare funding should be dramatically increased. As the number of working parents rises, there is a greater need for childcare services. Many parents cannot afford the high cost of these services, and therefore loans and grants must be provided for them. Additionally, Sen. Kerry discusses the need to also help childcare facilities especially with labor costs and building costs.

Conservative Viewpoint

Jefferson B. Sessions (R-AL). Mr. President, I am inclined to want to say: Here we go again. We have a good bill, founded on, and built upon, a welfare reform bill that passed a number of years ago that has had extraordinary success. We now have about half as many people in America on welfare as there were before.

I guess the average American would think we have saved money, but, of course, that is not so. The way we give money to the states, fundamentally, is they get the same amount of money, no matter how many people are on the rolls, and they get to focus that money more on the people who are on welfare. And we have not saved money.

In addition, we have come up with a new welfare reform bill that I believe does a lot of good things. It will encourage work. It will encourage family formation. It will encourage stable family units and be positive in a number of different ways. So I think it is a good bill.

But even though the number of people on welfare is down, even though that number has continued to drop during the times of economic activity that we have seen in the recent past, we are not saving any money.

The bill itself, the fundamental bill, has a $1 billion increase in funding. And now, on top of that, we have a $6 billion childcare program added on top.

Now, having served on the Budget Committee, as I know the presiding officer has, we wrestled hard with these numbers. We wrestled hard with these numbers, and we criticized ourselves, and we told ourselves—over and over again—we have to start restraining what we do in terms of spending.

We have had people on the other side complain mightily about budget deficits over and over again. Oh, they are concerned about our budget deficits. But when we have a bill to add a huge new spending program to a welfare bill that, truthfully, ought to come in flat, at least, if not reducing the amount of welfare—since we have half as many people on welfare as we used to have—we now tack on to that $1 billion fundamental welfare reform a $6 billion childcare reform.

To my knowledge—I am on the Health, Education, Labor and Pensions Committee—we have not discussed childcare in our committee. I do not believe there has been any formal or thorough hearings in the Finance Committee. Just boom, right on top of this bill, $6 billion. Sock it to the taxpayer.

Oh, they say it is going to be paid for by customs user fees. Every bill that comes through here that is unfunded they say it is going to be paid for by customs user fees. Surely, we will have some revenue come out of customs user fees, but it is just revenue, just money that is coming into our government when we are in a time of substantial deficit.

So we are going to spend that, not to fund programs we have out there now that need it, but we are going to spend that new money, they tell us, in this bill on an entirely new childcare program.

Let me show this chart. This chart gives an indication that this Congress has not been insensitive to childcare in America. And let me say this, something we do not think about: We have fought in this Congress, and we need to reauthorize this year, the child tax credit, which provides $1,000 per year for every child in America so families can use that money for childcare or anything else they need—$1,000 per child. For a three-child family, $3,000. They have that money they can utilize as they choose.

Not only that, we are reducing the marriage penalty. When people get married, they pay more taxes. Not only that, we have reduced the 15 percent bracket, or expanded the 10 percent bracket, so that more people will be paying income tax rates at 10 percent rather than 15 percent. It is a substantial reduction for them, a one-third reduction in the amount of income tax lower income working Americans will be paying.

Those are good things we have done without any bureaucracy or anything of that nature.

Look at this chart. This shows the various childcare programs we have in America. Total childcare spending, federal and state—about $6 billion of it is state—$23 billion per year. Now, I am telling you, that is a major commitment by this Congress and the American people to deal with childcare.

But there is a limit to what we do here. We have reduced people on welfare by 50 percent. Are we saving any money for the taxpayers? No. We are adding a $1 billion increase in this bill to help that remaining 50 percent to be positive contributors, to have education and training and jobs and other assets and childcare.

I wish we had the money to fund everybody who wanted to have childcare, to just let them have it. I wish we had the money. I wish we had the money to do a lot of things around here, but we are in a period of deficit. We need to maintain integrity in spending.

The Congressional Record. March 30, 2004: S3324–S3335.

Liberal Viewpoint

John Kerry (D-MA). Mr. President, with most of the country's attention focused on the war in Iraq, important issues at home are falling through the cracks. Today, I rise to talk about one of the needs of working moms and dads and their children—child care. We have a shortage of childcare in this country, and it is a problem for our families, a problem for our businesses, and a problem for our economy. The Census Bureau estimates that there are approximately 24 million school age children with parents who are in the workforce or pursuing education, and the numbers are growing. There has been a 43 percent increase in dual-earner families and single parent families over the last half a century. As parents leave the home for work and education, the need for quality child care in America continues to increase.

As the ranking Democrat of the Committee on Small Business and Entrepreneurship, I think we can foster the establishment and expansion of existing child care businesses through the Small Business Administration, SBA. Today, with Senators Harkin, Landrieu, Pryor, Lieberman, Daschle, Bingaman, and Johnson, I am introducing the Child Care Lending Pilot Act of 2003, a bill to create a three-year pilot that allows small, non-profit child care providers to access financing through SBA's 504 loans.

There is a real need to help finance the purchase of buildings, to expand existing facilities and improve the conditions of established centers to meet the demand for child care. It is appropriate to provide financing through the 504 program because it was created to spur economic development and rebuild communities, and child care is critical to businesses and their employees. Financing through 504 could spur the establishment and growth of child care businesses because the program requires the borrower to put down only between 10 and 20 percent of the loan, making the investment more affordable. Another advantage of 504 loans is that they have terms of up to twenty years, with fixed interest rates, allowing small businesses to keep their monthly payments low and predictable.

As anyone with children knows, quality childcare comes at a very high cost to a family, and it is especially burdensome to low-income families. The Children's Defense Fund has estimated that child care for a four-year-old in a child care center averages $4,000 to $6,000 per year in cities and states around the nation. In all but one state, the average annual cost of child care in urban area child care centers is more than the average annual cost of public college tuition.

These high costs make access to child care all but nonexistent for low-income families. While some states have made efforts to provide grants and loans to assist childcare businesses, more must be done to increase the supply of childcare and improve the quality of programs for low-income families. According to the Child Care Bureau, state and federal funds are so insufficient that only one out of ten children in low-income working families who are eligible for assistance under federal law receives it.

For parts of the country, when affordable child care is available, it is provided through non-profit child care businesses. I formed a task force in my home state of Massachusetts to study the state of child care, and of the many important findings, we discovered that more than 60 percent of the child care providers are non-profit and that there is a real need to help them finance the purchase of buildings or expand their existing space. Child care in general is not a high-earning industry, and the owners don't have spare money lying around. Asking centers to charge less or cut back on employees is not the way to make child care more affordable for families and does not serve the children well. An adequate staff is needed to make sure children receive proper supervision and support. Furthermore, if centers are asked to lower their operating costs in order to lower costs to families, the safety and quality of the child care provided would be in jeopardy.

The Congressional Record. April 8, 2003: S4958–S4974.

ADOPTION AND SAFE FAMILIES ACT

The Adoption and Safe Families Act (ASFA) was signed by President William J. Clinton in 1997 to attempt to correct problems within the foster care system. The act was a continuation from previous legislation in 1980 that did not anticipate adoption of minority children and children with special needs. The Adoption and Safe Families Act passed with an overwhelming majority in both the Senate and the House of Representatives with only seven congressmen voting against it.

Support for the Adoption and Safe Families Act was overwhelmingly bipartisan. Many congressmen, including Sen. Jay Rockefeller (D-WV), point to the inherent problems within the current foster care system. Furthermore, the act places more emphasis for foster care agencies to place children within the biological family. ASFA significantly reduces mandatory time that children are required to spend in foster care and thus speeds up the adoption process. Finally, ASFA requires the state to create a permanent plan of placement for children and imposes time limits on reunification efforts. By passing this act, many children and families were helped.

Even though the Adoption and Safe Families Act enjoyed great support in 1997, many Democrats, such as Rep. George Miller (D-CA), believe that the bill was not strong enough. Six years following the passage of the act, Rep. Miller points out the same problems are faced by the foster care system. Problems of inefficiency, fund abuse, and child abuse still continue to plague the foster care system. Rep. Miller believes that the foster care system needs to be strengthened further, not only from a financial standpoint but also for the children's sake.

Conservative Viewpoint

Jay Rockefeller (D-WV). Mr. President, I am proud and pleased to be part of the successful effort to pass the Adoption and Safe Families Act of 1997. Having worked to achieve the objectives of this bill for many years, I am very grateful to everyone involved in reaching today's result—the final passage of a significant bill that will help children and families in true need across the country for many years to come.

This legislation is the culmination of extensive bipartisan negotiations between the House and Senate over the course of this year to enact the most effective ways to ensure the health, safety, and stability of America's most vulnerable population: abused and neglected children. The product of intense debate and sometimes difficult concessions on all sides, this bill has emerged as a positive first step in fixing our nation's broken child welfare system. At the same time this process has demonstrated the undeniable benefits of bipartisan cooperation and compromise, it has also highlighted the mountain of work still left to be done on behalf of abused and neglected children. In that regard, I hope the Adoption and Safe Families Act of 1997 will be a cornerstone for future efforts on behalf of abused and neglected children, especially those children whose special needs present formidable barriers to their safe adoptive placement.

The Adoption and Safe Families Act of 1997 is most significant in its focus on moving children out of foster care and into adoptive and other positive, permanent placements. If American child welfare policy does not succeed in providing a real sense of belonging and identity to children living in the foster care system, we will be denying these young people the fundamental supports they need to become satisfied and caring adults. It would be a tragedy to write these children off as a lost generation, just another group of children from broken homes and a broken system who just didn't get enough support to make a difference.

In my role as chairman of the National Commission on Children, I had the unique opportunity to travel across the country and speak with hundreds of children, parents, and caregivers about how to effectively address their most basic needs and about how the Government can help to foster their most fundamental aspirations. Because of that commission, I spent a day in LA juvenile court and saw the system at its worst, overwhelmed and ineffectively serving children. But I also met a dedicated advocate, Nancy Daly, and she introduced me to the Independent Living Program and other efforts that can work to serve children. We've stayed in touch, working on these issues together ever since.

At the heart of the recent debate about the best policy for adoption and child welfare, dozens of complex questions have been raised about how federal taxpayer dollars should be spent and who is worthy of receiving them. As we struggle with these difficult issues, which often pit social against fiscal responsibility, I keep returning to the same fundamental lesson I have learned from the families with whom I have spoken over the years: If we cannot build social policy that effectively protects our children, we have failed to do our job as a government and a society.

. . .

The Adoption and Safe Families Act of 1997 will fundamentally shift the focus of the foster care system by insisting that health and safety should be the paramount considerations when a state makes any decision concerning the well-being of an abused and neglected child. This legislation is designed to move children out of foster care and into adoptive and other permanent homes more quickly and more safely than ever before. For the first time, this legislation requires states to use reasonable efforts to move eligible foster children toward adoption by introducing a new fast-track provision for children who have been subjected to severe abuse and other crimes by their parents. In such severe cases, this bill would require that a permanency hearing be held within thirty days. In the case of an abandoned infant where reasonable efforts have been waived to reunite the family, that child could be moved into a safe and permanent home in a month's time.

While this legislation appropriately preserves current federal requirements to reunify families when that is best for the child, it does not require the states to use reasonable efforts to reunify families that have been irreparably broken by abandonment, torture, physical abuse, murder, manslaughter, and sexual assault. In cases where children should not be reunited with their biological families, the Adoption and Safe Families Act of 1997 requires that the states use the same reasonable efforts to move children toward adoption or another permanent placement consistent with a well thought-out and well-mentioned permanency plan.

In addition, the act encourages adoptions by rewarding states that increase adoptions with bonuses for foster care and special-needs children who are placed in adoptive homes. Most significantly, the legislation takes the essential first step of ensuring ongoing health coverage for all special-needs children who are adopted. Without this essential health coverage, many families who want to adopt children with a range of physical and mental health issues, would be unable to do so. I am delighted to see that medical coverage, which has always been a vital part of any program that substantively helps children, is also a key component of this bipartisan package.

Ensuring safety for abused and neglected children is another significant goal of this legislation. The Adoption and Safe Families Act of 1997 seeks to accomplish this goal by ensuring that the safety of the child is considered at every stage of the child's case plan and review process. Moreover, the bill requires criminal background checks for all potential foster and adoptive parents.

The legislation also substantially cuts the time a child must wait to be legally available for adoption into a permanent home by requiring states to file a petition for termination of parental rights for a child who has been waiting too long in a foster care placement. At the same time that it speeds adoptions where appropriate, it also gives states the discretion to choose not to initiate legal proceedings when a child is safely placed with a relative, where there is a compelling reason not to go forward, or where appropriate services have not been provided in accordance with the child's permanency plan.

At the same time that this bill imposes tough but effective measures to decrease a child's unnecessary wait in foster care, it reauthorizes and provides $60 million in increased funding for community-based family support and court improvements over the next three years, collectively referred to as the "Promoting Safe and Stable Families Program." As part of a balanced bipartisan package, these programs will support a range of fundamental state services to help children and families and to provide necessary services to adoptive families. This legislation also takes care to assure that children who have gone through adoptions that have been disrupted or whose adoptive parents die will remain eligible for federal support.

For West Virginia, and every state, this legislation means positive change. Our state currently has about three thousand children in foster care. Under this new legislation, the emphasis will shift the primary focus to their health and safety and to finding them a stable, permanent home. Throughout these debates, I have listened to West Virginia leaders, including Chief Justice Margaret Workman, who testified before the Senate Finance Committee, and Joan Ohl, our West Virginia Secretary of Health and Human Resources. I have visited agencies in my state that provide the full range of services from family supports to adoption, and I have been in touch with social workers and families. I know that the provisions of this legislation will challenge my state, but I am equally confident that its leaders are ready to make the necessary changes to do more for the thousands of children in West Virginia who are depending upon us. . . .

The Congressional Record. November 13, 1997: S12668–S12675.

Liberal Viewpoint

George Miller (D-CA). Mr. Speaker, today the ACLU and several child advocacy groups brought a suit requesting the court to hold accountable those county and state officials responsible for oversight of California's foster care system. Plaintiffs charged that negligence, mismanagement, and abuse and neglect of children are routinely committed by the very state agency charged with protecting children and ensuring their safety and well-being.

In the following article in today's *Los Angeles Times*, one of the plaintiffs reports that the suit will demand all appropriate mental health services; multidisciplinary assessments of the needs of each child; case plans; and providers to ensure that no child will be neglected. Judging from recent news reports, this same lawsuit could be brought against most state child welfare agencies.

The federal child welfare law that I authored in 1980 requires states to comply with a number of core requirements intended to protect children placed in foster care as a condition of receiving federal foster care funds. Yet twenty years after enactment of P.L. 96-272, many of the same shortcomings as prompted the passage of the law are affecting hundreds of thousands of children in foster care placements, raising serious questions about the diligence of the states and the federal government in enforcing the law and protecting the children.

The situation described in the *Times* article is not unique to California, which has had a very troubled history in foster care for decades. In Florida, in the District of Columbia, in New York, and in many other jurisdictions, allegations about inappropriate services, improper placements, inadequate staff training and compensation coupled with massive caseloads and staff turnover are commonplace. And yet the Congress has not taken a broad look at how best to assist in the improvement of accountability and services in the nation's foster care system.

The time has come for a broad review that brings together experts and practitioners and advocates to help shape a thoughtful critique of current practice and make recommendations for the federal, state and local governments. This is not only a family crisis and a children's crisis; it is a fiscal crisis, because we are spending billions of dollars a year on a system that, despite efforts at reform, continues to fail the children in its custody.

The Congressional Record. July 18, 2002: E1304–E1305.

INTERRACIAL ADOPTION

Interracial adoption occurs when a child of one race or ethnic group is placed with adoptive parents of another group. Since there are a disproportionate number of minority children within the foster care system, interracial adoptions have increased. The increase does not come without controversy.

Proponents of interracial adoption argue that time of adoption is decreased. By letting minority children wait for minority adoptive parents, the children will prolong their time in the foster care system dramatically. Furthermore, proponents argue that adopting a child from another race or culture is culturally rewarding.

Opponents of interracial adoption argue that it is a bad idea to mix cultures. Race matching in adoption is the only way to ensure a child's healthy development. Furthermore, opponents of interracial adoption add that psychological effects that the child faces among its peers in school are damaging. Even though many would like to think that race does not play a factor in our society, it is not the case.

Conservative Viewpoint

Deborah Price (R-OH). It is a good day for this Congress. I would urge all my colleagues to cast a vote in strong support of adoption and in support of keeping loving families together. Vote "yes" on the rule and the bill and vote "no" on any attempt to weaken this legislation.

Madam Speaker, I rise today to express my concerns regarding the modified closed rule for H.R. 3286. While I applaud the fact that this legislation would make it possible for more families to provide a loving and permanent home for adoptive children, I am concerned that this bill might not recognize that cultural sensitivity, without delaying adoption, is important to give the child the full measure of their background.

Madam Speaker, approximately one-half of the children awaiting adoption today are minorities. In my home state of Texas, the number of children under the age of eighteen living in foster care in 1993 was 10,880. This represents an increase of 62.4 percent from 1990, and the number continues to climb. Similarly, the number of children living in a group home in 1990 was 13,434. Approximately one half of these 13,434 children are minorities. There are wonderful foster care parents but these numbers of children in nonpermanent homes are way too high.

The sponsors of this legislation argue that current law, which states that race cannot be used as the sole factor in making an adoption placement but can be used as one of multiple factors in the decision, has resulted in adoptions being delayed or denied because of race. This of course is the result of local agencies misinterpreting the law. Should we not penalize directly the agencies incorrectly using the law? According to the sponsors, because of the inherent bias among many social workers, the real-world outcome of current law is that race ends up becoming the sole factor when placements are made. I have worked with social workers and they consistently overall try to work in the best interest of the child.

While I do not believe that race should be the sole criteria in adoption placements, I do believe that we should be sensitive to cultural backgrounds. Had I been permitted, I would have offered an amendment to this bill which would have required that in making adoptive parent placements, the state or appropriate entity shall make every effort to ensure that a prospective adoptive parent is sensitive to the child's ethnic or racial background. It should not, however, delay drastically such adoption.

Adoptive parents and children need not be of the same race. However, it is important that adoptive parents are sensitive to the cultural backgrounds of the children they adopt. It is important that such children grow up in an environment that is respectful and appreciative of the child's heritage. Unfortunately, our society is not color blind, and therefore states and agencies must ensure that adoptive parents of a different race from the minority and Indian children are sensitive to the issues that may arise as the child gets older, including discrimination and questions the child may have about his or her cultural background.

In no way, however, should this policy result in children languishing in foster homes for extended periods of time or in adoptions being delayed or denied when loving, caring parents are ready to adopt.

The Congressional Record. May 9, 1996: H4766–H4775.

Liberal Viewpoint

John McCain (R-AZ). Mr. President, earlier this year I introduced the Adoption Antidiscrimination Act of 1995, S. 637, to ensure that adoptions are not denied or delayed on the basis of race, color, or national origin. I am pleased that the House passed an almost identical provision in its welfare reform bill, H.R. 1. It is my hope that the members of the conference committee on welfare reform will recognize the importance of this issue, and incorporate interracial adoption provisions in the conference report.

In the late 1960s and early 1970s, over ten thousand children were adopted by families of a different race. This was before many adoption officials decided, without any empirical evidence, that it is essential for children to be matched with families of the same race, even if they have to wait for long periods for such a family to come along. The forces of political correctness declared interracial adoptions the equivalent of cultural genocide. This was, and continues to be, nonsense.

Sound research has found that interracial adoptions do not hurt the children or deprive them of their culture. According to Dr. Howard Alstein, who has studied 204 interracial adoptions since 1972, "We categorically have not found that white parents cannot prepare black kids culturally." He concluded that "there are bumps along the way, but the trans-racial adoptees in our study are not angry, racially confused people" and that "They're happy and content adults."

Since the mid 1970s, there have been very few interracial adoptions. African American children who constitute about 14 percent of the child population currently comprise over 40 percent of the one hundred thousand children waiting for adoption in foster care. This is despite twenty years of federal efforts to recruit African American adoptive families and substantial efforts by the African American community. The bottom line is that African American children wait twice as long as other children to be adopted.

Last year, Senator Metzenbaum attempted to remedy this problem by introducing the Multiethnic Placement Act of 1994 [MEPA]. Unfortunately, the bill was weakened throughout the legislative process and eviscerated by the Clinton administration Department of HHS in conference.

.   .   .

The legislation that was finally signed by the president does precisely the opposite of what was originally intended. This is because it contains several huge loopholes that effectively permit continuing the practice of racial matching. For example, it states that an agency may not "delay or deny the placement of a child for adoption or into foster care solely on the basis of [race, color, or national origin]." This language can be used by those opposed to interracial adoptions to delay or deny placements by using race, color, or national origin as only part of their rationale.

An even bigger loophole is contained in the "permissible consideration" section of MEPA which states that an agency "may consider the cultural, ethnic or racial background of the child and the capacity of the prospective foster or adoptive parents to meet the needs of a child of this background as one of a number of factors used to determine the best interests of a child." While this language may appear innocuous, it can be used by those who are committed to racial matching to delay or deny a placement simply by claiming that an interracial adoption is not in the best interests of the child.

The U.S. Department of Health and Human Services (DHHS) has issued guidelines for implementing the Multiethnic Placement Act. Again, on their face, the guidelines do not appear to be objectionable. However, consistent with the underlying MEPA law, they continue to allow race to be a major consideration that may be used by those who wish to stop interracial placements. Consequently, the National Council for Adoption and Institute for Justice have informed the department that its guidelines do not adequately address this issue. They continue to believe that new legislation is necessary.

Clearly, we need to fix last year's flawed legislation. In considering the House provisions on this issue, the conferees should prohibit, under any circumstances, an agency that receives federal funds from delaying or denying the placement of a child on the basis of the race, color or national origin. Racial or cultural background should never be used as a basis for denying or delaying the placement of a child when there is at least one qualified household that wants the child.

The Congressional Record. September 19, 1995: S13770–S13804.

SELECTED READING

Childcare Funding

"Child Care." 2006. www.policyalmanac.org/social_welfare/childcare.shtml.

"Child Care Bureau." Administration for Children and Families. 2006. www.acf.hhs .gov/programs/ccb/policy1/misc/approp06.htm.

Kaplan, Jan. "Child Care Funding and Policy Issues." January 2002. www .financeproject.org/Publications/childcarefundingpolicyissues_trn.htm.

Mezey, Jennifer. "Making the Case for Increasing Federal Child Care Funding." Center for Law and Social Policy. October 16, 2003. www.clasp.org/publications/CC_ fact_sheet.pdf.

National Head Start Association. 2006. www.nhsa.org.

Adoption and Safe Families Act

"Adoption and Safe Familes Act of 1997." University of Michigan. 2006. www.ssw .umich.edu/icwtp/legalIssues/c-asfa1997.pdf.

"ASFA." 2006. www.ncsacw.samhsa.gov/files/508/ASFA_Brochure.htm.

Moye, Jim. "It's a Hard Knock Life: Does ASFA Adequately Address Problems in the Child Welfare System?" 2006. www.law.harvard.edu/students/orgs/jol/vol39_2/ moye.pdf.

"The Impact of ASFA." National Institute of Corrections. 2006. www.nicic.org/ Library/021325.

Welte, M. Carmela. "Adoption and Safe Families Act: Has It Made a Difference?" CASANet Resources. Summer 2003. www.casanet.org/library/adoption/ asfa-has-made-a-difference.htm.

Interracial Adoption

"Interracial Adoption." National Adoption Information Clearinghouse. 2006. interracial.adoption.com.

Shokraii, Nina. "Adopting Racism." 2006. www.foundationforlargefamilies.com/ nina.html.

Stevenson-Moudamane, Veronica. "Parenting across the Color Line: Books on Trans-racial Adoption, Brief Article." *Black Issues Book Review*. January 2001. www .findarticles.com/p/articles/mi_m0HST/is_1_3/ai_71317392.

"The Adoption History Project." 2006. darkwing.uoregon.edu/~adoption/topics/ transracialadoption.htm.

"Transracial Adoption." The Multiracial Activist. 2006. www.multiracial.com/issues/ issues-transracialadoption.html.

6

Education

A free public education system is one of the hallmarks of American democracy. Not only is it critical for the development of a civic-minded polity, one key to representative democracy, but it is also a primary mechanism Americans use to climb the social ladder. Education is also a way to fuel economic development. Not only can good science education help develop more and better scientists and engineers, but virtually any area of competency developed through teaching can produce a population better equipped for a modern workplace. School is also a primary place where children are socialized—where they are introduced, for example, to basic notions like equality and fairness.

Because its implications are significant and multifaceted, political debates around education policy are often quite heated. The content of science education, especially in biology classes, has been fiercely debated for a hundred years, for example, and the issue of religion in schools has been another contentious focal point. President Eisenhower considered a robust education system as critical to winning the Cold War against the Soviet Union, and civil rights activists saw schools as a vehicle for ending racism in America. In the past few decades, a range of education issues have become the primary areas of debate, and we have chosen a number of these issues to focus on below.

SCHOOL VOUCHERS

The school voucher program is one approach promoted by many conservatives to improve the American educational system. Proponents argue that a primary reason that American schools are failing is a lack of competition. Since there is no incentive for administrators and teachers to improve the learning environment, schools do not strive to improve their "product" in the way businesses do. The idea behind the voucher program is to make schools more like companies in a free market. Instead of simply paying the school system directly, the government would give part of the funding to the students' family as a voucher. That family can then "spend" the voucher by selecting among the public and private schools within the region or city, and the schools would then receive this money from the government. This would force schools to compete for students, and to do so they would increase the quality of education in their schools. Students from bad schools would shift to better schools, and therefore failing schools would have to reform to maintain government funding.

Opponents to this plan argue that the analogy between business and education is misplaced. People who enter education as a profession are not guided by a drive to beat opponents. Even if it works—that is, even if students move from worse to better schools—the failing schools would lose much-needed funding and their best students, both of which are critical for building better educational programs. Many of these opponents argue that instead, some parents will take the government money and use it to send their children to religious schools. In other words, they argue, the voucher program is really just a backdoor strategy for producing government funds for religious schools.

NO CHILD LEFT BEHIND

Another approach to improving American schools is called "outcomes-based education," in which uniform standards are created for educating students and students are tested on their ability to meet these standards. These standards can also be used to measure the performance of teachers as well as to pressure schools to improve the quality of education. The No Child Left Behind Act of 2001 (NCLB) employs this approach. Supported by some conservatives (it was promoted by President Bush during his first year in office) and liberals (one of its main supporters was also Sen. Edward Kennedy of Massachusetts), the law requires each state to develop an accountability system. This system includes assessing yearly progress toward set educational goals. The state determines proficiency levels that students are required to meet, notably in reading, math, and science. Students are then tested in these areas during particular stages of their education. If these standards are not reached widely enough within a school, penalties are imposed on the school. Proponents argue that the system produces accountability, which in turn produces various forms of pressure on schools to excel.

Opponents argue that NCLB produces many unwanted consequences. They claim, first and foremost, that having the success of teachers and schools linked to student performance on standardized tests, and especially having that performance linked to funding as well as other incentives, encourages educators to teach to the test. Instead of educating students, which is understood as providing a broad and rich background that cannot always be quantified, teaching becomes focused on test preparation. Conservatives have also complained that standardized tests undermine local control over education. Liberals claim that the emphasis on reading, math, and science has led to a significant reduction in the teaching of the arts and social sciences, and has produced a deemphasis on physical education, a serious problem in a period of rising obesity. Critics also complain that the program is not adequately funded, undermining its effectiveness.

SCHOOL FUNDING INEQUITIES

The problems related to the funding of NCLB are closely related to the unequal funding of school systems across America. Generally speaking, school systems in poorer municipalities receive less money per student than those in middle-class and wealthier districts. The main reason for this inequity is the source of the funding. Public schools are funded primarily by local property taxes and state taxes, and approximately 10 percent of the money is given by the federal government. Since property tax is higher in wealthier municipalities, these local governments are able to provide more school funding. Poor communities are rarely able to compete in providing funding for modern equipment, teacher salaries, and the various other factors that differentiate the quality of education that students receive. The primary mechanism for producing more equity in funding therefore comes from state and federal programs.

However, liberals and conservatives are deeply divided on how much these governments should spend. Generally, fiscal conservatives argue for reducing taxes and government spending on social programs, including education. In contrast, liberals argue for a progressive tax policy, in which those who are wealthy pay a higher percentage of their income in taxes to use for social programs, including education. Since the 1980s, state funding for education has declined, partially because many states have reduced state taxes, thereby dropping revenue that could be spent on education, but also because the federal government has reduced the amount of money it has been allocating to state governments. As that money has been reduced, and as states have had to cover the costs of more programs alone, states have been forced to cut funding to education.

SEX EDUCATION

Liberals and conservatives generally agree that sex education is an important tool for reducing teenage pregnancy rates and curtailing the spread of sexually transmitted diseases. Both also generally agree that teenagers should be encouraged to delay becoming sexually active. But from that point forward, the opinions of the two groups diverge radically.

Conservatives generally support abstinence-only education. They argue that teaching teenagers about contraception gives them a false sense of security, since condoms can fail and other methods are dangerous in short-term, monogamous relationships. Moreover, teaching students how to use contraception implicitly promotes sexual activity, giving it a form of legitimacy. They therefore argue for education that focuses entirely on encouraging students to abstain from sex until they are married. Any mention of contraceptives, they argue, should focus on their rate of failure. This program is used in many states and it is promoted by the federal government through the Section 510 Abstinence Education Grant Program, which gives block grants to states to promote abstinence-only programs in schools.

Liberals counter that abstinence-only education is unrealistic. They argue that many teenagers are likely to have sex regardless of what educators tell them, and therefore abstinence-only education might leave them utterly unprepared for moments when they actually need to understand how to protect themselves. For this reason, liberals generally promote comprehensive sex education. This approach also encourages students to delay having sex, but for those who choose to have sex anyway, they encourage minimizing the number of sex partners and using contraceptives to protect themselves.

FAITH-BASED INITIATIVES

In 2000, George W. Bush campaigned for president as a "compassionate conservative," a term coined by Marvin Olasky that means using culturally conservative methods to resolve social issues usually addressed by liberals. For example, Bush argued that faith-based community organizations could often do a better job of dealing with issues like drug addiction than government organizations. After entering office, the Bush Administration created the White House Office of Faith-Based and Community Initiatives (OFBCI), which distributes billions of dollars in competitive grants to provide social services. Centers for this office have been established in a number of departments of the executive branch, including the Department of Education. The program has then given government funds to a range of education programs, which have included sex education programs that employ abstinence-only techniques, programs to teach people the value of het-erosexual marriage, and church-based organizations that mentor children at risk.

The liberal criticisms have been on exactly these types of programs funded by OFBCI. They argue, first and foremost, that grant recipients often use the money to promote their religious beliefs, which liberals argue vio-lates the First Amendment. An example was a funded mentoring program, MentorKids USA, which a federal court found was allowing only devout Christians to become mentors, and that part of their mentoring responsi-bility was to read the Bible to the children and show them God's redemp-tive plan for all. Liberals also claim that since these organizations are taking government money but hiring people based on religious background, they are violating employment laws by discriminating against job applicants who do not hold the same religious beliefs.

CONCLUSIONS

Debate on education policy covers a wide range of issues, including the controversies discussed in this chapter. In the end, because public education is funded primary by local and state taxes, many education issues play out differently from state to state and community to community. But since the education system has such a profound impact on American society, the na-ture of these debates is likely to continue to evolve and change form in the coming decades.

SCHOOL VOUCHERS

In the 2000 presidential election, the issue of school vouchers was hotly de-bated between the presidential hopefuls. While George W. Bush strongly supported school vouchers, the former vice president, Al Gore, was against the limited educational strategy. School vouchers would take kids out of public schools and place them into private schools. Money that is currently spent on the child's education would be given to the parents in the form of a voucher, which would be used at a school of their choice.

Proponents of school vouchers argue that school choice gives people the option of selecting a school for their child. School choice would provide greater opportunity for kids to succeed in school and grant the parents more control over their child's education. Proponents such as Rep. Martin R. Hoke (R-OH) argue that school choice will only increase the competition among schools and therefore will benefit the child's education. Proponents cite many successful trial voucher programs that were implemented around the United States as cases to make the voucher program and school choice a national initiative.

Critics of the voucher program strongly oppose it because it gives taxpayer money to private schools that are often religious. The issue of separation of church and state is critical within the school choice debate. Liberals such as Sen. John Corzine (D-NJ) argue that vouchers will not only hurt the child's progress, but they will also hurt the public school system. By taking money from the public school and putting it into a private school, the improvement of public schools is impossible.

Liberal Viewpoint

John S. Corzine (D-NJ). Our government promises every child in the United States a free and appropriate public education. The very idea that federal funds that should be going to our nation's public schools to fulfill that promise will instead be siphoned away to private schools is of great concern to me.

As a product of public schools, and the child of a public school teacher, I am a strong supporter of the public school system. I often say that while we cannot be a nation of equal outcomes, we can and must be a nation of equal opportunities. Our public schools are the key to equal opportunity for all American children.

Although the voucher program we are discussing today would only impact the District of Columbia, it clearly would have national implications. It is a calculated first step toward broader voucher programs, which would drain resources from our public schools—the very schools that are free and open to all children, and accountable to parents and taxpayers.

Simply put, vouchers are not the answer to our educational ills—they are bad education policy driven by ideological goals.

Wouldn't our energy be better focused on strengthening our public schools, which can and do succeed with adequate resources? To succeed, schools need high-quality teachers, a rigorous curriculum, high expectations, parental involvement, and effective management. All of these require adequate resources.

In 2001, Congress passed the No Child Left Behind Act, which was intended to reform public education by establishing high standards for every student, providing federal incentives to boost low-performing schools, and creating accountability.

Unlike vouchers, which even supporters acknowledge would reach only a small fraction of all children, No Child Left Behind was intended to implement proven, effective reforms in all schools not just for a few students, but for all students.

But the administration and this Congress are not living up to the promise of No Child Left Behind and are under-funding it by over $8 billion. This leaves millions of children behind and places additional burdens on already burdened State and local education budgets.

And, on top of under-funding No Child Left Behind, we are now considering giving funds to schools that are not even subject to its provisions.

As we know, No Child Left Behind would ensure oversight and accountability, including testing standards and teacher qualification standards. But the voucher program we are considering today does not provide the same system of accountability or oversight of these private schools, nor does it set the same criteria for the very people that will be teaching our children.

In fact, this bill allows any private school to apply to participate in the program, but there is no evaluation process before they are accepted to participate. This leaves District of Columbia children vulnerable to poor-performing schools.

I ask proponents of the bill: How can we ask our public schools to fulfill the significant mandates of No Child Left Behind, when we are refusing those schools adequate funds and at the same time giving federal money to schools that are not even required to abide by many of its mandates?

Proponents of the voucher program say that it provides parents with "choice" that they do not currently have. This is simply not true. The District of Columbia already offers three alternatives to traditional public schools. First, D.C. has the largest number of public charter schools per capita in the nation. If we pass this voucher program, these charter schools will remain under-funded. Yet we still want to give private schools money.

Second, D.C. has established fifteen public transformation schools that have, for the first time ever, succeeded in raising the scores of low-income children in low-performing schools. Again, however, the very programs in these transformation schools that have succeeded are now seeing cuts in funding. Yet we still want to give private schools money.

Finally, D.C. allows parents who are not content with their neighborhood school to send their child to out-of-boundary schools that are accountable to public education standards. Yet we still want to give private schools money.

If this is not school choice, then what is? Why can't we give these types of schools a chance to succeed rather than undermining them and draining funds from their already successful programs? Proponents of vouchers also claim that the program in this bill is a pilot program and should be given a chance. But Milwaukee and Cleveland both tried to implement a voucher program, and a GAO study of the programs in these two cities found no or little difference in voucher and public school students' performance.

Our cities have tried vouchers and have not succeeded. Our children should not be guinea pigs for programs that have simply not been proven effective at raising academic achievement.

I am not the only one opposed to this program. My friend and colleague in the House of Representatives, Eleanor Holmes Norton, along with the majority of the D.C. City Council and School Board, also oppose any voucher program. In addition, the residents of the District of Columbia are overwhelmingly opposed to private school vouchers.

Let's not turn D.C. into a laboratory for school vouchers. Vouchers are not the solution to improving educational opportunity in D.C. or anywhere else in America. Let's instead focus on fulfilling the promise of No Child Left Behind by fully funding it, and giving our public schools the resources they need to truly succeed.

The Congressional Record. October 3, 2003: S12442–S12443.

Conservative Viewpoint

Martin R. Hoke (R-OH). Mr. Speaker, we all know that a quality education is the greatest investment we can make in our children as well as in our nation's future. It is often remarked that a nation's most valuable asset is its youth, and as the father of three young children, I know full well the truth of that observation.

School choice is an innovative and overdue idea. At present, the public schools have a monopoly in education because their consumers, students, and their parents, are forbidden to choose which school to attend unless they can afford private or parochial schools. Not surprisingly, this Government monopoly has failed to provide a quality service to its captive consumers.

School choice would allow parents to take the money they already spend on taxes for education and invest that money in the school they believe will best educate their child. Essentially, the funds go where the child goes. The child would be able to go to a public or private school, including a religious one. By putting power in the hands of parents, schools would be forced to compete for students. Competition, in turn, will force school administrators to make much needed reforms in order to attract even more customers.

The Congressional Record. January 17, 1995: E107–E109.

NO CHILD LEFT BEHIND

During the 2000 presidential campaign, Vice President Al Gore and Governor George Bush debated heavily the future of the American education system. The No Child Left Behind Act was Bush's solution to the educational crisis in America. He felt that the No Child Left Behind Act would hold schools accountable and allow the federal government to eliminate federal education funding when schools do not meet the set standards. The No Child Left Behind Act implements a national standardized test for all students, regardless of learning disabilities, mental disabilities, or ESL (English as a second language) status. If a school does not continue to meet a standard set or improve on its testing results, the president felt that No Child Left Behind would be an equitable way of enforcing the standards and bettering our school system to match that of the Europeans while opponents have seen this as neglecting analytical thinking, literature, and the social sciences. Many claim that No Child Left Behind has forced schools to teach standardized-test skills rather than actually teach the curriculum at large. Since it's been signed into law, many schools have lost their funding. At the time of its introduction, it was heavily supported by the Republican Party and heavily opposed by the Democratic Party. Currently, No Child Left Behind is still heavily questioned by educators and politicians alike, and has helped to foster the debate about the school voucher program.

Liberal Viewpoint

Edward M. Kennedy (D-MA). Mr. President, for families across this country who have school-age children, they have been involved over the period of these recent days and weeks preparing their children to attend, by and large, the public schools of our country. Over 90 percent of the children in this country go to the public schools. A little less than 10 percent go to private schools.

Over these last several months, we have had, with President Bush, a bipartisan effort which resulted in what was called the "No Child Left Behind Act." That legislation recognized that what is really needed for the neediest children in this country is school reform. But we also need investment, school reform and increased resources.

For a long time, the Title I program was criticized because it provided resources without really providing the kind of accountability that is so important. So there was a bipartisan effort to provide for that kind of accountability.

. . .

I was asked over the recent month of August as I went around Massachusetts, is: What is going to be the administration's response to the children being left behind with the budget that the administration recommended to the Congress for funding of No Child Left Behind? Will politicians be accountable? There are 10.3 million children who fall into what we call the

Title I category. Over 6 million of those children are going to be left behind under the administration's budget. We do not expect that money in and of itself to be the answer to all of the problems, but it is a pretty good indication of the priorities of a nation and the priorities of an administration. And this chart is a pretty clear indication of the recent history of increased funding for education. We are talking here about the total education budget. In 1997, a 16 percent increase; 12 percent in 1998; 12 percent in 1999; 6 percent in the year 2000; 19 percent in 2001; and 16 percent in 2002. However, it is only 2.8 percent under this administration's budget, the lowest we have seen over the last seven years.

Again, money is not everything, but we did make a commitment to the parents, to the families, to the schools. There are tough criteria for all of those groups. We have seen, in the efforts made by Senator Harkin in the Appropriations Committee, the recommendation that it will be higher than this program. It will be some $4.2 billion, and it will raise this percentage up to about 6 percent. 2.8 percent is the recommendation that is being made by our Republican friends in the House of Representatives. By and large, the best judgment we have is that this will be the figure coming from the House, and we will be somewhat above, and the conference will come out lower, certainly, than what we have seen in recent years.

What has resulted from this—from the fact that we have not seen adequate funding of the program? We recognize in the No Child Left Behind Act that one of the most important necessities is a well-qualified teacher in every classroom in the country. There is virtually no increase in funding for teacher training. So the 18,000 teachers that would have been trained if there had been a cost of living increase will not receive the training.

Mr. President, 20,000 students will be cut from the college Work-Study Program; 25,000 limited-English-proficient children cut from the federal bilingual program; 33,000 children cut from after-school programs; there is virtually no increase in the Pell grants; and there is no increase in student loans.

What has the administration requested of the Congress? Why do I take a few moments of the Senate time today? I want to point out what is happening in this debate regarding funding of education because tomorrow in the House of Representatives, they will mark up a recommendation by this administration for $4 billion in new funding for private school vouchers. We understand, this is for private schools, 10 percent of the education, $4 billion. Yet just 2.8 percent increase for the public schools, where 90 percent of the children go.

There are a number of reasons we should be concerned. I think most of us believe that we should not be taking scarce funds from the public school children and putting them into private schools. That is in effect what this is doing. If we had the $4 billion, we would be able to increase the total number of poor children to be covered under the Title I program to about two-thirds of those that are being left behind this year. However, the administration said no; we will have $4 billion over a five-year period to be used for the private schools, for just 10 percent of the children.

The reason we raise this issue is in case we have these resources again, we will have an opportunity, hopefully, to debate this, and it ought to be directed toward the public school system.

But beyond that, some of the things that concern us is that with the $4 billion, there is virtually no requirement that we have accountability. The administration made a great deal about accountability, to make sure that we know where the money is invested, what the results will be on the standardized systems to be able to tell if children are progressing. In my own state of Massachusetts, we have seen important progress where we have had accountability and support, including the recent announcement of the MCAS [Massachusetts Comprehensive Assessment System] results in the past week, in which we have seen continued progress in math and continued progress made in English. Not all the problems are resolved, and there are still painful problems in terms of disparity, but we have seen progress made because of accountability.

The administration has talked about accountability. But for their $4 billion, there is no accountability to any schools to ensure that they do what all the public schools do, and that is, to have the examinations.

There is no accountability to ensure that private schools accept all the children. In the public school system there has to be acceptance of all of the children, but the private schools do not have to do that.

In private schools, there is no accountability to ensure teachers will be highly qualified teachers. We wrote in that legislation that in a four-year period there will be highly qualified teachers in the classrooms. We fund a variety of programs regarding recruitment, training, and retention, and we give maximum flexibility to local communities to be able to do that. But there is no requirement with that $4 billion that they use those funds for highly qualified teachers in the classrooms. And there is no requirement to give the parents the critical information they need and which we have insured under this legislation.

So we are puzzled. We heard both the president and our good friends on the other side saying accountability was the key element. We agree that was enormously important—we are going to have accountability and resources. However, now we have the administration coming back with $4 billion more. Instead of allocating that to the 90 percent of the schools that will train the children of America, the public school systems which returned to school this past week—no, they will use that money, the $4 billion, in the private schools for vouchers. They have basically retreated on each and every one of these principles. It seems a very important mistake and one which we will have the opportunity, hopefully, to debate.

With those resources, if the Bush budget took that $4 billion in new funding for private schools over five years along with the cut in public schools, had that $4 billion been available for public schools, it would mean the upgrading of the skills of 1 million teachers across this country. It would upgrade the skills of 1 million teachers. You could provide 5.2 million more children with after-school learning opportunities.

I just point out about the after-school programs, because of all of the federal programs that are out there that go through the process and are considered to be quality programs, when they get in line for the funding, the after-school programs are number 1. Do we understand that? There is a greater need, in terms of limited resources for these programs, than for any other federal program. People understand that if you are going to provide after-school programs and supplementary services for the children who need them, this is the way to try to do it. We are seeing the results of success academically as well as in terms of the social progress the children have made.

This is what you would be able to do. You could provide 5.2 million more children with after-school learning opportunities. You could provide a Pell Grant to five hundred thousand more college students—those students who are able, gifted, talented, motivated young people whose parents have limited resources and income. They will not go on to college because they are not eligible for the Pell grants. With these resources, 5 million more children would receive increased college aid.

As we continue this debate and discussion about funding education, it is enormously important that the American people understand whose side we are on. We on this side of the aisle believe very strongly that with scarce resources in our budget, these resources ought to be used to provide more highly qualified teachers in every classroom, smaller class sizes, after-school programs, supplementary services, and information to parents so they know what is happening in those schools—all of those for the children in this country. We believe that is where the needs are. That is what we ought to be doing with scarce resources, not siphoning off $4 billion for the 10 percent of children who are attending private schools.

We will have an opportunity, when this comes before the Senate, to debate it further. But we want the parents of children going to public schools, who are facing increasing pressure—as we have seen all across this country as States have cut back in support and help to local communities, increasing the size of their classes, reducing the after-school programs, cutting out a number of subjects such as music programs, and cutting back on the number of teachers' aides and teachers' assistants—to know that we understand this is not a time to abandon our public schools. This is a time to invest in our future.

One final point. We have had a great deal of discussion and debate about national security and national defense. I would like to make the point that ensuring that we are going to have well-qualified children in schools that are going to meet standards is an essential aspect of our national security and national defense. And we should not shortchange that investment any more than we do our Defense Department.

The Congressional Record. September 4, 2002: S8150–S8152.

Conservative Viewpoint

President George W. Bush. We've got large challenges here in America. There's no greater challenge than to make sure that every child—and all of us on this stage mean every child, not just a few children—every single child, regardless of where they live, how they're raised, the income level of their family, every child receive a first-class education in America.

. . .

And we owe the children of America a good education. And today begins a new era, a new time in public education in our country. As of this hour, America's schools will be on a new path of reform and a new path of results.

Our schools will have higher expectations. We believe every child can learn. Our schools will have greater resources to help meet those goals. Parents will have more information about the schools and more say in how their children are educated. From this day forward, all students will have a better chance to learn, to excel, and to live out their dreams.

I want to thank the Secretary of Education, Rod Paige, for being here and for his leadership. I asked Rod to join my administration because I wanted somebody who understood what it meant to run a school district in Washington, D.C. I didn't need somebody that based his knowledge on theory; I wanted somebody who based his knowledge on experience. And Rod was a teacher, a school board member, and the superintendent of the Houston Independent School District. He did a fine job there, and he's doing a fine job in Washington.

. . .

First principle is accountability. Every school has a job to do, and that's to teach the basics and teach them well. If we want to make sure no child is left behind, every child must learn to read, and every child must learn to add and subtract. So in return for federal dollars, we are asking States to design accountability systems to show parents and teachers whether or not children can read and write and add and subtract in grades three through eight.

The fundamental principle of this bill is that every child can learn, we expect every child to learn, and you must show us whether or not every child is learning. I read a quote one time from a young lady in New York. She said, "I don't ever remember taking an exam. They just kept passing me along. I ended up dropping out in the seventh grade. I basically felt nobody cared."

The story of children being just shuffled through the system is one of the saddest stories of America. "Let's just move them through." It's so much easier to move a child through than trying to figure out how to solve a child's problems. The first step to making sure that a child is not shuffled through is to test that child as to whether or not he or she can read and write or add and subtract.

The first way to solve a problem is to diagnose it. And so, what this bill says, it says every child can learn. And we want to know early, before it's too late, whether or not a child has a problem in learning. I understand taking tests aren't fun. Too bad. We need to know in America. We need to know whether or not children have got the basic education.

No longer is it acceptable to hide poor performance. No longer is it acceptable to keep results away from parents. One of the interesting things about this bill, it says that we're never going to give up on a school that's performing poorly, that when we find poor performance, a school will be given time and incentives and resources to correct their problems. A school will be given time to try other methodologies, perhaps other leadership, to make sure that people can succeed. If, however, schools don't perform, if, however, given the new resources, focused resources, they are unable to solve the problem of not educating their children, there must be real consequences. There must be a moment in which parents can say, "I've had enough of this school." Parents must be given real options in the face of failure in order to make sure reform is meaningful.

And so, therefore, this bill's second principle is, is that we trust parents to make the right decisions for their children. Any school that doesn't perform, any school that cannot catch up and do its job, a parent will have these options: a better public school, a tutor, or a charter school. We do not want children trapped in schools that will not change and will not teach.

The third principle of this bill is that we have got to trust the local folks on how to achieve standards, to meet the standards. In Washington, there's some smart people there, but the people who care most about the children in Hamilton are the citizens of Hamilton. The people who care most about the children in this school are the teachers and parents and school board members. And therefore, schools not only have the responsibility to improve; they now have the freedom to improve. The federal government will not micromanage how schools are run. We believe strongly—we believe strongly the best path to education reform is to trust the local people. And so the new role of the federal government is to set high standards, provide resources, hold people accountable, and liberate school districts to meet the standards.

I can't think of any better way to say to teachers, "We trust you." And first of all, we've got to thank all the teachers who are here. I thank you for teaching. Yours is indeed a noble profession, and our society is better off because you decided to teach. And by saying we trust local folks, we're really saying we trust you. We trust you. We want you to have as much flexibility as possible to see to it that every child that walks in your classroom can succeed. So thank you for what you do.

And a fourth principle is that we're going to spend more money, more resources, but they'll be directed at methods that work, not feel-good methods, not sound-good methods, but methods that actually work, particularly when it comes to reading. We're going to spend more on our schools, and we're going to spend it more wisely.

If we've learned anything over the last generations, money alone doesn't make a good school. It certainly helps. But as John mentioned, we've spent billions of dollars with lousy results. So now it's time to spend billions of dollars and get good results.

As John mentioned, too many of our kids can't read. You know, a huge percentage of children in poverty can't read at grade level. That's not right in America. We're going to win the war overseas, and we need to win the war against illiteracy here at home, as well. And so this bill—so this bill focuses on reading. It sets a grand goal for the country:

Our children will be reading by the third grade. That's not an impossible goal. It's a goal we must meet if we want every child to succeed. And so, therefore, we tripled the amount of federal funding for scientifically based early reading programs.

We've got money in there to make sure teachers know how to teach what works. We've got money in there to help promote proven methods of instruction. There are no more excuses, as far as I'm concerned, about not teaching children how to read. We know what works, the money is now available, and it's up to each local district to make sure it happens. It's up to you, the citizens of Hamilton, to make sure no child is left behind. And the federal government can spend money, and we can help set standards, and we can insist upon accountability. But the truth of the matter is, our schools will flourish when citizens join in the noble cause of making sure no child is left behind.

This is the end of a legislative process. Signing this bill is the end of a long, long time of people sitting in rooms trying to hammer out differences. It's a great symbol of what is possible in Washington when good people come together to do what's right. But it's just the beginning of change. And now it's up to you, the local citizens of our great land, the compassionate, decent citizens of America, to stand up and demand high standards, and to demand that no child—not one single child in America—is left behind.

Public Papers of the President: George W. Bush. January 8, 2002: 26–29.

SCHOOL FUNDING INEQUITIES

Even though school attendance is compulsory within the United States, a variation in age requirements as well as funding is common. Since school funding is provided by federal, state, and local taxes, there are many disparities nationwide and even statewide. School districts are often controlled by school boards who control the local curricula, teaching, and most importantly funding. Studies have shown that school funding varies between rural and urban communities as well as city and suburban communities.

Republicans such as Sen. William Frist (R-TN) believe that school testing and accountability are the primary responsibility of a school system. Many Republicans believe that increasing funding for education is not the answer. Instead, many believe in using the money already allocated to be more effective.

Many Democrats point to racial lines and disparities in school funding. Since most of the funding comes from property taxes, children living in poor neighborhoods are at a major disadvantage. Per-child spending is significantly lower in inner city schools than it is in suburban school systems. School funding disparities have also increased in the age of No Child Left Behind legislation. Federal funding is taken away from schools that do not meet the necessary testing standards.

Liberal Viewpoint

Paul D. Wellstone (D-MN). I have heard many senators say: We are for the testing for the accountability, but we are also going to invest in these children and make sure there are the resources. That is point one.

Point two: Senator Dodd and Senator Collins came to this Chamber with a very important amendment which authorized a dramatic increase in resources for the title I program. It was a bipartisan amendment. There were, I believe, seventy-nine senators who voted for this amendment.

· · ·

This amendment says that by 2005—we committed in that amendment that we would spend $24.72 billion for title I which would go to the benefit of children for extra reading help, for after-school, for prekindergarten, all of which is critically important.

So what this amendment says is that the tests we are authorizing need not be implemented unless we, in fact, appropriate the money at the level we said we would. This was the amount the Dodd amendment authorized. We have been saying to our states: We are going to get you the resources. So what we are saying in this amendment is that states do not have to do this unless we make the commitment to the resources.

I have heard people talk about the need to walk our talk. I have heard senator after senator say that they are for accountability but they are for resources. I do not know how senators can vote against this proposal. We said we were for authorizing this money. This amendment is a trigger amendment. It says that we make this commitment to $24.72 billion for title I. And this amendment says, if we do not do this, then the new tests need not be implemented.

If the States or school districts want to say we do not want to do this because you have not lived up to your commitment, they do not have to do it.

· · ·

Now just a little bit about what this really is all about. This is the heart of the debate. Right now, title I is a program for children from disadvantaged backgrounds. It is the major federal commitment. We are funding it at a 30 percent level. The title I money is used for extra reading help. It can be used for pre-kindergarten. It can be used to help these children do better.

What this amendment is saying is, it does not do a heck of a lot of good to test the children all across the country when we have not done anything to make sure they have the best teachers; that the classes are smaller; that the buildings are inviting; that they come to kindergarten ready to learn; that they get additional help for reading.

The testing is a snapshot. It is one piece of the picture. It does not tell us anything about what happened before or what happens after. What good does it do to have so many children in America right now who are crowded into dilapidated buildings, into huge classes, who have four teachers a year, who do not have the same resources and benefits as a lot of other children, who come to kindergarten way behind, and we are going to test them and show that they are not doing well, which we already know, but we are not going to have the resources to do anything to help them after they don't do well on the tests. Or even more importantly, we are not going to have the resources to help them to make sure that when we hold them accountable, they have the same opportunity as every other child in America to do well.

· · ·

It is quite one thing to say all of us in America live in a national community and when it comes to discrimination, when it comes to human rights, when it comes to civil rights, when it comes to a basic diet that every child should have, no state, no community should be able to fall below that. That is one kind of argument. But now we are going to tell every school district they have to do this? It is absolutely amazing to me that we are doing so.

The point is, don't anybody believe that the test we make every child take means that child now is going to have a qualified teacher. It doesn't do anything about that. A test doesn't reduce class size. A test doesn't make sure the children come to kindergarten ready. Part of the crisis in education is the learning gap by age five. Some children come to kindergarten, then they go on to first grade, second grade, third grade. Now we are going to test them, age eight.

One group of children, to be honest with you, actually has had seven years of school. They came to kindergarten. Then they had the three years plus that. Now they are third graders. Before that, they had three years of enriched child care. They came to kindergarten having been widely read to. They know colors and shapes and sizes. They know how to spell their name. They know the alphabet. They are ready to learn. They have had the education. And then a lot of other children haven't. And they are behind, way behind. This is during the period of time of the development of the brain, the most critical time. Then they fall further behind.

Testing doesn't change any of that. Testing doesn't do anything about making sure there is the technology there. Testing doesn't do anything about whether or not you have forty or fifty kids crowded into a classroom. But if we were to make a commitment to some title I funding, then we could get some additional help for reading; some additional help for after school; for teachers to have assistance helping them with children, one-on-one help; pre-kindergarten.

· · ·

Senators, if we are going to say that it will be a national mandate that every child in America will be tested and we will hold the children and the schools and everyone else accountable, then it should be a national mandate that every child should have the same opportunity to learn and do well in America. That is what this amendment is about.

· · ·

We are not doing anything about rebuilding crumbling schools. Shame on us.

We are not doing anything about reducing class size. Shame on us.

Now what we are going to do is test these children and show these children in America again how little we care about them.

· · ·

I am not surprised by a recent study by the Education Trust Fund which shows the extent of the gap between low-income and high-income districts. There are not too many senators who have children in low-income districts.

The study found that nationally low-poverty school districts spend an average of $1,139 more than high-poverty school districts. In 86 percent of the States, there is a spending gap favoring wealthier students. The widest gap is in New York where the wealthiest districts spend on average $2,794 more per student.

As the Center for Educational Policy concludes: "Policymakers on the State and national levels should be wary of proposals that embrace the rhetoric of closing the gap but do not help build the capacity to accomplish this goal."

That is what this amendment is about. This testing is nothing but the rhetoric of closing the gap. We are not closing the gap because we are not providing the resources. This amendment says we go on record, we are committed, we are going to say to any State and school district: If we do not live up to our commitment and provide the resources in 2005, which we have gone on record in supporting, then you do not have to do the testing.

． ． ．

Again, we went on record. We said we were for this authorization. This amendment just says let's do it. My colleagues say tests have their place. By the way, I want to also print in the Record—I hope every senator will read this. This is a high stakes testing position statement. This is a statement by health care professionals which include people such as Robert Coles, a psychiatrist who has written probably forty books about children in America. The man has won every award known to humankind; Alvin Poussaint, another talented African-American psychiatrist; Debbie Meyer who has done more good work in inner-city New York City than anybody in the country.

Do my colleagues want to know what they say in the statement? They say two things. One, which ties into this amendment, is that we must make sure we live up to the opportunity-to-learn standard; that every child has the same opportunity to learn.

What I want to point out is they say from a public health point of view: What are you doing to these kids? They are talking about the stress on eight-year-olds taking all these tests, and they point out what is happening to schools.

． ． ．

One hundred percent of major city schools use title I to provide professional development and new technology for students; 97 percent use title I funds to support after-school activities; 90 percent use title I funds to support family literacy and summer school programs; 68 percent use title I funds to support preschool programs.

The Rand Corporation linked some of the largest gains of low- and moderate-income children doing better in education to investment in title I.

In my home state of Minnesota, the Brainerd Public School system has had a 70 to 80 percent success rate in accelerating students in the bottom 20 percent of their class to the average of their class following 1 year of intensive title I–supported reading programs.

· · ·

Mr. President, do you know that in my state of Minnesota, in St. Paul, schools where we have less than 65 percent of the students who are eligible for the free or reduced school lunch program, receive no title I money. We have run out. I could not believe it. I heard the Secretary of Education and some of my colleagues saying we have spent all this title I money; we have thrown dollars at the problem.

First of all, we are not funding it but at a 30 percent level and, second, title I represents about one-half of 1 percent of all the education dollars that are spent, but it is key in terms of the federal government commitment. I am suggesting that it can make a huge difference.

The problem is, we have had a dramatic expansion in the number of children who need help. The GAO study said that, but a lot of states, such as the state of Minnesota, in a school that has 64 percent of the children who are low income or who qualify for the reduced or free school lunch program get no help. Can my colleagues believe that?

· · ·

We are saying to the teachers: Teachers, you are afraid to be held accountable, so now we will hold you accountable with these tests. Teachers are not afraid to be held accountable. And the teachers and the parents and the schools, especially the schools with low- and moderate-income children, already know what is working and what is not working. They already know they don't get the resources. They already know the children come to kindergarten way behind. They already know the buildings are dilapidated. They already know the classes are too large. They already know they don't have beautiful landscaping. They already know they don't have the support assistance they need from additional staff. They know all of that. They are just wondering when we will live up to our words and provide some assistance. That is what they wonder.

In my opinion, we are playing politics with children's lives. We all want to have our picture taken next to them; we all want to be in schools with them; we are all for them except when it comes to reaching in the pocket and investing in resources.

I believe what we are doing to poor children in America, unless we pass this amendment, is we are going to test children and show they are not doing as well. Why would anybody be surprised?

The children in the inner city of south Minneapolis or west St. Paul are not doing as well as the children in the affluent suburbs with a huge disparity of resources and a huge disparity of life chances. It is staring us in the face in terms of what we need to do. We have not made a commitment to them, and now we are going to club them over the head with tests and humiliate them.

The Congressional Record. June 7, 2001: S5907–S5954.

Conservative Viewpoint

William H. Frist (R-TN). Mr. President, I rise in opposition to the Wellstone amendment. I look forward to the debate over the next several hours. I think the amendment comes back to some of the fundamental questions asked about this bill. It will give members on both sides of the aisle the opportunity to address the fundamental concept of the bill, the structure of the bill, the why of the bill.

It comes down to accountability, to flexibility, being able to figure out what the problems are. We all recognize there is a problem with education in this country. After diagnosing it, we need to intervene in a way that we can truly leave no child behind.

This amendment addresses two issues: the whole concept of accountability using assessments and dollars and cents. The amendment states that no State shall be required to conduct any assessments in any school year by 2005 if the amount appropriated to carry out this part for fiscal year 2005 is not equal to or exceeds $24 billion.

That summarizes the amendment. It can be broken into two arguments. One is money and how important money is, and is money the answer. The other is assessment and the testing. It is a useful component of what is proposed by President Bush and what is in the underlying bill today, as amended, accountability and assessment—that measuring success or failure is important if you want to intervene and make a difference.

. . .

The comment of the senator from Minnesota is, why test somebody if you know they are not doing well? The implied corollary is, forget the test, dump more money and make that cure the system—as if throwing more money will make sure we leave no child behind.

On the first part of that argument, I think testing is important. I say that as somebody who has a certain parallel, and the parallel of my life, obviously, is medicine. The symptoms are there. The symptoms today are, we are failing, by every objective measurement we use today, versus our counterparts in other countries internationally. Whether we look at the 4th grade or the 8th grade or the 12th grade, we are failing as a society in educating our children. I suppose that is what the senator from Minnesota meant when he said we know we are leaving children behind.

As a physician, when someone comes to your office and complains of fatigue, they do not feel quite right, perhaps shortness of breath, as a physician and as a nation, it is hard for you to know how to address the symptoms of a problem until a diagnosis is made.

We know children are being left behind. By any measure, there is a huge achievement gap, which is getting worse in spite of more money, in spite of good intentions, in spite of additional programs. That gap is getting worse, and we are leaving the underserved behind.

How do we correct that? Our side of the aisle worked with the other side of the aisle in a bipartisan way, to pass a bill through the Health, Education, Labor, and Pensions Committee, that injects strong accountability into the bill.

I thought we had gone long beyond the accountability argument. Apparently we have not. I think it is important to go through this diagnosing, the assessments, so we can intervene and improve the education of our children. We need to be able to determine through assessments how well each child progresses, or, unfortunately, does not progress and falls behind—from the third to the fourth grade; from the fourth to the fifth grade; from the fifth to the sixth grade; from the sixth to the seventh; from the seventh to the eighth.

. . .

Why do we need more assessments? If you assess a student in the seventh grade—say a young girl in the seventh grade—and that test shows she is not only last in the class, but last in the community. You find out in the seventh grade that she cannot read because she has been last in the class, and because she has been ushered along and advanced from year to year. Or you find she cannot add and subtract in the seventh grade.

. . .

As a physician, what is it similar to? I mention somebody coming through that door to see, not Senator Frist, Dr. Frist; they come in and have these vague complaints. If I don't do tests—I can take a pretty careful history. But until I do the physical exam, until I do some tests—noninvasive tests, very simple tests—EKG, a scan called a MUGA scan, fairly simple tests today—I am not going to be able to specifically know whether the problem is with the lungs or with the heart or whether that problem is due to lack of conditioning or if it is due to general fatigue.

So if I have the seventh grade girl there, not only should we have made the diagnosis earlier, but we need a test that can sufficiently make the diagnosis: Is it mathematics? Is it reading? Is it lack of resources? Is it lack of an ability to use a computer or type on a keyboard? We have to make the assessment. Then once, with that patient coming in, I identify the heart, I know how to intervene. I have taken the blood pressure, I find it is high blood pressure, there is something I can do to intervene. But if it is just fatigue, until I know their blood pressure is up, how can I give a pill to bring the blood pressure down?

You can argue there is not enough money in the world to treat everybody's hypertension, and you can argue you cannot give everybody the full battery of tests and give everybody a heart transplant or everything they need. But that is not an argument to me, or it defies common sense to say you should not come back and do the tests in the first place and ask the question and make the specific diagnosis. In fact, I argue if you have dollars, or a pool of dollars—it doesn't even have to be a fixed sum—if you want the best value for that dollar, instead of taking all that money and throwing it at the fatigue of the patient with a whole bunch of potential treatments that may make you feel good, or invent programs to put them in, why not step back, invest that $1 in making the diagnosis, in figuring out the problem, because that will set you, I believe, in a much more efficient way to determine treatment over time.

. . .

I say there is absolutely no difference with how we should address our education system today—if we look at accountability, we want better results, we want better value, we are failing, today, to say assessments are important, measurable results that can be looked at, that can be used and thrown into our own individual database at a local level in order to decide how to address that specific problem, whether it is the seventh grade girl or whether it is a school we see is failing miserably year after year, in spite of putting more resources in and getting more teachers and smaller class size and better books and more technology—that is the only way to get the answer.

Then you start drawing this linkage between dollars. We always hear from the other side of the aisle—this is a good example. I looked at this. I don't know if it is $24 million or $24 billion or $24 trillion. To me, it doesn't matter. But it really drives home the point that there is a perception that you can throw money at a problem without making a diagnosis, without figuring out what the fundamental disease is—not the symptoms, we know what the symptoms are—but without figuring out what the disease is you will never have enough money.

Although you can always argue for more money and, boy, I tell you, we have really seen it in this bill. If there is one very valid criticism of this bill it is that every amendment that comes down here, we come down to vote on, every amendment coming from the other side requires more money. It is more money for programs, more money for technology, more money for teachers, more money for assessments.

Focusing on money as the only response takes the target off what the American people care about. It takes the spotlight off what the president of the United States cares about, what the president of the United States has demonstrated the leadership at the highest levels about, and that is the child. That is the seventh grade girl who is sitting in that classroom who is failing and we are not willing to come in and do the reform.

Reform is a scary word. Reform means change to some people. But we have to recognize when you say improve accountability, or reform, or measurable results—all of that basically says we have to change what we are doing, figure out what is wrong, and fix it. And you cannot just say throw money at the problem. You have to have the reform. That is where the assessment, accountability, measurable results, the figuring out what the problem is, is so critically important.

· · ·

We cannot argue with what is underlying this amendment, that you don't do the test because somebody has the symptoms. I argue you have to do the test. That is first and foremost in order to figure out what the disease is, to treat it, to get the best value for the dollar that we put in, that we make available. When we hear the rhetoric on the floor of playing politics with children's lives, they have to be very careful, again, because the debate is so much further along than where it was 6 months ago, I think in large part because of President Bush and his leadership, putting this issue out front.

Let's not use that language of playing politics with children, but get reform and improvement in the system by putting additional resources in as we go forward, which this President and this Congress clearly have shown a willingness to do. But let's not just put more money in and then do away with tests, which in essence is what this amendment does.

The latest results of the National Assessment of Educational Progress have shown—they show it again and again—that money is not the answer and that new programs are not the answer.

· · ·

We have heard it on the floor again and again. We spent $150 billion on literally hundreds of federal elementary and secondary education programs over the last thirty-five years. In terms of progress compared to others, we have not seen it.

That is why this bill is on the floor. That is why it is critical that we address it in a way that recognizes not just the money but the modernization, the demanding of accountability, the raising of expectations for all children, for all schools, and for all teachers. The answer is not just more dollars.

. . .

In the bill, there are also rigorous corrective actions for schools that fail to meet those standards. Again, senators have worked very hard in a bipartisan way to make sure that accountability is fashioned in such a way that you just do not make the diagnosis but you set up a system in which there can be early intervention and treatment.

. . .

In the same way, when we come to this underlying question of measuring what one is learning or not learning, I would argue that it is necessary. We haven't been doing it in the past. We have to make the diagnosis. Again, it comes back to the individual child. It comes back to the parent. That is why we need to step in. That is why, when people use the word "mandate," I think it is important for us to say at least the value of testing is agreed upon, and the individual child or that individual parent will know where the deficiencies are and how they can improve. Is it math—adding or subtracting? Is it science? Is it how to use a computer? We don't know today.

. . .

Annual testing is simply the only way to get away from the symptoms of things not going quite right. To be specific, fortunately we know what can be done.

If you have $1—whatever it is, a federal, or a local dollar, or a dollar at school—you know how best to invest that dollar, and not just throw a dollar at the symptoms. But you will know how to invest that dollar, and it can be accomplished through this legislation. It is already in the legislation.

I want to make sure we don't, with this particular amendment, allow the opportunity to strip away all accountability in the bill. That is the heart of this bill.

We are going to talk flexibility and local control and decision-making at the local level involving the parents. But the heart of this bill comes back to accountability.

This amendment basically gives the opportunity to say, let's just cut the heart out of this bill; let's cut out the accountability provisions; get rid of it, and we can feel good; and let's in fact throw a lot more money at it. That is simply not the approach of the President of the United States, which says spend more money but link it to modern situations and accountability.

· · ·

I believe these accountability provisions increase choice for students. They increase the opportunity to empower people to make decisions that will benefit their education, again from the standpoint of the parents, and the education of a family as we go forward so that we can truly leave no child behind.

Let me simply close by saying that money is not the answer. That is what we come back to. We talk a lot about the accountability. Money is important. But as we look to the past, and federal education, state education, and local education, spending has increased dramatically. Total national spending on elementary and secondary education has increased by about 30 percent over the last 10 years. Federal spending on secondary and elementary education has increased by 180 percent. Federal spending is only 6 percent of the overall pie. The federal role has increased by 180 percent over the last decade. Over the past five years, federal funding for elementary and secondary programs has increased by 52 percent.

Yet in spite of all of those increases—people can say that is not near enough, or maybe some people would say that is way too much—over time, test scores have been national. The achievement gap between the served and the underserved, the rich, the poor—however, you want to measure it—has gotten greater in spite of this increased spending.

The Congressional Record. June 7, 2001: S5907–S5954.

SEX EDUCATION

Sex education in school has been a highly polarizing issue within the United States. The promotion of abstinence-only education has been credited to the religious right movement in the United States. It has been widely criticized by the medical community for misleading students.

Republicans such as Rep. Joseph Pitts (R-PA) advocate for abstinence-only education. They believe that if kids are given information about contraception, it will lead to sexual activity among teenagers. Abstinence-only education advocates abstaining from sex until marriage by either completely avoiding the topic of contraception or only discussing their failure rate. In addition, "abstinence pledges" are often made as commitments by young adults to abstain from sexual activity until marriage.

Democrats such as Rep. Louise M. Slaughter (D-NY) believe that abstinence-only education is extremely detrimental. Just because kids are not taught about it in school does not mean that the topic of sex does not come up in other forms of media. Furthermore, many argue that abstinence-only education prevents kids from getting the necessary health information to make wise decisions. The abstinence-only program has also been widely criticized for exaggerating the failure rates of condoms and other contraception.

Conservative Viewpoint

Joseph R. Pitts (R-PA). Mr. Speaker, I rise today in strong support of the funding for abstinence-until-marriage education in this bill, and I thank the chairman for his leadership on this important issue.

Today, the results of a landmark Zogby International survey assessing parental attitudes on sex education have been released to the public. The Zogby poll reveals strong parental approval for character-based, abstinence-until-marriage programs and proves that parents soundly reject the goals and content of so-called "comprehensive" sex education. The results are available online at www.whatparentsthink.com

According to the Zogby poll, 73.5 percent of parents approve or strongly approve of abstinence-centered sex education. 61.1 percent of parents disapprove or strongly disapprove of so-called "comprehensive" or "safe sex" education. 75.3 percent of parents disapprove or strongly disapprove of the Centers for Disease Control (CDC) sex education curriculum.

When parents are accurately informed about what "comprehensive" sex education actually entails, which includes distributing condoms in schools, they make it clear that they do not want their children to be inundated with "safe sex" propaganda. Instead, parents want their children to be taught self-respect, self-control and abstinence-until-marriage.

This survey marks the first time parents have been polled using the exact language from comprehensive sex education guidelines. The major weaknesses of previous polls are their misleading questions and fuzzy interpretations. In this poll, Zogby used exact definitions and verbatim wording from the comprehensive sex education curricula developed and endorsed by such groups as the Sexuality Information and Education Council of the United States (SIECUS) and Planned Parenthood.

The Zogby organization also found that: All demographic groupings strongly disapprove of comprehensive sex education—especially non-white minorities (Hispanics and Asians). And 70 percent of parents strongly disapprove of their teens getting contraceptives without their approval.

Mr. Speaker, America's parents have spoken. They want abstinence-until-marriage education. This bill ensures that the values many American parents hold dear—the values of abstinence and marital faithfulness are not determined by taxpayer-funded "safe-sex" propaganda in schools.

The Congressional Record. February 13, 2003: E263–E264.

Liberal Viewpoint

Louise M. Slaughter (D-NY). President Bush promotes the unproven abstinence only sex education programs, denying our nation's young people critical information on ways to prevent pregnancy and sexually transmitted diseases, including HIV/AIDS, even though we know that over 60 percent of 12th graders report having had sexual intercourse.

In fact, recent analysis of abstinence only programs found that such programs can actually reduce the use of condoms when program participants become sexually active, increasing their risk of pregnancy.

In my opinion, the president's "abstinence only" programs should be more accurately labeled "ignorance only," and we are placing the very lives of our youth in danger. This is unconscionable.

When the nation is in such a severe budget crunch and running skyrocketing deficits, George Bush's decisions to spend millions upon millions of dollars on a program that is not only unproven but potentially harmful is dumbfounding. Moreover, he is also exporting this dangerous ignorance policy to other countries around the world.

· · ·

The Congressional Record. June 22, 2004: H4734–H4735.

FAITH-BASED INITIATIVES

The first action President Bush took when he entered office was to enact the Faith-Based Initiatives policy. Faith-based initiatives were subsidies by the government to provide social services for communities. This is the first time federal monies have been used for religious-affiliated organizations. The initiative required that faith-based organizations follow nondiscriminatory regulations and the Equal Opportunity Act. President Bush felt that the faith-based initiative was a good way to more heavily involve the community while providing federal funds for much-needed social programs.

The opposition to this came in two forms: the first from the Christian right and the second from House Democrats. The objections by the Christian right focus on taking away the organizations' ability to combine scripture with social programs. The basis of these programs has always had a religious connotation, providing guidance as well as help. Under the new federal statute, no longer can groups tie their religious foundations to their community service. House Democrats objected for a different reason. They believed that faith-based initiatives would drown out federal money for federal social welfare programs such as Medicaid, Medicare, and the welfare program. They felt that the faith-based initiative was a breach between the church and the state.

Liberal Viewpoint

Chet Edwards (D-TX). Mr. Speaker, in today's *Washington Post*, President Bush was quoted as saying those who disagree with his faith-based initiatives "do not understand the power of faith." He then referred "to the skeptics of faith in our society."

Mr. Speaker, I personally respect the president and his right to offer his proposals. However, I do not think it is fair to question the religious faith of decent Americans who happen to disagree with his policy proposals. Challenging people's religious faith because of public policy differences is not a way to bring Americans together; rather it is a prescription for religious divisiveness.

Numerous groups such as the Baptist Joint Committee and the American Jewish Committee differ from the president on faith-based initiatives, not because they question the power of faith, but because they want to prevent government from regulating our faith.

As we proceed in the debate on faith-based initiatives, I urge all sides to focus on the specific issues at hand and not to challenge the religious faith of those with differing views of conscience.

The Congressional Record. June 6, 2001: H2893–H2894.

Conservative Viewpoint

Mark Souder (R-IN). Earlier this week, President George Bush announced his faith-based initiatives office and different proposals that he will be sending down to Congress. Earlier today, the gentleman from Oklahoma (Mr. Watts), who has been a leader in this effort, and Senator Rick Santorum, along with the gentlewoman from Kentucky (Mrs. Northup) and myself, and Senators Tim Hutchinson and Sam Brownback held a press conference with a number of leaders from Michigan, Florida, and other places around the United States to highlight some of these initiatives.

There are a number of questions that I wanted to address here as we prepare to analyze and hopefully report the president's package and add different things we have considered here in the House and Senate to it as well.

First and foremost, this is not a new idea. Former Congressman and Senator Dan Coats, when he was in the House, had a number of these initiatives. In the Senate, the Agenda for American Renewal. Former Secretary of Housing and Urban Development Secretary Jack Kemp had a number of faith-based initiatives there because a lot of people would not reach out and care for those with AIDS. In the early stages of the AIDS crisis, as people were dying, there were all sorts of false rumors around and many people did not care for them. Without the faith-based communities, if the government had not reached out to the faith-based communities and involved them, there would have been many people dying of AIDS who would not have received any assistance whatsoever. Nobody objected to the faith-based communities coming and working.

Similarly in homelessness, the federal dollars, the state dollars, and the local dollars were not enough to address the homeless questions. So, under HUD, they expanded into the faith-based organizations back in the Bush administration. That was continued under Secretary Cisneros and continued under Secretary Cuomo. It is not fair to say that these things are suddenly new and that President Bush is trying to insert religion into the national debate. It has been there.

The difference is, instead of an afterthought, President Bush wants to make it a focus. He is saying that all these flowering organizations that are developed in every neighborhood, particularly those that are hurting the most, there are people making a difference and we need to tap into that.

The Congressional Record. January 31, 2001: H135–H136.

SELECTED READING

School Vouchers

Coulson, Andrew J. "School Voucher." School Choices. 1998. www.schoolchoices.org/roo/vouchers.htm.

Peters, Tom. "Against School Vouchers." 1996. users.ox.ac.uk/~mert2049/atheistground/peters-againstvouchers.shtml.

"Policy Debate: Do School Vouchers Improve the Quality of Education?" Economics Resource Center. 2002. www.swlearning.com/economics/policy_debates/vouchers.html.

"School Vouchers." National Education Association. 2006. www.nea.org/vouchers/index.html.

Smoke, Kurt L. "Why School Vouchers Can Help Inner-City Children." August 20, 1999. Manhattan Institute for Policy Analysis. www.manhattan-institute.org/html/cb_20.htm.

No Child Left Behind

Bush, George W. "Foreword." 2006. www.whitehouse.gov/news/reports/no-child-left-behind.html.

"Fact Sheet: No Child Left Behind Act," The White House. www.whitehouse.gov/news/releases/2002/01/20020108.html.

"No Child Left Behind." Department of Education. 2006. www.ed.gov/nclb/landing
.jhtml.

Novak, John R. "Penalizing Diverse Schools?" December 2003. www.asu.edu/educ/
epsl/EPRU/documents/EPRU-0312-48-RW.pdf.

Rueter, Ted. "Disastrous No Child Left Behind Act Should Be Repealed." September
9, 2005. DePaw University. www.collegenews.org/x4814.xml.

"States Rebelling Against No Child Left Behind." *Fox News*. February 17, 2004.
www.foxnews.com/story/0,2933,111675,00.html.

School Funding Inequities

Lefkowits, Laura. "School Finance: From Equity to Adequacy." March 2004. www
.mcrel.org/PDF/PolicyBriefs/5042PI_PBSchoolFinanceBrief.pdf.

"New Report Finds NJ Charter Schools Suffer From Severe Inequities in Funding."
U.S. Charter Schools. March 1, 2006. www.uscharterschools.org/cs/n/view/
uscs_news/861.

Richards, Cindy. "Tax Swap Is Only Way to Fix Schools." *Chicago Tribune*. October
11, 2006. www.suntimes.com/news/richards/91362,CST-EDT-CINDY11.article.

Singer, Alan. "Eliminate Funding Inequities." April 1, 2004. www.people.hofstra.edu/
faculty/alan_j_singer/Publications/Newsday/ND%20Equal%20Education%
20LI%204%1%200.pdf.

Timar, Thomas. "Study Finds Inequities in Targeted Aid for Education." July
14, 2004. www.news.ucdavis.edu/search/news_detail.lasso?id=7087.

Sex Education

Connolly, Ceci. "Some Abstinence Programs Mislead Teens, Report Says." *Washington Post*. December 2, 2004. www.washingtonpost.com/wp-dyn/articles/
A26623-2004Dec1.html.

"Doctors Denounce Abstinence-Only Education." *MSNBC News*. July 5, 2005. www
.msnbc.msn.com/id/8470845.

Maynard, R.A., ed. *Kids Having Kids: A Robin Hood Foundation Special Report on the
Costs of Adolescent Childbearing*, New York: Robin Hood Foundation, 1996.

Monbiot, George. "Joy of Sex Education." *The Guardian*. May 11, 2004. education
.guardian.co.uk/schools/comment/story/0,,1214047,00.html.

Pardini, Priscilla. "Abstinence-Only Education Continues to Flourish." Winter 2002.
www.rethinkingschools.org/archive/17_02/Abst172.shtml.

Faith-Based Initiatives

Cooperman, Alan. "Losing Faith in the President." *Washington Post*. October 17, 2006.
www.washingtonpost.com/wp-dyn/content/article/2006/10/16/AR2006101601101
.html.

"Faith-Based Initiatives." www.faithbasedcommunityinitiatives.org.

Mabrey, Vicki. "Faith Based Prisons." *ABC News*. January 27, 2006. abcnews.go.com/
Nightline/story?id=1550733.

Paulson, Amanda. "A Tighter Rein on Faith-Based Initiatives." *Christian Science Monitor*. June 12, 2006. www.csmonitor.com/2006/0612/p03s02-usju.html.

"The Faith-Based Initiative Two Years Later: Examining Its Potential, Progress, and Problems." March 5, 2003. pewforum.org/events/index.php?EventID=41.

White House Office of Faith-Based and Community Initiatives. 2006. www.white-house.gov/government/fbci.

7

Housing

The U.S. Department of Housing and Urban Development (HUD) defines an "unaffordable housing burden" as expenditures on housing that total more than 30 percent of a household's income. Housing costs that exceed this amount may compromise a family's ability to afford other basic necessities such as food, clothing, child care, and health care. Studies indicate that approximately one-third of Americans spend at least 30 percent of their income on housing and that nearly half of the working poor spend 50 percent of their income on housing. Thus, access to affordable housing is emerging as an increasingly prevalent problem. The federal government has strikingly dissimilar responses to citizens' housing needs. All homeowners who qualify receive a tax deduction to offset their housing costs, but only 25 percent of persons eligible to receive housing assistance actually obtain the benefit, primarily due to inadequate funding and the lack of available low-income housing units. The recent focus on deficit reduction, tax cuts, the fight on terrorism, and the Iraq war has led to a reduction in welfare spending, increasing the need of the poor for housing assistance and concurrently curtailing the development of low-income housing units.

AFFORDABLE HOUSING

Contrasting ideologies held by liberals and conservatives result in divergent ideas regarding the appropriate strategies for addressing housing issues. Liberals and conservatives disagree about whether housing should be considered a "right" or a "privilege," the causes of the affordable housing shortage, and the appropriate governmental response to the lack of affordable housing. Liberals consider housing a basic human right and believe that all U.S. citizens are entitled to affordable housing. In contrast, conservatives stress the individual's obligation to put forth the needed effort to develop the skills and earning power necessary to compete in the private housing market. Conservatives believe that the federal government has already met its basic obligation to citizens by ensuring that all Americans have an opportunity to secure quality housing if they wish.

Liberals have identified a worsening "housing crisis" that they believe is caused by the lack of affordable housing stock and the failure of wages and benefits to keep up with the sharp rise in housing prices. Not surprisingly, conservatives dispute liberals' claims that there is not enough affordable housing to go around. Instead, they attribute the problem to deviant and unproductive lifestyle choices, a lack of commitment to work, under-education, and failed policies on the local level. Conservatives think housing assistance is detrimental to self-sufficiency because it buffers recipients from the negative consequences of their poor decisions and suggests that society will always take care of them. Conservatives further maintain that housing assistance, which is provided without time limits and with few or no strings attached, contributes to dependency. The observation that most vouchers are allocated to single mothers provokes conservative objections that these programs encourage out-of-wedlock births.

Both liberals and conservatives acknowledge that the federal government should play a prominent role in improving housing options for low- and moderate-income citizens, but they disagree about the extent of government involvement necessary. Conservatives contend that historical far-reaching federal involvement in housing assistance programs has discouraged the development of private housing stock by increasing competition with private developers. Furthermore, stringent government control and oversight of public housing programs has weakened local initiative to resolve housing issues in a manner that meets their unique needs. Conservatives call attention to the fact that federal policies aren't the primary determinant of the availability of affordable housing. They contend that local policies such as rent control, zoning requirements that segregate usage, and mandates for low housing density levels are the primary determinants of the availability of affordable housing and housing prices.

According to conservatives, the private sector is better suited to addressing housing issues. They support the use of housing vouchers that allow low-income consumers to exercise their choice based on the assumption that this will drive the housing market in the direction it needs to go. However, conservatives acknowledge middle-class apprehensions that the movement of low-income residents into their neighborhoods often lowers property values and increases crime.

Liberals, on the other hand, feel that the free market cannot be the sole provider of housing due to its lack of responsiveness to persons who cannot pay the fair market price. Strong government intervention in the free market to "level the playing field" so poor people can compete in the private housing market is encouraged. In addition, liberals support the development of mixed-income public housing developments to avoid creating a concentration of poverty and the accompanying concentration of social problems. Many liberals consider redesigned public housing developments to be the simplest, most cost-effective means for housing the poor. Liberals have historically supported public housing, which has served as a major technique for housing people of diverse backgrounds, including African Americans, large families, people with disabilities, and the elderly.

URBAN RENEWAL AND GENTRIFICATION

Urban renewal—the redevelopment of unsafe, dilapidated, or inadequately planned neighborhoods and communities—emerged as a strategy for revitalizing central cities that were losing residents to the suburbs. Urban renewal consists of a series of programs and policies that rely on public investment to stimulate larger-scale, private investment. Public improvements to the infrastructure (roads, parks) are intended to lure private investment. While earlier projects focused on large-scale development, changes in voter and policy-maker priorities have shifted the focus to smaller projects that rely on a comprehensive array of interventions to strengthen and revitalize communities. Problems addressed include substance abuse, failing schools, and the lack of child care. Local flexibility and participation from residents, policy makers, and business leaders are considered paramount.

"Gentrification," the replacement of run-down housing with upper-scale offices and condominiums, is often a controversial by-product of urban renewal projects. Liberals object to urban renewal projects that displace poor residents without providing alternative affordable housing options. Liberals contend that the resulting increases in property values often price the poor out of their neighborhoods. They argue that many of the houses that are demolished could actually be rehabilitated to provide housing to the poor. They also charge that many lots are simply left undeveloped. Redesigned urban renewal projects that focus on revitalizing the existing physical environment and housing stock receive much more favorable ratings from liberals.

Bipartisan efforts to improve the effectiveness of urban renewal have led to the development of enterprise zones and enterprise community programs designed to help distressed areas. The federal government collaborates with residents, businesses, community-based organizations, and local government officials by providing tax incentives and block grant programs to promote development. This strategy is consistent with conservative values and beliefs. A strong belief in the efficacy of the free market leaves conservatives with fewer reservations regarding the upscale development of formerly dilapidated areas. The resulting economic development and increased tax base is assumed to benefit and trickle down to poor residents. Finally, the prominent role localities assume in supporting economic and housing development to reduce social problems is unlikely to result in long-term dependence on the federal government.

CONCLUSIONS

The lack of affordable housing is emerging as a major political issue. The real estate boom that benefited many Americans and led to skyrocketing housing costs left many Americans with large housing burdens that often interfere with their ability to purchase other necessities. In addition, many Americans in the inner city and rural areas are not sharing in the nation's general economic prosperity due to disinvestment in their communities. Liberals and conservatives disagree about the severity of the problem, with liberals identifying the problem as a "crisis." A review of congressional debate suggests that to obtain bipartisan support, housing assistance and community development proposals will need to incorporate aspects of both political ideologies. Such proposals will likely combine tax incentives to promote industry participation, block grants to fund programs that improve schools and address social problems, close collaboration with the business sector, and an emphasis on local control and flexibility.

AFFORDABLE HOUSING

With housing prices skyrocketing beyond the means of the average worker, many people rent their home. With time and a lot of saving, people slowly move toward the opportunity of house ownership. To help, the United States government provides subsidies to make housing more affordable to its citizens. These subsidies take the form of tax breaks or housing subsidy programs. Housing subsidy programs are divided into three types: public housing, tenant-based housing, and project-based housing. President George W. Bush believes in everyone's opportunity to achieve "the American Dream," which begins with home ownership. Since he has been president, President Bush has increased homeownership through favorable tax cuts and mortgage programs. President Bush firmly believes that by increasing home ownership, he is strengthening the community as well as the U.S. economy.

Democrats such as Rep. Eva M. Clayton (D-SC) appreciate President Bush's rhetoric when it comes to affordable housing, but they are waiting for positive results. So far, they are yet to come. Rep. Clayton points out the disparity in majority and minority homeownership and the widening gap between the two figures. Rep. Clayton urges Congress to start paying attention to the affordable housing problem and pledge the necessary funding to fix it. Affordable housing should not simply be a ploy to get reelected; rather, it should employ bipartisan legislation to fix the problem.

Conservative Viewpoint

President George W. Bush. For millions of individuals and families, the American Dream starts with owning a home. When families move into a home of their own, they gain independence and confidence, and their faith in the future grows. The spread of ownership and opportunity helps give our citizens a vital stake in the future of America and the chance to realize the great promise of our country.

From the earliest days of our nation, homeownership has embodied the core American values of individual freedom, personal responsibility, and self-reliance. A home provides children with a safe environment in which to grow and learn. A home is also a tangible asset that provides owners with borrowing power and allows our citizens to build wealth that they can pass on to their children and grandchildren.

The benefits of homeownership extend to our communities. Families who own their own homes have a strong interest in maintaining the value of their investments, the safety of their neighborhoods, and the quality of their schools. Homeownership is also a bedrock of the American economy, helping to increase jobs, boost demand for goods and services, and build prosperity.

More Americans than ever own their own homes, but we must continue to work hard so that every family has an opportunity to realize the American Dream. In 2002, I announced a goal to add 5.5 million new minority homeowners by the end of the decade. Since then, we have added 2.3 million new minority households. My Administration has also set a goal of adding 7 million new affordable homes to the market within the next 10 years. In my FY 2006 budget, I proposed a single family housing tax credit and two mortgage programs—the Zero Down payment mortgage and the Payment Incentives program—to help more families achieve homeownership. In 2003, I signed the American Dream Down Payment Act, and I have proposed more than $200 million to continue the American Dream Down

Payment Initiative to provide down payment assistance to thousands of American families. By promoting initiatives such as financial literacy, tax incentives for building affordable homes, voucher programs, and Individual Development Accounts, we are strengthening our communities and improving citizens' lives.

Public Papers of the President: George W. Bush. May 25, 2005: 885–886.

Liberal Viewpoint

Eva M. Clayton (D-SC). Mr. Speaker, over the last few days, the president has been promoting an initiative to increase homeownership opportunities for minorities and reduce barriers. The president's interest and participation is welcome.

Mr. Speaker, those of us in the Congressional Black Caucus have been working hard for years to correct the inequities and eliminate the disparities of housing opportunities for people of color and are pleased that the president has recognized the need for such an effort.

All we can say is WOW. More than a year ago, the Congressional Black Caucus and the Congressional Black Caucus Foundation launched an ambitious initiative called With Ownership Wealth, or WOW for short.

The president's new plan echoes and amplifies many of our initial goals but may not have realized the objectives we share in common. To the extent the president is joining the lead of the Congressional Black Caucus Foundation and comprehensive group of sponsors which include the housing financing industry, the insurance industry realtors and nonprofit organizations, including faith-based organizations, as well as community development organizations, it is indeed a step in the right direction.

. . .

Mr. Speaker, representing a district in North Carolina that is not only predominantly rural but also is heavily populated by Afro Americans and other minorities I welcome the president's stated intention to step up to help create greater wealth in communities where housing needs are so critical. At a minimum, the administration announcement should increase interest of our industry players and minority homeownership acquisition.

That said, I must point out that just as there is a great gap between majority and minority homeownership, so too there is a gap between the president's words or his promise or his intention and his administrative work. The president's announcement this week does not mention that his budget has slashed rural housing programs essentially from the 2002 level, including a 12.4 percent reduction in funds for guaranteeing homes for single-family housing and 11.4 percent cut in the Department of Agriculture direct loan for single family housing and a whopping 47.4 percent for direct loan for rental housing.

There is a significant gap between the promise and the reality. Mr. Speaker, African Americans nationwide have a home ownership rate of 48 percent compared with the majority rate of 73 percent. Politicians of both parties, Democrat and Republican, wax rhapsodically, eloquently. They say great words, great phrases about the American dream. They talk endlessly about the American dream and the right to own a home, and they also talk about the United States being the land of opportunity. For many, yes, but not for all.

It is time that the reality mirrors the rhetoric and the deeds match the words with action. It is time now that we indeed make it a reality that the American dream to own a home is made available not only to those with a lot of money, but also those who have moderate resources should not be denied, or those of African American or other minorities. It should be the right for all Americans to have that.

· · ·

The land of opportunity should mean something more than words, and I hope that the president's promise to reduce the barriers and to make home ownership available for minorities is indeed a reality, and that resources would indeed follow the commitment.

The Congressional Record. June 20, 2002: H3766–H3770.

URBAN RENEWAL AND GENTRIFICATION

Gentrification has been a highly contentious issue, especially in urban areas. The practice of gentrification renovates deteriorating, low-cost housing. In turn, the property value increases dramatically and wealthier residents move in. The original tenants who lived in the often subsidized housing are left to find another place to live.

Urban renewal mostly takes place within city limits as the old and deteriorating neighborhoods are rebuilt. The sudden interest in urban living in the United States has invigorated the practice of gentrification as the median income in the newly built communities has risen. Supporters of gentrification argue that the process allows the neighborhoods to be renovated. As a result, there is a decrease of crime, street sanitation is improved, and new jobs are created.

There are many attempts to control gentrification. Affordable housing, exclusionary zoning, rent control, and community land trusts are just some of the solutions employed by different communities throughout the country. Democrats argue that the practice of gentrification is damaging because it forces the low-income tenants to leave their homes. Many people are unable to find apartments that are within their previous budget and as a result, more problems are created. Furthermore, gentrification also creates a racial divide because most tenants forced out of their home are black and the new tenants tend to be white.

Liberal Viewpoint

Paul D. Ryan (R-WI). Mr. Speaker, today we are voting on H.R. 4923, the Community Renewal and New Markets Act, which includes a provision to create several very large investment companies targeted toward the inner cities and rural communities.

The American Private Investment Companies' (APIC) proposed goal of bringing large-scale businesses to economically distressed communities is a laudable and important goal. However, the APIC proposed under the Community Renewal and New Markets Act accepts the various impediments to investing in the inner city and rural communities and simply offers businesses a subsidy for risky investment. Further, the legislation duplicates several existing programs, including Small Business Investment Companies (SBICs), which are also expanded under this bill. The proposal has not been adequately scored to take government loan guarantee risk into consideration, and is to be administered by the Department of Housing and Urban Development (HUD), which is inadequately prepared for the responsibility.

A lack of capital is not keeping businesses from investing in these areas, especially not the large-scale, established businesses that the APIC program would target—the problem is the high cost of doing business. Instead of attacking the fundamental problems of these areas, a program such as APIC reduces urban and rural areas' incentives to change what makes investment in these communities difficult in the first place—penalizing tax rates, burdensome regulatory policies, a lack of pubic infrastructure, and high crime rates.

Further, a lack of venture capital is not an issue. The companies the APIC proposal targets are not entrepreneurial start-ups, nor are they small businesses. They are companies like Safeway or Wal-Mart. Location of venture capital is also not an issue. In today's information economy where technology facilitates long-distance interpersonal communication, venture capital flows to where it can earn a high rate of return, whether the investment is in Chicago or the Appalachian Mountains.

At least eight federal programs already exist that have similar goals as the APIC program. We understand each program is structured slightly differently and awards loans and grants differently than APICs, but the outcome remains the same. These include Community Development Block Grants (CDBG) Section 108 Loan Guarantees, Community Development Financial Institutions (CDFIs), SBICs, and the Business and Industry Loan program administered by the USDA.

The APIC proposed creates quasi-GSEs, by relying on government subsidies to back "private" loans. This is not a private market initiative. HUD is granted authority to create a secondary market in APIC debt, similar to how Ginnie Mae guarantees mortgage debt. Creation of this secondary market further lowers the cost of capital, but increases taxpayer risk.

In fact, under H.R. 4923, APICs are expected to lose $6 million for every $1 billion invested. CBO believes that this loss could be greater if the true value of risk is calculated. In addition, CBO wrote that although the APIC legislation "authorizes the appropriation of $36 million annually for the subsidy cost of loan guarantees and $1 million annually for administrative expenses . . . based on the experience of similar loan guarantee programs administered by the SBA. CBO estimates that the subsidy cost to guarantee $1 billion in loans under the APIC program would cost about $50 million annually." Based on SBA programs, "CBO expects that APIC borrowers would default on between 25 and 30 percent of the guaranteed loans." To put this in perspective, CRS contrasts the expected 3.6 percent subsidy rate with both CDFIs and SBICs. CDFIs have a FY1999 subsidy rate of over 39 percent and SBICs have a subsidy rate of 25 percent (as of 1996). . . .

Finally, HUD is a highly political department and has demonstrated a lack of success in handling new programs, such as the community builders program. Unlike the Treasury Department or the Small Business Administration (SBA), HUD has no expertise in managing a large-scale business investment program. For the reasons outlined above, we believe that the APIC program is not the preferred means of addressing poverty and unemployment in economically distressed urban and rural areas. Its band-aid approach as a government subsidized investment program does not reduce the cost of business in these areas, aside from reducing the cost of capital for large companies who can easily find funds in the private market. The best way to promote economic growth is to reduce federal, state and local tax and regulatory burdens, which would encourage local entrepreneurs—with their own capital at risk—to determine what works best in their community.

The Congressional Record. July 25, 2000: H6797–H6841.

Conservative Viewpoint

Phillip English (R-PA). Today, Mr. Speaker, we will vote on landmark legislation that will provide our communities with the tools they need to revitalize our cities and many of our depressed rural areas. This is the day we will provide communities the tools they need to once again become self-reliant, and with that we give people more control over their own futures.

The Community Renewal and New Markets Act breathes new life into areas that have become America's forgotten communities. With this legislation, we empower impoverished cities and towns to rise above the perils of poverty. We give them the mechanisms needed to mold faith, family, hard work, and cooperation into opportunity, while expanding the community leaders' ability to attract new investment and grow existing businesses.

This bipartisan community renewal initiative will provide poor inner cities and rural areas with workable mechanisms that allow them to evaluate the needs in their communities and address them. This bill creates forty renewal communities with targeted progrowth tax benefits, homeownership opportunities, and other incentives that address the principal hurdles facing budding small businesses: raising capital and maintaining cash flow.

In a renewal community, individuals would not pay capital gains taxes on the sale of renewal community businesses and business assets held for more than five years. Small businesses would also be able to expense up to $35,000 more in equipment than they are able to under current law. And those who revitalize buildings located in these renewal communities will receive a special deduction.

Beyond that, this bill will stimulate state efforts to build the necessary infrastructure and rebuild economically depressed areas by accelerating the scheduled increase in the amount of tax exempt private bonds. Even more importantly, we will increase the amount of low-income tax credits a state can allocate. This translates into more and better housing opportunities for low-income families.

Today, through a variety of incentives, we will create a fertile environment for growth, with targeted pro-growth tax benefits, regulatory relief, savings accounts, and homeownership opportunities, as well as provide for the inclusion of local faith-based organizations. This is an opportunity for Congress to aid in lifting up those who have already been left behind during a time when many are enjoying the benefits of a prospering economy.

The Congressional Record. July 25, 2000: H6797–H6841.

SELECTED READING

Affordable Housing

Block, Dorian. "Affordable-Housing Plan Riles Residents." *Boston Globe.* October 2, 2005. www.boston.com/news/local/articles/2005/10/02/affordable_housing_plan_riles_residents.

Fireside, Daniel. "Burlington Busts the Affordable Housing Debate." *Dollars & Sense.* 2006. dollarsandsense.org/archives/2005/0305fireside.html.

National Low Income Housing Coalition. 2005. www.nlihc.org .

Sard, Barbara. "2006 Annual Housing Conference—Presentation by Barbara Sard, Center on Budget and Policy Priorities." Center of Budget and Policy Priorities. September 20, 2006. www.knowledgeplex.org/showdoc.html?id=206915.

U.S. Department of Housing and Urban Development. Office of Policy Development and Research. 2006. www.huduser.org.

Urban Renewal and Gentrification

"Gentrification." Now Public. 2006. www.nowpublic.com/tag/gentrification.

Hampson, Rick. "Studies: Gentrification a Boost for Everyone." *USA Today.* April 19, 2005. www.usatoday.com/news/nation/2005-04-19-gentrification_x.htm.

Kennedy, Maureen, and Paul Leonard. "Dealing with Neighborhood Change: a Primer on Gentrification and Policy Choices." Brookings Institution. April 2001. www.brookings.edu/es/urban/gentrification/gentrificationexsum.htm.

Levy, Diane, Jennifer Comey, and Sandra Padilla. "In the Face of Gentrification: Case Studies of Local Efforts to Mitigate Displacement." Urban Institute. 2006. www.urban.org/publications/411294.html.

Newman, Kathe, and Elvin Wyly. "Gentrification and Resistance in New York City." July–August. 2005. www.nhi.org/online/issues/142/gentrification.html.

8

Elderly Issues

Many Americans are unaware that federal expenditures for social insurance programs such as Social Security and Medicare are twice as large as those for public assistance programs like Temporary Assistance for Needy Children (TANF) and Medicaid. In fact, Social Security is the largest social program, accounting for slightly over 21 percent of the federal spending in 2004. Established in 1935, Social Security was designed as a pay-as-you-go program. This means that the benefits of current recipients are funded by the payroll taxes of today's workers, who contribute 12.4 percent of their earnings, up to a maximum of $90,000. While self-employed individuals must pay all 12.4 percent themselves, workers employed by others contribute 6.2 percent and their employers match their contributions. Workers also contribute 2.9 percent of their earnings in Medicare taxes, with employees paying 1.45 percent and employers matching this contribution on all earnings. Social Security and Medicare payroll taxes are set aside in trust funds to be paid out to beneficiaries as needed.

Demographic changes resulting from lower fertility rates and increased longevity have fueled projections that the Social Security and Medicare trust funds will eventually go bankrupt due to the shortage of workers to support the large retiring baby boom generation. The dependency ratio, defined as the number of current workers available to support program beneficiaries, has steadily increased. In 1960, there were four workers for each retiree; today, there are approximately three workers per retiree; and by 2030 there are expected to be only two workers per retiree.

Recognized as the most consistent and informed voting block, senior citizens wield substantial political power. Therefore, revamping Social Security and Medicare can be a dicey political proposition. To react to this challenge, following his election in 2000, President George W. Bush appointed a bipartisan Social Security Commission to propose strategies for restoring the program's solvency. In his second term, Bush selected Social Security reform as his number one domestic policy objective. Although Bush pledged not to change benefits for current or near retirees, he accepted the commission's recommendation to partially privatize the program. Bush proposed that workers under the age of fifty-five be allowed to deposit a portion of their payroll taxes into Private Retirement Accounts (PRAs), which are expected to yield higher returns.

SOCIAL SECURITY REFORM

Bush's proposal to fundamentally alter the traditionally sacrosanct Social Security program resulted in a hailstorm of criticism from liberals and moderate Republicans. The disagreement between conservatives and liberals regarding Social Security reform is illustrative of their fundamentally different political ideologies. Liberals would like to expand government's support of senior citizens and guarantee them a basic standard of living, which may require additional expenditures. However, conservatives hope to reduce government's role in the provision of health care to seniors and place more of the responsibility and control for their well-being on senior citizens themselves. Conservatives are also committed to relieving American's tax burden and allowing them to keep more of their money and use it to build wealth.

Both liberals and conservatives acknowledge that Social Security needs to be fixed, but they disagree about the extent of the problem. According to conservatives, Social Security is in "crisis" and the system is poised to go bankrupt by 2013 if changes are not made. In response, liberals accuse conservatives of manufacturing a "phony crisis" to create public support for their political goal of privatizing the program. Liberals estimate that Social Security will collect enough money until 2042 to pay 75 to 80 percent of eligible beneficiaries. Therefore, they believe the program is in need of only minor adjustments to maintain its solvency.

Liberals predict that privatization will place the entire system at risk because the diversion of contributions to private accounts will deplete $1 to $2 trillion from the trust funds. Redirection of worker contributions to private retirement accounts will result in significantly less money being deposited into the trust funds. Analysts agree that these so-called transitional costs will range from $1 to $2 trillion, and assert that the costs will need to be covered either by cutting benefits or borrowing money, since it is unlikely that Congress will raise taxes. Liberals caution that the deficit incurred could be substantial enough to cause stock market prices to tumble, interest rates to climb, and economic growth to stagnate. Liberals further warn that higher-yield investments entail greater risks, and that private retirement accounts may expose retirees to unnecessary risk. They cite incidents such as the Enron scandal and periodic downturns in the stock prices as evidence that rising stock values are not guaranteed. Liberals object to benefit levels being tied to stock values and investor luck. According to liberals, the major beneficiaries of Bush's plan will be the Wall Street firms who manage millions of private accounts and the corporations who utilize these funds. Conservatives respond that Wall Street will see only minor profits from these accounts.

Conservatives argue that Social Security benefits received during retirement years yield below-market returns on the payroll taxes paid. They maintain that returns of 1 percent or 2 percent (and 0 or negative in some cases) will not provide sufficient income for future retirees. Conservatives are convinced that payroll deductions slow economic growth by decreasing the amount of discretionary income that workers have to save and invest. They predict that that the diversion of payroll taxes to private retirement accounts will provide millions of low-income workers with the opportunity to invest in the stock market, encouraging a culture of savings. This will build wealth across the board and help reduce the growing wealth gap.

Liberals, on the other hand, blame slow economic growth on the massive deficits incurred under the Bush Administration, which they say are draining off capital that could be invested in economic growth. Liberals observe that the administration of millions of private retirement accounts entails higher administrative costs for employers and workers. Such costs can siphon funds from the accounts of low-income workers, leaving them less money to invest. Small businesses may be hurt by the increased administrative costs and paperwork. Finally, liberals charge that conservatives have ulterior motives for advancing privatization of Social Security. They accuse conservatives of promoting privatization to achieve their political aims of reducing the size of government and shifting policy toward greater personal responsibility. Some liberals have faulted conservatives for proposing privatization to "starve" the federal government of needed revenue with the intent of compelling more fiscal conservatism.

Moderate Republicans were uncomfortable with the diversion of money from the trust funds into private retirement accounts. They dissented from the more conservative members of their party, objecting to the dismantling of the basic principles on which Social Security was founded and the revocation of the guaranteed monthly income. Instead, moderate Republicans proposed alternative strategies for restoring the program's solvency, which do not deplete the trust fund or reduce benefits. For example, one proposal involved the use of revenues generated from "value added taxes" (taxes on products coming into the United States) to generate program revenues as an alternative that is used by many other nations.

MEDICARE REFORM

According to many analysts, there is even greater reason to be concerned about the status of Medicare. Experts predict that spending for Medicare will outpace Social Security expenditures in 2020. Although spending for Medicare is expected to grow exponentially, costs for Social Security will level off around 2030. The Medicare Modernization Act of 2003 (Medicare reform) established the program's first prescription drug benefit and expanded medical savings accounts, renamed Health Savings Accounts (HSAs). These accounts allow workers and their employers to select insurance plans with higher deductibles and place the savings from lower premiums into tax-sheltered savings accounts owned by the employee. Finally, the act allows private health plans to compete directly with traditional fee-for-service Medicare programs on a trial basis.

Liberals and conservatives vehemently disagree about whether or not the system is actually broken. According to liberals, the program's structure is basically sound, although it needs fine-tuning to control escalating costs and reflect the realities of the medical marketplace. Liberals accuse conservatives of exaggerating Medicare's problems to obtain the American public's support for privatization. Conservatives, on the other hand, protest that Medicare costs rise unpredictably each year partly due to overuse of services by seniors. They call for immediate reform to forestall exponential growth in costs, predicted to total $3.5 trillion by 2030.

Liberals and conservatives advance vastly different proposals for Medicare reform. Liberals hope to strengthen the traditional Medicare program and establish prescription drug coverage for all beneficiaries— significantly expanding the government's role in the provision of health care coverage to senior citizens. In contrast, conservatives are intent on containing program costs through increased competition and worker management of their own money through tax-preferred medical saving accounts. According to conservatives, HSAs and vouchers would provide incentives for consumers to select the most efficient and cost-effective health plans, consequently lowering health insurance costs and encouraging price competition in physician and hospital services. Finally, conservatives seek to create a limited program to direct competition between the traditional Medicare program and private plans.

Neither liberals nor conservatives are satisfied with the resulting reform package. Liberals grumble that the program amounts to a "pharmaceutical give-away" favoring drug manufacturers and insurance companies. Liberals charge that private sector reforms are not actually intended to save money, but are a deliberate attempt to remove seniors from traditional Medicare and push them into private sector plans. They fear that many seniors will be forced into HMOs and that many rural areas will not have enough private insurance companies to implement the market-based reforms. Finally, liberals also think many seniors are not in a position to compare assorted medical plans and will ultimately be confused by too many choices.

On the other hand, conservatives feel that the legislation does not go far enough to encourage private sector competition. They also object to the addition of prescription drug coverage on the grounds that it amounts to a "costly new government entitlement" that increased the role and size of government. They fear that prescription drug costs will spiral out of control and significantly increase the deficit.

PRESCRIPTION DRUG COST CONTROL

Although the Medicare Modernization Act of 2003 establishes payment levels for most health care service providers, it prohibits the federal government from engaging in direct negotiations with pharmaceutical companies to secure lower drug prices for beneficiaries. Liberals are outraged that the United States is the only government in the world denied the right to negotiate drug prices. They accuse conservatives, who insisted on inclusion of this provision, of caving in to the powerful drug lobby and showing favoritism to pharmaceutical companies who contributed to their campaigns. Since its passage, liberals have vowed to repeal this provision and have introduced legislation to allow the federal government to negotiate prices directly with private drug companies. They have also backed proposals to legalize the importation of drugs from Canada and to create a government-run prescription plan.

However, conservatives are strongly opposed to "price controls" in any form, believing that they stifle innovation, discourage research, and cause shortages in supply. Citing the widely publicized price overruns of the defense department, conservatives contend that government bureaucrats cannot be trusted to negotiate drug prices. The government, they maintain, does not need to be involved for large groups to take advantage of their buying power to negotiate lower prices. They prefer that large employers and special-interest organizations negotiate directly with drug companies for lower prices.

Conservatives also claim that price controls at the state level have restricted access to new drugs and fueled higher prices for uninsured and privately insured individuals. They allege that price controls in Europe have also resulted in higher costs to citizens compared to savings on prescription drugs. Conservatives warn that drug companies that charge lower prices will have fewer resources for innovation, capital investments, research, and quality control. Conservatives believe that drug costs can be held down through competition among private firms. Competition, they believe, will lead to more efficiency, cost savings, and the elimination of waste. They prefer to provide workers with additional money for prescription drug coverage in the form of tax credits or vouchers that seniors can use to select coverage from competing health plans.

However, liberals counter that price controls will not put a significant dent in the pharmaceutical industry's incredibly high profits. In fact, they predict that price reductions will positively impact sales because more people will be able to afford to use drugs as prescribed. Thus, liberals forecast the effects of price reductions will actually be offset by increases in sales.

CONCLUSIONS

Nowhere is the conflict of ideology between liberals and conservatives more evident than in the debate surrounding the reform of Social Security and Medicare. Conservatives' vision of an "ownership" society in which workers keep more of their money through tax cuts is the foundation for their preference for retirement and medical savings accounts. In contrast, liberals' emphasis on societal obligations to assist its most vulnerable members motivates their calls for expanded benefits on the federal level. The federal government, liberals say, is the only entity that has the power and resources available to guarantee all members of society a basic level of well-being.

SOCIAL SECURITY REFORM

In his 2005 State of the Union address, President George W. Bush alarmed the country when he described Social Security as "headed for bankruptcy." While most Americans are aware of Social Security's financial crisis, there is confusion over the dimensions of the crisis as well as the necessary measures of solving it. Social Security is a welfare program initiated by Franklin D. Roosevelt in 1935 during the Great Depression. It uses the payroll of current workers paid to the government to pay the benefits of today's recipients. Social Security has usually run a surplus because there were more workers paying taxes than people receiving benefits. The surplus is expected to disappear as the number of people over the age of sixty-five increases much faster than the number of working Americans. Many predictions hold the year 2042 as the year when Social Security will run out of money.

Like many conservatives, President George W. Bush has advocated a partial privatization of Social Security. In his opinion, the program should incorporate federal assistance along with individual choice. President Bush has strongly endorsed individual savings accounts, as they give individuals more financial freedom over their income.

Many opponents of privatization have continued to criticize the president's plan. They believe that privatization is the first step towards the elimination of Social Security. Liberals such as Sen. Richard J. Durbin (D-IL) argue that privatization will decrease payroll taxes from individuals, but their return will diminish as well. Regardless of the viewpoint, Social Security continues to be the subject of widespread debate.

Conservative Viewpoint

President George W. Bush. This past week, I addressed the nation to talk about the challenges facing Social Security. The Social Security system that Franklin Roosevelt created was a great moral success of the twentieth century. It provided a safety net that ensured dignity and peace of mind to millions of Americans in retirement.

Yet today, there is a hole in the safety net for younger workers, because Congress has made promises it cannot keep. We have a duty to save and strengthen Social Security for our children and grandchildren.

In the coming week, I will travel to Mississippi to continue to discuss ways to put Social Security on the path to permanent solvency. I will continue to assure Americans that some parts of Social Security will not change. Seniors and people with disabilities will continue to get their checks, and all Americans born before 1950 will also receive their full benefits. And I will make it clear that as we fix Social Security, we have a duty to direct extra help to those most in need and make Social Security a better deal for younger workers.

We have entered a new phase in this discussion. As members of Congress begin work on Social Security legislation, they should pursue three important goals. First, I understand that millions of Americans depend on Social Security checks as a primary source of retirement income, so we must keep this promise to future retirees as well. As a matter of fairness, future generations should receive benefits equal to or greater than the benefits today's seniors get.

Second, I believe a reformed system should protect those who depend on Social Security the most. So in the future, benefits for low-income workers should grow faster than benefits for people who are better off. By providing more generous benefits for low-income retirees, we'll make good on this commitment: If you work hard and pay into Social Security your entire life, you will not retire into poverty.

This reform would solve most of the funding challenges facing Social Security. A variety of options are available to solve the rest of the problem.

And I will work with Congress on any good-faith proposal that does not raise the payroll-tax rate or harm our economy.

Third, any reform of Social Security must replace the empty promises being made to younger workers with real assets, real money. I believe the best way to achieve this goal is to give younger workers the option of putting a portion of their payroll taxes into a voluntary personal retirement account. Because this money is saved and invested, younger workers would have the opportunity to receive a higher rate of return on their money than the current Social Security system can provide.

Some Americans have reservations about investing in the markets because they want a guaranteed return on their money, so one investment option should consist entirely of Treasury bonds, which are backed by the full faith and credit of the United States Government. Options like this will make voluntary personal retirement accounts a safer investment that will allow you to build a nest egg that you can pass on to your loved ones.

In the days and weeks ahead, I will work to build on the progress we have made in the Social Security discussion. Americans of all ages are beginning to look at Social Security in a new way. Instead of asking whether the system has a problem, they're asking when their leaders are going to fix it. Fixing Social Security must be a bipartisan effort, and I'm willing to listen to a good idea from either party. I'm confident that by working together, we will find a solution that will renew the promise of Social Security for the twenty-first century.

Public Papers of the President: George W. Bush. April 30, 2005: 715–716.

Liberal Viewpoint

Richard J. Durbin (D-IL). Mr. Speaker: the president of the United States is on the road today. He is taking his case for privatization of Social Security around the United States. It is an interesting debate. It is a good debate because it gets down to the heart of the question.

I joined with some Democratic Senate leadership—Harry Reid, Byron Dorgan, and several other colleagues—and we went on the road last week to New York, Philadelphia, Phoenix, and Las Vegas to talk about this issue. We are engaging the American people because we believe it is an important debate.

I think we should start the debate by agreeing on some very basic points, and the first point on which we should agree is that at the end of the debate, Social Security will still be there, it will survive, and we are all committed to it. Any proposal that comes from anyone of either political party that weakens Social Security and lessens the likelihood that it will be there as a safety net for America should be summarily rejected.

That is why we on the Democratic side have said we want to sit down with President Bush and the Republican leadership to make Social Security strong, but first we have to take privatization of Social Security off the table because privatization of Social Security, as the president is proposing, will weaken Social Security, it will not strengthen it. It takes trillions of dollars out of the Social Security trust fund, a trust fund that has already been raided by politicians for years. It would be devastated by taking out this much money.

The president is calling for taking the money out of the Social Security trust fund that is going to be used to pay off retirees in the years to come.

How do they make up for this? The president's White House proposes cutting the benefits for retirees as much as 50 percent. So if someone is receiving $1,200 today, had the president's plan been in effect from the beginning of Social Security, they would be receiving around $500.

It is a dramatic cut the president is talking about. It would push many senior citizens into poverty, not to mention add dramatically to our national debt, a debt which is already too large, will be increased this year by our deficit spending, and a debt which is financed by foreign countries. China, Japan, Korea, and Taiwan hold America's mortgage.

President Bush's privatization plan means that mortgages will grow substantially, from about $8 trillion to at least $15 trillion by the president's calculations. That means our children, who are supposed to be benefited by this so-called privatization, will not only have to gamble their retirement in the stock market, but also face the payment of this debt. That is fundamentally unfair.

Many people have said: Why don't the Democrats come forward with a plan on Social Security? I will tell my colleagues the Democratic plan in three words: Social Security first. If any plan to strengthen Social Security does not guarantee that this safety net and the benefits people can count on for retirement will be there in the years to come, it is not a plan we should even consider. Privatization cannot meet that guarantee.

The Congressional Record. March 9, 2005: S2305–S2306.

MEDICARE REFORM

Medicare is the largest welfare program in the United States. It is a health insurance program for people over the age of sixty-five as well as those who are disabled or meet specific criteria. Medicare was started in 1965 under President Lyndon B. Johnson and has been continually growing. In recent years, critics have contended that Medicare is expensive, ineffective, and in need of serious modernization.

President George W. Bush has welcomed bipartisan efforts in Congress to reform Medicare and he has also created his own solution. President Bush claims that his new Medicare program has encompassed more people into Medicare than ever before and more are enrolling each week. By enrolling into President Bush's Medicare plan, seniors receive cheaper drugs due to competition. Not only will the price of drugs decrease with the Bush plan, monthly premiums should decrease as well.

Democrats such as Rep. Sherrod Brown (D-OH) strongly oppose President Bush's plan to revamp Medicare. They argue that the "reformed" plan strongly benefits the pharmaceutical companies and leaves the average American behind. Rep. Brown claims that the Bush Medicare plan actually increases premiums instead of downsizing them. In addition, House Democrats are criticizing the Bush Administration for increased HMO profits that result from the Bush plan. Even though drug price reduction was the original purpose of Medicare more than forty years ago, the same problems continue to plague American seniors today.

Conservative Viewpoint

President George W. Bush. When I came into office, I found a Medicare system that was antiquated and not meeting the needs of America's seniors. The system would pay tens of thousands of dollars for a surgery but not a few hundred dollars for the prescription drugs that could have prevented the surgery in the first place. So working with Congress, we passed critical legislation that modernizes Medicare, provides seniors with more choices, and gives seniors better access to the prescription drugs they need.

Since the program went into effect six weeks ago, more than twenty-four million people with Medicare now have prescription drug coverage, and hundreds of thousands more are enrolling each week. The competition in the prescription drug market has been stronger than expected and is lowering costs for taxpayers and seniors alike. This year, the federal government will spend 20 percent less overall on the Medicare drug benefit than projected just last July. The average premium that seniors pay is a third less than had been expected—just $25 per month instead of $37 per month. And the typical senior will end up spending about half of what they used to spend on prescription drugs each year.

· · ·

Still, when you make a big change in a program involving millions of people, there are bound to be some challenges, and this has been the case with the new drug coverage. Some people had trouble the first time they went to the pharmacy after enrolling. Information for some beneficiaries was not transferred smoothly between Medicare, drug plans, and the States.

And in the early days of the drug coverage, waiting times were far too long for many customers and pharmacists who called Medicare or their drug plans to seek help.

· · ·

Despite early challenges, the results so far are clear: The new Medicare prescription drug plan is a good deal for seniors. If you're a Medicare recipient and have not yet signed up for prescription drug coverage, I encourage you to review your options and choose the plan that is right for you. Americans who have parents on Medicare should encourage and help them to sign up. Citizen groups, faith-based organizations, health professionals, and pharmacies across America are working to help answer questions. Seniors can also get information 24 hours a day by calling 1-800-MEDICARE or by visiting the official Medicare web site at medicare.gov.

Prescription drug coverage under Medicare has been available for just a few weeks, but its benefits will last for decades to come. I was proud to sign this Medicare reform into law. And because we acted, millions of American seniors are now saving money, getting the life-saving drugs they need, and receiving the modern health care they deserve.

Public Papers of the President: George W. Bush. February 11, 2006: 231–232.

Liberal Viewpoint

Sherrod Brown (D-OH). Madam Speaker, it is easy to understand why President Bush and the Republicans have had such a hard time selling the Medicare law to the American people. Their Medicare law has more than its fair share of dirty laundry, as we can see from this chart. Cost estimates hidden from Congress, the administration violated ethics laws, members of Congress strong-armed to change their vote. We know this Medicare bill was passed in the middle of the night. The roll call was kept open an unprecedented three hours. One member was literally bribed on the House floor, he claimed, the next day, or they attempted to bribe him on the House floor, a Republican leader attempting to bribe a Republican member.

· · ·

The administration then turned around, spending tens of millions of dollars on infomercial-style ads making Medicare almost look like an item for sale on the Home Shopping Network. That bad process, the middle-of-the-night, the bribery, the campaign contributions, the sleazy kind of tactics to get this bill passed the expenditure of tax dollar money to sell a bad product to the American people, that whole process that bad process resulted logically in a bad product.

The drug benefit offers a part-time response to a full-time problem, requiring year-round premium payments for drug coverage that ends in August. And the Medicare law is confusing, handing seniors a stack of discount cards and saying if they cannot figure this out, here is an 800 number. The Medicare law does nothing to contain the skyrocketing cost of prescription drugs. Instead, instead, the Republicans and the president went out of their way to write the drug industry a blank check. No surprise there. This bill means $180 billion, with a "b," in extra profits above and beyond what the drug companies' record profits already are, $180 billion in extra profits for this drug bill; and, again no surprise, to complete the circle, the drug companies have given President Bush and Republicans in Congress tens of millions of dollars for their campaign.

· · ·

I want to get started by talking for a moment about the Bush Medicare premium hike. We heard about it. It was in the papers. Despite the Bush administration's efforts to keep it as quiet as possible, they released the information about the biggest Medicare hike in history, a 17.4 percent premium hike. They released it on the Friday before Labor Day, hoping people would not notice. But the biggest premium increase in Medicare history, they just cannot keep it quiet. So the news that Saturday was all about the Bush administration's plans, President Bush's plans to impose a 17.4 percent Medicare premium increase. The Republican spin machine is nothing if were not tenacious; so faced with bad news, they did what they always do, they blame the Democrats or they blame someone else. In this case they tried to convince us that Democrats are really the reason the premium hike happened. The fact is Republicans control the House, they have for 10 years, the Republicans control the Senate, the Republicans have had the White House. During the Clinton years, premiums stayed almost even for the last four years of the Clinton years, the second term of the Clinton administration, and now they have jumped up.

In fact, before the Bush Medicare bill became law, the nonpartisan Medicare trustees estimated the monthly premium increase for next year would be $2. After the Bush Medicare bill became law, the premium increase jumped to $11.60. That is per month. That is not much to a member of Congress, but a senior citizen whose Social Security only went up 2, 2¼, 2½ percent, when faced with a 17 percent increase, well over $100, that is a serious amount of money. Five times larger than the premium increase estimated before the Bush Medicare law.

So where is that money? Where is that billions of dollars, the 17 percent increase, the billions of dollars that seniors have to pay out of their pockets? Whose pockets is that money going into? Where does that money go?

The fact is much of it is going into the pockets of Medicare insurance HMOs. The Medicare law creates a $23 billion slush fund that HMOs can use to lure seniors out of traditional Medicare into their private insurance plans. Seniors already spend 25 percent of their income on out-of-pocket health care costs. The Bush Medicare law hands them a giant increase in their Medicare premiums.

HMO profits already this year have jumped 50 percent over last year. Now we are giving them this $23 billion. And here is how it works: Last March the government, taxpayers, gave the first $229 million payment to insurance company HMOs. In April, taxpayers gave another $229 million payment to insurance company HMOs. In May and June, all the way through this year and all the way through next year, $229 million every month from taxpayers to insurance company HMOs. But do my colleagues know something? Seniors do not get the prescription drug benefit until 2006. So $229 million for twenty-two straight months go from seniors through this premium increase and taxpayers directly into the pockets of insurance company HMOs before they even get a drug benefit.

So it makes us wonder why. And the answer to the question why is insurance companies and drug companies wrote this Medicare bill, insurance companies and drug companies benefit from this Medicare bill, and the president and Republican leaders get major campaign contributions from the drug and insurance industry. It is all pretty simple. It is also corrupt. It is also outrageous. It is also morally reprehensible. And it is also something that we all need to think about when we make a decision this fall, come November 2.

The Congressional Record. September 28, 2004: H7718–H7724.

PRESCRIPTION DRUG COST CONTROL

Prescription drug prices have been a hotly contested issue in the United States. The cost of prescription drugs in the United States is significantly higher than in other countries since many other countries have price controls. Many people from the United States travel to Canada or Mexico to buy generic drugs for about half the cost.

Pharmaceutical companies argue that the high prices are necessary to fund further research. Since many of the clinical trials are unsuccessful, their funding must be obtained from the drugs already on the market. Furthermore, many conservatives such as Rep. Philip M. Crane (R-IL) are concerned about the safety of drugs imported from the neighboring countries. He argues that the United States Food and Drug Administration has many stringent rules and more control over what goes on the market than does

Canada or Mexico. As a result, generic drugs that are obtained from Canada or Mexico may be more harmful for the patient.

Democrats such as Rep. Rahm Emanuel (D-IL) believe in the necessity of drug importation. Citing several drug examples, Emanuel argues that drugs are much cheaper if they are imported from other countries. More importantly, drug importation would allow those who could not afford drugs access to these drugs. Both the Senate as well as the House of Representatives have passed legislation to legalize drug importation; however, the Bush Administration and the Food and Drug Administration have strongly opposed it.

Conservative Viewpoint

Phillip M. Crane (R-IL). Mr. Speaker, as the Congress continues to debate the question on how to provide seniors with affordable prescription drugs, I wanted to bring to my colleagues attention the article "Prescription Drug Costs: Has Canada Found the Answer?" by William McArthur, M.D. Dr. McArthur is a palliative care physician, writer and health policy analyst in Vancouver B.C. Some of our colleagues have been touting the affordability of prescription drugs in Canada and in some cases sponsoring bus trips for seniors across the border to obtain these drugs. We should be skeptical of this approach because, in reality, the Canadian government drug mandates harm patients and increase the costs in other sectors of the health care system.

The Canadian bureaucracies cause significant delays in access to new and innovative drugs. First, at the federal level, Canadians wait up to a year longer than Americans do for approval of new drugs. Then the delays continue at the provincial level where various government "gatekeepers" review the "therapeutic value" of prescription drugs before they are included in the formulary. The length of the delays varies widely. The government officials in Nova Scotia approve drugs for its formulary in 250 days, while the wait in Ontario is nearly 500 days.

Canadian patients are often forced to use the medicines selected by the government solely for cost reasons. Patients who would respond better to the second, third, or fourth drug developed for a specific condition are often denied the preferred drug, and are stuck with the government-approved "one size fits all" drug.

I urge my Colleagues to read this article and keep in mind that while prescription drugs appear to cost less in Canada than in the United States, there is a costly price associated with the Canadian system that ultimately translates into a lack of quality care for patients.

The Congressional Record. October 4, 2000: E1673–E1674.

Liberal Viewpoint

Rahm Emanuel (D-IL). Mr. Speaker, people from around the world come to America for their medical care. Yet Americans are forced to travel around the world for their prescription drugs and medications. Today, in the *Washington Post*, there was a poll conducted by the *Washington Post* and ABC News showing more than two-thirds of Americans think it should be legal to purchase medications from Canada and Europe and other industrialized nations.

I think this is significant given on the eve that the conference on prescription drugs is meeting to know where the American people are on the major issue of allowing them to purchase medications from either Europe or Canada, allowing competition to pervade in the prescription drug area, allowing choice to consumers. Two-thirds of the Americans think it is the right thing to do.

In the meantime, millions of Americans are forced to either cut their medications in half, skip a month, forgo their prescription drugs entirely, or cut their pills, as I said, in half. Yet of those who choose not to do that, many are forced to go to Canada to buy their medications.

. . .

You take the cancer drug Tamoxifen, $360 in the United States; Canada, $33, a life-saving medication for women with breast cancer. You go down the list, line by line. Last week, *USA Today* ran an article going line by line over major medications, and they were all somewhere between 40 to 50 percent cheaper in Canada than they are in the United States.

And the irony of all of that is many of those medications were developed with U.S. taxpayer dollars. So what have we provided? Not only do we fund the research and development of these new life-saving medications, we are provided the unique opportunity of paying the most expensive prices in the world for medications that were originally developed with U.S. tax dollars.

Many in the industry not only now are limiting sales, they argue about the safety of these medications purchased from Canada. Yet today, we import $15 billion worth of medications from around the world. Nobody argues about their safety. And the most telling example about the issue of Canada is that in October 2000 when the United States Government needed a vaccine for anthrax, where did they turn because there was a shortage here in the United States?

They turned to Canada. If it was so unsafe for our consumers to go to Canada to buy medications, where did the United States Government go in dire need? They went to Canada because the system in Canada is comparable to our system.

The facts are that the claims made by the FDA and the pharmaceutical companies about the dangers of these drugs simply do not hold. They did not hold when the United States Government needed them, and they do not hold today when our seniors and others are forced to go to Canada to get life-saving medications.

This system is not some great beyond that we do not know. Today in Europe the system of parallel trading exists, free trade where people in Germany or France or England or Ireland buy medications wherever they need them in Europe. That system exists, and it is the most competitive market in the pharmaceutical industry.

What I am suggesting, what others in bipartisan fashion have passed in July, the legislation known as market access, are suggesting is allow the United States to participate in that market access. Allow the barriers to come down, allow the market to organize and properly manage itself and prices in the United States would come down, rather than allowing a 40 to 50 percent disparity between the prices in Canada and Europe between the United States. That is what would happen if we passed this legislation today.

For too long, if we take a look at it, in Families USA, the fifty most commonly used drugs by our seniors have risen 3½ times the rate of inflation. Between 2000 and 2003, seniors' expenditures on prescription drugs increased by 44 percent.

The costs of medications are too expensive. Eli Lilly and the other pharmaceuticals are limiting the sales to Canada in an attempt to cut off the seniors. And what does the United States Congress do and what does the United States Senate do? When they passed a prescription drug, when it came to the issue of price and affordability, the Congress did nothing. And so people are forced to take action in their own hands and go to Canada.

The Congressional Record. October 20, 2003: H9709–H9710.

SELECTED READING

Social Security Reform

Bixby, Robert L. "Social Security Reform." The Concord Coalition. 2005. www .concordcoalition.org/issues/socsec/doc/050203testimonyexecsummary.htm

"Common Sense on Social Security." April 13, 2006. www.sscommonsense.org/page18 .html.

Guthrie, Ben. "Editor's Note: Why Liberals Should Support Social Security Reform." *Stanford Review* 34:8 (2005). Last update: October 6, 2006. www.stanfordreview.org/ Archive/Volume_XXXIV/Issue_8/Opinions/Opinions4.shtml.

Rodriguez, Ciro D. "Protecting Our Future: Preserving Social Security." *Senior Journal.* October 12, 2006. www.seniorjournal.com/NEWS/SocialSecurity/SocSecReform/ 03-14-02DemView.htm.

"Social Security." Social Security Reform Center. Last updated: October 12, 2006. www
.socialsecurityreform.org/index.cfm.

Medicare Reform

"Medicare." Centers for Medicare and Medicaid Services. 2006. www.cms.hhs.gov.

"*Medicare Reform: The Real Winners.*" CBS News. November 20, 2003. www.cbsnews
.com/stories/2003/11/20/opinion/main584722.shtm.

"The Official U.S. Government Site for People with Medicare." Medicare. 2006. www
.medicare.gov.

Potts, Laurine E. "Medicare Criticized." *American Journal of Nursing* 69:11 (1969),
2346.

"Strengthening Medicare: A Framework to Modernize and Improve Medicare." The
White House. 2006. www.whitehouse.gov/infocus/medicare.

Prescription Drug Cost Control

Adams, Michael. "Importation of Prescription Drugs from Canada Rises Despite
FDA's Best Efforts to Protect Big Pharma's Profits in the U.S." *News Target.* 2005.
www.newstarget.com/001493.html.

Baldauf, Sarah. "Prescription Drug Imports: Two Shots of Good News." *U.S. News.*
www.usnews.com/usnews/health/articles/061006/6health.htm.

Frank, Richard G. "Prescription Drug Prices." *New England Journal of Medicine*
351:14 (September 30, 2004): 1375–77.

"Importing Prescription Drugs." United States Food and Drug Administration.
2006. www.fda.gov/importeddrugs.

"Would Prescription Drug Importation Reduce U.S. Drug Spending?" Congressional
Budget Office. April 29, 2004. www.cbo.gov/showdoc.cfm?index=5406&sequence=0.

9

Civil Rights

On the subject of civil rights, modern conservatives and liberals agree on most issues of major importance. It is commonly held that all people, regardless of race, gender, or numerous other characteristics, are equal under the law. While conservatives and liberals have disagreed in the past, current positions held by both parties are very similar on a number of issues under the banner of civil rights. However, it is useful to consider the specific stances conservatives and liberals have on various issues. To that end, the issues of civil rights (as a whole), gay marriage, the Equal Rights Amendment, affirmative action, and hate crimes will be analyzed according to the division between conservative and liberal perspectives.

The issue of civil rights is an extremely broad topic that is difficult to analyze by typical standards. However, conservative and liberal positions on this issue have undergone significant changes over time. Throughout much of U.S. history, equality in civil rights of both genders and all races has been suppressed in favor of a supposed "stability." This resulted in neither equality nor stability for race relations in the United States.

It is not productive to indict either liberals or conservatives for suppressing civil rights, as various leaders of liberal and conservative inclinations have supported repressive legislation against civil rights equality. In essence, both conservatives and liberals today agree on the need for equality in civil rights for most groups. What has changed is that conservatives have expressed concerns recently about classifying groups under social dichotomies (sexual orientation, etc.) as opposed to more typical physical classifications that have been addressed in many cases (race, gender, etc.).

In contrast to this, liberals have typically supported open recognition of civil rights protection to groups of diverse individuals. This stance goes back hundreds of years, to early advocates of class equality in Europe. Some of the early efforts at achieving more equality and civil rights include the efforts of participants in the French Revolution and the various reform periods in Britain afterward. However, as people have gained more rights on a class basis, battles have continued to be fought along social fronts.

GAY MARRIAGE

In the area of civil rights, one of the most divisive issues currently is the debate over gay marriage. This debate polarizes conservatives and liberals across the political spectrum, but it is important not to completely define conservatives and liberals alone in this issue. To the extent that libertarian thought is present in both the liberal and conservative viewpoints, not all conservatives are against gay marriage. In addition, due to varying interpretations of religious canonical texts (the Bible, among others), not all liberals can be classified as being in total support of this issue. Therefore, to define this issue, a multitude of views must be accepted, even in the overall scheme of two distinct political identities of conservatives and liberals.

The liberal argument in favor of gay marriage is that it is a natural continuation of individual rights. As prejudices against homosexuality and homosexual behavior are broken down, acceptance into society necessitates acceptance into traditional societal structures. To this end, a legal definition of marriage that allows homosexuals to enter into marriage is necessary for social acceptance. In addition, the fiscal benefits of marriage are noteworthy and currently left out in the case of homosexual partners. As such, it is necessary to support gay marriage for the rights of homosexual couples to achieve the same benefits and opportunities currently available for heterosexual couples.

Conservatives take a different perspective on this issue, depending on their affiliation with a more libertarian-based conservative view or a more religious-based conservative view. Those conservatives who share a more libertarian-based conception of conservatism view the issue of gay marriage as a potential for individual empowerment, a key concept under libertarianism. However, conservative support under these ideals extends toward individual empowerment only, dictating that civil unions are a viable bridge to garner bipartisan support. Conservatives embracing a more religious-based view are more skeptical of gay marriage as it runs into conflict with various canonical precepts from the Bible and other religious texts. However, conservatives embracing a more religious-based interpretation of their conservatism have signaled in some cases that a compromise of civil unions is possible. This possibility offers the best chance of success in this politically charged debate.

EQUAL RIGHTS AMENDMENT

The Equal Rights Amendment is a fairly old idea, developed in the early part of the twentieth century. This proposed amendment came on the heels of the Nineteenth Amendment to the Constitution, guaranteeing women the right to vote. The ERA has, at its heart, a commitment to guarantee equal rights under virtually all circumstances and conditions to women and men alike. While quite promising for its commitment to continue the reforms in women's rights started at the beginning of the twentieth century, it has gained a number of problematic aspects to both liberals and conservatives as time has passed.

The amendment was originally proposed in the U.S. Congress by two Republicans. It faced opposition at that time from labor unions and women's advocates who did not want women to lack significant protections under the law. They believed that women's protections would be potentially lessened with this amendment. These protections include specific laws regulating limits of heavy work and other physical constraints. However, in following years, support and opposition switched party affiliations, as liberals and conservatives find themselves arguing over this issue for different reasons than before.

Currently, a liberal perspective endorses this issue as a necessary means toward women's equality in various aspects of life, both social and economic. This amendment would, in theory, make federal laws more gender-neutral and work to eliminate existing provisions that have been accused of being discriminatory on the basis of gender. Such views are held by people such as Supreme Court Justice Ruth Ginsberg, who advocated similar arguments in a 1977 report, "Sex Bias in the U.S. Code."

The conservative argument against this amendment has many important aspects. A primary concern for conservatives is that this amendment could have many unpredicted consequences. Some of these consequences have already been seen in various legal cases that have invoked the ERA in specific instances. Such examples include arguments in favor of same-sex marriages, abortion rights, and intervention of traditionally single-sex institutions using the ERA as a qualifier for these arguments. A more central concern for many conservatives, especially those with a libertarian perspective, is the issue of increased government intervention via Congress and federal courts due to passage of the ERA. As the ERA is enforced on a federal level, it would allow government much more influence in people's activities. While this intrusion may be made with the best intentions, it is still an intrusion on people's rights, according to many conservatives.

AFFIRMATIVE ACTION

This is possibly the most divisive civil rights issue of our time. This issue stems from the concept that traditionally excluded minority groups require special consideration or compensation to more quickly achieve equality with a majority typically embodied by white males. However, this contention itself and the measures proposed to compensate or provide special consideration to minorities have been under serious debate since affirmative action was first proposed. Therefore, it is necessary to understand the variance between the conservative and liberal perspectives on this issue.

The liberal stance on this issue is characterized by a pattern of arguments in favor of affirmative action on the basis that various minority groups are currently "underrepresented" in education and various career fields. Affirmative action is viewed as one of the primary tools in reducing this inequality by offering incentives and special opportunities to minority applicants for college and/or jobs, or outright quota requirements for certain companies found in noncompliance with affirmative action ideals. While other tools for reducing inequality exist, liberals argue that affirmative action offers the quickest method for inequality reduction and the most "bang for the buck" to limit and roll back inequality.

The conservative position has typically maintained that affirmative action is a good idea, but suffers from flawed implementation. While reducing inequality is a noble idea, offering governmental support and pressure for colleges to employ and accept more minorities has many questionable side effects. One basic example is that this increases government influence on college applications. In addition, affirmative action sets potentially economically inefficient behaviors into place. Minority individuals who now have increased artificial incentives to attend college and apply for newly available jobs may not have the educational or fiscal ability to sustain their involvement in college. Admittedly, this is a position of concern early in the affirmative action process. As minorities become more integrated into middle- and upper-class society, they have more educational and fiscal ability to sustain their involvement in college and the job environment.

Overall, affirmative action offers substantial promise toward encouraging more minority involvement in typically out-of-reach environments of higher education and certain career fields. However, it is important to note significant issues of concern with affirmative action. In addition, if the economic incentives for minority involvement in education and careers are unnaturally skewed, people will get involved in education without sufficient long-term resources, leading to a severe waste of money. Either way, affirmative action must be undertaken carefully so as to not encroach on individuals and schools while still encouraging minority involvement in new and exciting areas previously unavailable to them.

HATE CRIMES

Both liberals and conservatives hold an interest in the issue of hate crimes and the legislation in prevention and/or punishment of these crimes. On this issue, significant bipartisan support has been seen in numerous cases. In cases where gender or race has been a factor, both conservatives and liberals have joined forces in favor of prosecuting these crimes. However, concerns have been raised by conservatives about the overzealousness of applying hate crime status to crimes that may have only dubious attachment to any bigoted intent.

These concerns stem from a conservative distrust in government application of broad-reaching law. Though laws against hate crimes have been made with good intentions, the possibility of abuse under these laws is present, but not sufficiently discussed, according to various conservatives. According to many conservatives, hate crime law is applied on an ambiguous basis such that crimes involving a victim that is gay, African American, or some other minority can be too easily classified as hate crimes, although the direct evidence of a true "hate crime" is minimal.

However, liberals have argued that conservative concerns about the potential risks of the broad application of hate crime law are exaggerated. Instead, hate crime law must be overly broad due to the nature of hate crimes. Hate crimes are especially heinous and difficult to discern. Therefore, without broad laws that place more resources and powers in the hands of law enforcement to prosecute hate crimes, these crimes are more likely to continue.

This issue is not likely to be solved any time soon due to the nature of objections and defenses of this legislation. This legislation touches on a number of very sensitive spots in American history and liberal/conservative ideology. While defending vulnerable minorities is important, defending the rights of innocent people who could too easily be accused of a hate crime is important as well. While a solution to this issue is not easy to develop, it must embrace both the rights of victims and those accused of the crime so as to supplement standards of equal legal rights, instead of potentially supplanting them.

CONCLUSIONS

Civil rights remain some of the most debated rights in America today. While agreement has been reached on a number of issues, divisions still remain as conservative and liberal ideologies conflict on many civil rights issues where the national government is directly involved. Therefore, it is necessary for future attempts at solving civil rights issues to take into account cautionary measures toward government involvement. These cautionary measures will better preserve individual rights, which is of great importance to both liberals and conservatives.

GAY MARRIAGE

The same-sex marriage debate has been a long-standing issue within the Bush Administration. It can be defined as the union between two people of the same gender.

Currently, same-sex marriage is legal in Belgium, Canada, Spain, the Netherlands, and the state of Massachusetts. Many U.S. states recognize civil unions or domestic partnerships between homosexual couples, which allow them to receive some of the benefits enjoyed by married couples.

President Bush and other opponents of gay marriage base their justifications against same-sex marriage on religion. They argue that marriage is a sacred institution between a man and a woman, and gay marriage goes against tradition, procreation, and conventional meanings. In fact, in 2006, President Bush wanted to amend the U.S. Constitution and limit the definition of marriage to a man and a woman. Many argue that legalization of gay marriage would lead to an increase of gay couples in the United States and also redefine family values and the notion of a "traditional" family. Conservative and moderate Christians believe that same-sex marriage goes against the Bible. Furthermore, opponents believe that same-sex marriages would corrupt the current church beliefs by forcing them to perform marriages that they do not agree with.

Proponents of same-sex marriages argue that the separation of church and state within this country prohibits religion to be used as an argument. Supporters continue to argue that marriage is a right and therefore should not be limited to heterosexual couples. Rep. James McGovern (D-NJ) argues that an amendment would bring forth more discrimination and intolerance among citizens. He believes that homosexual couples should be able to enjoy the same rights heterosexual couples do. Despite contrary beliefs, McGovern argues that same-sex marriages are not a threat to heterosexual marriages, and therefore should be celebrated as well. Furthermore, proponents believe that a law such as this should not be defined by the federal government but rather by the states. The constitutional amendment to protect marriage did not pass.

Conservative Viewpoint

Samuel D. Brownback (R-KS). Mr. President, if members of the Senate vote as their states have voted on this amendment, the vote today will be 90 to

10 in favor of a constitutional amendment. Forty-five states have defined marriage as the union of a man and a woman.

I want to show my colleagues an outdated map. It shows the number of states that have weighed in on the topic of marriage. Yesterday, Alabama voted by 81 percent to define marriage as the union of a man and a woman. The dark green states are those that have already passed; light green are those where it is pending, and only five states have not defined marriage as a union between a man and a woman. So if senators would represent their states, this amendment would pass 90 to 10. It would pass with the definition of marriage as the union of a man and a woman. And if anybody wants to define it otherwise, it will have to go through the state legislature, not the courts.

So there is nothing to oppose in this amendment. If your state wanted to go at it by a different route, it says it has to go through the legislature. It can't be forced by the court. What is wrong with that?

I find it a sad prospect that we might not be able to pass this 90 to 10. Marriage is a foundational institution. It is under attack by the courts. It needs to be defended in this way by defining it as the union of a man and a woman as 45 of our 50 states have done. If it is going to be defined otherwise, it must be done by the legislatures and not by the courts.

This morning, we are going to vote on a constitutional amendment to define marriage as the union of a man and a woman. This is about who is going to determine the definition, whether it is the courts or the legislative bodies. The amendment is about how we are going to raise the next generation. How are they going to be raised? It is a fundamental issue for our families and for our future. It is an issue for the people. It is not an issue that the courts should resolve. Those of us who support this amendment are doing so in an effort to let the people decide.

There has been a lot of eloquent debate about this constitutional amendment. I have been on the Senate floor most of the time. I have heard very little debate against the amendment. I have heard a lot of people complaining that we ought to take up something else, that this is not so important. I look at it and say, we have this many states that have deemed it important enough that they would put it on their ballots. This is important. We have had basically one, two, maybe three speakers say they really question the amendment, but most of them say we shouldn't spend our time on this amendment. We shouldn't spend our time on the estate tax. They don't mention the native Hawaiian bill that is coming up, or suggest that we should not spend our time on that.

We are going to have this vote. People are going to be responsible for this vote. We are making progress in America on defining marriage as the union of a man and a woman, and we will not stop until it is defined and protected as the union of a man and a woman. We have far more states now that have voted on this issue than the last time we voted on it. We now have far more court challenges taking place to this fundamental definition of how we look at the union of marriage.

Marriage is about our future. I continue to be struck by the opponents of this amendment who say it is an effort to promote discrimination. The amendment is about promoting our future, our families, how we raise that next generation, and about allowing a definition of a fundamental institution to be made by the people rather than by the courts.

I have shown a number of charts demonstrating that the best situation for our children to be raised is in a home with a mother and father. Children need these two parents. It is not that you can't raise good children in a single-parent household; you can. Many struggle heroically to do so. Yet we know from all the data that the best place is with a mother and father. Children do best academically and socially, and they are more likely to be raised in financially stable homes when a mother and father are both present.

More importantly, they have the security of knowing there are two people in their lives who provide security and stability, two people who provide something, each differently, but that is very important. These two people become one. They are united. They become one bonded together. This past weekend, my mother-in-law and father-in-law celebrated fifty-six years of marriage. While often they may disagree with one another—sometimes pretty heatedly, sometimes one could call it almost barking at each other—they are inseparable. They are one. It is a beautiful thing to see. It is the way that we should uphold these institutions. Their children and their grandchildren and great-grandchildren get to see these two people, two old trees leaning against each other, holding each other up, physical bodies not anything near what they used to be, but supporting and helping and setting a foundation for all future generations to look at and say: That is the way it ought to be done.

Life hasn't always been easy for them. There have been difficulties through time. They have had some hardships, working together. My father-in-law has done very well, served in Korea, during which time they were separated by many miles. My parents have been married over 50 years. You look at them and say: That is the way it should be, where two become one. Out of that union comes more people, more children raised with a solid set of foundational values that you hope can be good citizens. We are all going to have difficulties and problems, but isn't that something that we can do and we should do for the next generation?

We have an important issue in front of us, the definition of marriage. We have a country that is watching and that knows what they believe marriage should be defined as, the union of a man and a woman, as forty-five states have defined it. The courts are moving otherwise. We say let the legislatures decide, and that it is an important issue, meritorious of our vote.

To those who oppose this amendment, I think they will have to explain to a lot of people why they oppose marriage as the union of a man and a woman and why they don't think the state legislatures should be the ones responsible for defining this but, rather, that this should be defined by the courts. I don't think their position is across America. This is important. I hope my colleagues support this constitutional amendment.

The Congressional Record. June 7, 2006: S5517–S5534.

Liberal Viewpoint

James P. McGovern (D-MA). Mr. Speaker, I very much regret that the Republican majority in this House has brought this bill to the floor. This bill, to put it simply and bluntly, is about adding discrimination and intolerance to the United States Constitution. This is about the Republican majority's once again trying to divide and polarize the nation. It is about the Republican leadership's taking something that should be about love and turning it into a weapon of hate.

I am proud, Mr. Speaker, to be from Massachusetts, the home of the nation's first state constitution. In Massachusetts, over eight thousand same-sex couples have been married since May of 2004, when it became legal. I should advise my colleagues that Massachusetts has not fallen off the map into the Atlantic Ocean. The sun still rises and sets in the Commonwealth. The Red Sox still play at Fenway Park, and life goes on. The only thing that is different is that couples of the same sex who love each other, want to spend the rest of their lives together, and want to get married can do so. It means that men and women who happen to be gay are able to enjoy the same rights, privileges, and responsibilities as men and women who happen to be straight. And, Mr. Speaker, that is how it should be.

Those who have continued to advocate a ban on same-sex marriage are on the wrong side of history. There are some here who claim that they are on some sort of moral crusade to protect the institution of marriage. To them, I say worry about your own marriage. I do not need you to protect mine. I have been happily married to the same woman for seventeen years without the help or interference of Congress. What we should be protecting are the civil and human rights of all Americans.

The fact that same-sex marriage is legal in my home state has had no impact on my marriage except that we were invited to more weddings. Same-sex marriage is a threat to no institution, to no individual. The underlying bill before us would not only add discrimination to the Constitution for the first time in our history. It would repeal, it would actually take away, the rights of thousands of Americans. What do the supporters of this bill say to the gay couples in Massachusetts who are now legally married; our family members, our neighbors, our coworkers, the people who sit next to us in church? Do you say your marriage is now meaningless and we are going to take away your rights? Do you say we are sending you back to second-class citizenship? Do you say that we have so much hatred for who you are that we are willing to tarnish the United States Constitution?

Marriage law in this country has traditionally been left to the states. Indeed, even in Massachusetts the same supreme judicial court that the proponents of this bill decry recently ruled that a referendum banning same-sex marriage can go forward. That referendum is currently working its way through the process. And I believe, of course, that the referendum should and will fail, that the citizens of Massachusetts would not vote to turn back the clock. But that should be up to us, Mr. Speaker, not to the people of Colorado or Georgia or anywhere else.

In addition, this bill jeopardizes not just same-sex marriage in Massachusetts but domestic partnership and civil union laws in other parts of the country. The proposal before us is so poorly drafted that legal experts disagree on exactly what effect it will have on those laws. That means, of course, that the issue will end up back in the courts, which is ironic given the concept of court-bashing by the bill's supporters.

Mr. Speaker, the impact of this debate goes far beyond constitutional arguments. The proponents of this bill are contributing to a climate of intolerance. We will hear protests from the other side today that they have no problem with gay people. Yet here they are arguing that gay people do not deserve the same rights as everybody else.

Mr. Speaker, I am also terribly troubled by the hate spewing from some of the outside groups using the same-sex marriage issue to whip up emotions and raise money. Mr. Speaker, some of the rhetoric is just deplorable. But I doubt that we will hear any of the bill's supporters denouncing it here today on the floor.

My colleagues, discrimination is discrimination, and it should find no sanctuary in our Constitution or in our hearts. It should find no sanctuary on the floor of the people's House.

We all know why this proposal is before us. It is an election year, and if it is an election year, the Republican leadership will find a place on the agenda for gay-bashing.

This proposal is worse than a distraction. It is not an assault on our fellow citizens. It is an attack on a piece of their humanity, and I urge you to stand on the right side of history and to defeat this bill.

The Congressional Record. June 7, 2006: H5287–H5321.

EQUAL RIGHTS AMENDMENT

The Equal Rights Amendment was an amendment proposed to the U.S. Constitution to guarantee equal protection regardless of sex. The Twenty-eighth Amendment was first suggested in 1923 but the ratification process has been difficult to achieve. Though many people believe in equal rights, the amendment has not been able to obtain the necessary thirty-eight states out of fifty for ratification.

The biggest opposition to the Equal Rights Amendment came from a conservative Republican, Phyllis Schlafly. Arguments against the Equal Rights Amendment include many implications. First, opponents argue that the passage would obliterate traditional distinctions between sexes. In turn, women would have to register for the draft and would have to serve in combat just as their male counterparts do. Second, the ERA would also remove protective legislature in place for women in heavy industries. These include labor laws and health care benefits. Third, opponents of the ERA argue that the ERA would legalize same-sex marriages and dramatically increase abortion rates.

Supporters of the ERA strongly oppose the scare tactics. They argue that equality under law must be recognized in the U.S. Constitution. Supporters argue that the amendment would provide remedy for gender discrimination for both men and women and it will give equal status to women for the first time in U.S. history. The Equal Rights Amendment would clarify many judicial questions, as currently the courts do not sufficiently deal with gender discrimination. Furthermore, the supporters disagree that the ERA would invalidate state laws on abortion or even on same-sex marriages. They believe that it is the progressive nature of the state that decides the issues of abortion and same-sex marriage. The Equal Rights Amendment is a separate issue.

Liberal Viewpoint

Robert E. Andrews (D-NJ). Mr. Speaker, I rise before you today in strong support of the recent actions taken by the Illinois state legislature regarding the Equal Rights Amendment (ERA), a proposed amendment to the Constitution which would unequivocally guarantee equal gender rights under the law. As many of my colleagues are certainly aware, the Illinois State Assembly recently voted on and passed the ERA, clearing the way for their counterparts in the Senate to consider this crucial legislation at the conclusion of their current recess. If Illinois' state senate agrees to ratify the ERA, then only two more state ratifications will be necessary for this long overdue amendment to be added to our Constitution.

Some people have argued that the addition of an ERA amendment to the Constitution would simply be a change in semantics and nothing more. I strongly disagree. Presently, on average, women receive only 76 percent of the pay that men receive for comparable full time positions. Inequities such as these are inexcusable; they are disastrously damaging not just to women, but also to their families. Through the ratification of an Equal Rights Amendment, women would have an expanded legal basis to call for equal compensation for equal work.

Although the Equal Rights Amendment may have faded from the public spotlight at times, the movement to include women in the Constitution never died, and it is growing vigorously once again. Women had to wait until 1920 to be granted the right to vote under the Constitution. While this was certainly a monumental development, it has not produced full gender equality. The 14th Amendment, granting "equal protection of the laws," did not, and still does not, fully protect women from damaging gender discrimination. Only an Equal Rights Amendment would ensure the constitutionally guaranteed full equality that women deserve.

The ERA was originally passed by Congress in 1972, along with a seven-year time limit for ratification. In 1979, Congress extended the time limit for three more years, leaving the deadline at 1982. Within a decade of the initial 1972 passage, the amendment had been ratified by 35 states, three short of the necessary 38. For many years after that, the ERA was, for technical reasons, generally considered "dead." However, legal analyses indicate that with just three more state ratifications, the ERA may in fact meet the requirements to be added to the Constitution. As has been verified by several legal experts, the fact that the time limit appears in the proposing clause rather than the text of the legislation leaves this deadline open to adjustment. When Congress chose to extend the deadline in 1979, a precedent was set; subsequent sessions of Congress may adjust time limits placed in proposing clauses by their predecessors. These adjustments may include extensions of time, reductions, or elimination of the deadline altogether.

It is therefore possible for current or future sessions of Congress to eliminate the deadline originally placed on ratification of the ERA, thus allowing the amendment to be added to the Constitution once it is ratified by three more states. This "three state strategy" is a very real possibility, and I have introduced legislation into the House of Representatives, H. Res. 38, to ensure that action will be immediately considered by Congress once three more state legislatures ratify the ERA. Put simply, it is time for the Constitution to be amended to include an amendment which ensures gender equality for all Americans. Today, unlike some times in the past, the American people are decidedly ready for Constitutionally-guaranteed equal rights for men and women. A July 2001 nationwide survey by Opinion Research Corporation showed that 96 percent of American adults believe that male and female citizens of the U.S. should have equal rights, and 88 percent believe that our Constitution should explicitly guarantee those rights. Having the ERA in the Constitution will simply recognize what the American people already want—equal justice under the law.

Many leaders both here in Congress and in state legislatures are advocating for the "three state strategy," as well as a renewal of the ERA by Congress through a second passage of the amendment. I feel that anyone who is serious about guaranteeing equal rights to women should be supportive of both of these approaches. It does not matter how the ERA is eventually made part of the Constitution, as long as guaranteed gender equality rights are the end result.

As the Equal Rights Amendment reads, "Equality of rights under the law shall not be denied or abridged by the United States or by any state on account of sex." The ERA is unfinished business for the Constitution. It will be achieved, and present and future generations of women—and men—will thank us for it, and wonder why it took so long. It is simple justice, it is long overdue, and it is time.

The Congressional Record. June 5, 2003: E1162.

Conservative Viewpoint

James L. Buckley (R-NY). I find myself in full agreement with the finding that there still exist in our country a discrimination against women which can not be justified and which ought not to be tolerated.

. . .

In America, today we find three factors which affect the relative rights, prerogative duties, immunities and obligations of men and women. Some of these are cultural, others social, and the balance economic. I speak of distinctions based on sex, deference conferred because of sex, and discrimination which is predicated on sex. Only the last, I submit, is the proper target of the amendment now under consideration and of the enormous effort by the women of America to redress their longstanding and legitimate grievances. Yet the proposed equal rights amendment would have the inevitable effect of obliterating all of those differentiations—these distinctions, deferences, and discriminations—in the name of an abstract equality, of whether they in fact infringe the substantive rights of women.

It is because of this—because, quite specifically of my deep respect for women—that I cannot support the amendment; and I cannot support it because whatever the intentions of its sponsors, I think we will inevitably find it tugged and twisted and extended far beyond the limits of commonsense and reason. I am opposed to the proposed amendment, because in attempt to eliminate discrimination against women, it will at the same time inevitably strike down those distinctions and those deferences which our society now extends to women. It seems to me that the discriminations which all of us want to see ended can be more effectively accomplished in other ways.

. . .

The 14th Amendment of course is not the only legal remedy available to aggrieved women. Title VII of the Civil Rights Act of 1964, which Congress recently amended to provide greatly enlarged enforcement powers for the EEOC, provides yet another powerful tool for the relief of women discriminated against in the field of employment. Litigation under the 14th Amendment and under Title VII seems to me provide adequate remedies for the great majority of cases in which women are relegated to an inferior legal status.

. . .

I am therefore, encouraged in the belief that case-by-case approach will produce efficacious results. Certain advocates of the women's liberation tend to pooh-pooh the effectiveness of such piecemeal litigation. But experience will testify to the fact, I believe, that rights won by the gradual if admittedly sometime tedious process of litigation acquire more permanent constitutional security than the often ephemeral promises of vaguely worded statutes, fleshed out with grandiloquent humanitarian sentiments but very little else.

. . .

Whether the women of America want or need this kind of guardianship, however, is another matter altogether. I am unaware of any plebiscite granting representative authority to the women's liberation movement from any woman of America nor am I aware of any demonstrable indication that the women of America approve of what their self-appointed guardians would have delivered up for them. On the contrary, as the distinguished Senator from North Carolina has pointed out, the only detailed poll taken on the subject, the overwhelming majority of those polled revealed a singular indifference, if not hostility, toward the more obvious legal consequences that would flow from the passage of the equal rights amendment. Fully 77 percent of American women opposed equal treatment with respect to military service; 83 percent opposed the idea that a wife should be the breadwinner if she were a better wage earner than her husband; and 69 percent opposed the idea that a woman should pay alimony if she has money and her husband does not.

Yet, as I suggested earlier, if equal rights amendment were to be ratified, women would be drafted and could be required to serve in combat; states would be barred from imposing greater liability for support on a husband than on a wife merely because of his sex; criminal sanctions for failure to support one's family could not be sustained where only the male is liable for such support; and obligation for alimony could be placed on either spouse. Such changes in the law may bring joy to the hearts of the more militant advocates of the women's liberation movement, but they are not necessarily in the interests of most American women.

The Congressional Record. March 22, 1972: S9598.

AFFIRMATIVE ACTION

When the Supreme Court ruled in favor of affirmative action admission policy in higher education in 2003, the decision left many people dissatisfied with the judicial system. Barbara Grutter, a white student who had a high grade point average and high LSAT scores, alleged that her rejection from the University of Michigan's Law School stemmed from affirmative action.

The 5 to 4 decision in favor of the admission policy of the University of Michigan sparked many affirmative action debates throughout the country.

President George W. Bush came out against the affirmative action policy employed by University of Michigan. He believes that awarding extra points to students based solely on their race is discriminatory. Citing the U.S. Constitution, President Bush believes that all citizens should be treated equally. President Bush believes that increased school funding would allow more economically disadvantaged students to attend college. Furthermore, he strongly urges the University of Michigan and other like-minded schools to reconsider their admission policies.

Rep. Debbie Stabenow (D-MI) immediately spoke out against President Bush's attempt to overturn the admission policy. First, Rep. Stabenow made it clear that the Supreme Court case is not about racial quotas. Second, Rep. Stabenow contends that race is not the only factor taken into consideration upon university admission. Other factors such as athletic ability, past family attendance, economic status, and others are used to ensure a diverse environment. Furthermore, Rep. Stabenow urged the Bush Administration to examine its policy on equal opportunity to ensure that it is not only prevalent in the political discourse but in practice as well.

Conservative Viewpoint

President George W. Bush. The Supreme Court will soon hear arguments in
a case about admissions policies and student diversity in public universities.
I strongly support diversity of all kinds, including racial diversity in higher
education. But the method used by the University of Michigan to achieve
this important goal is fundamentally flawed.

At their core, the Michigan policies amount to a quota system that unfairly rewards or penalizes prospective students, based solely on their race.
So tomorrow my administration will file a brief with the Court arguing that
the University of Michigan's admissions policies, which award students a
significant number of extra points based solely on their race and establishes
numerical targets for incoming minority students, are unconstitutional.

Our Constitution makes it clear that people of all races must be treated
equally under the law. Yet we know that our society has not fully achieved
that ideal. Racial prejudice is a reality in America. It hurts many of our citizens. As a nation, as a government, and as individuals, we must be vigilant
in responding to prejudice wherever we find it. Yet, as we work to address
the wrong of racial prejudice, we must not use means that create another
wrong and thus perpetuate our divisions.

America is a diverse country, racially, economically, and ethnically. And
our institutions of higher education should reflect our diversity. A college
education should teach respect and understanding and good will. And
these values are strengthened when students live and learn with people
from many backgrounds. Yet quota systems that use race to include or ex-
clude people from higher education and the opportunities it offers are divisive, unfair, and impossible to square with the Constitution.

· · ·

The motivation for such an admissions policy may be very good, but its result is discrimination, and that discrimination is wrong.

Some states are using innovative ways to diversify their student bodies.
Recent history has proven that diversity can be achieved without using quotas. Systems in California and Florida and Texas have proven that by guaranteeing admissions to the top students from high schools. Throughout the
state, including low-income neighborhoods, colleges can attain broad racial
diversity. In these states, race-neutral admissions policies have resulted in
levels of minority attendance for incoming students that are close to and in
some instances slightly surpass those under the old race-based approach.

We should not be satisfied with the current numbers of minorities on
Americans' college campuses. Much progress has been made. Much more is
needed. University officials have the responsibility and the obligation to
make a serious, effective effort to reach out to students from all walks of life

without falling back on unconstitutional quotas. Schools should seek diversity by considering a broad range of factors in admissions, including a student's potential and life experiences.

Our Government must work to make college more affordable for students who come from economically disadvantaged homes. And because we're committed to racial justice, we must make sure that America's public schools offer a quality education to every child from every background, which is the central purpose of the education reforms I signed last year.

America's long experience with the segregation we have put behind us and the racial discrimination we still struggle to overcome requires a special effort to make real the promise of equal opportunity for all. My administration will continue to actively promote diversity and opportunity in every way that the law permits.

Public Papers of the President: George W. Bush. January 17, 2003: 71–72.

Liberal Viewpoint

Debbie A. Stabenow (D-MI). I rise to express my deep disappointment at news reports today that indicate the Bush administration will try to overturn the admissions policy at the University of Michigan, in my great state. As many people know, the Supreme Court will soon hear a case that will decide the future of racial diversity in all institutions of higher education. The University of Michigan's admissions policy so far has been upheld by the 6th Circuit Court of Appeals as constitutional. Unfortunately, those who want to dismantle all admissions programs that consider race have taken this all the way to the Supreme Court.

It is important to note this case is not about racial quotas. Let me say that again. It is important to note this case is not about racial quotas. The University of Michigan does not have racial quotas for admission. I am opposed to racial quotas and this, in fact, has been the law of the land since the Supreme Court's decision in the Bakke case in 1978.

The University of Michigan's undergraduate admissions policy simply takes into account student diversity as one of many factors that are considered for admission. Incidentally, the most important factors for admission are the applicant's grade point average and test scores. Race is one factor of diversity, but it is not the only factor. I think this oftentimes is missed in the discussion about the university's policies and what affirmative action means. There are several other factors the university considers, including if the applicant comes from a socially or economically disadvantaged background, if the applicant is a white student from a majority minority high school, if the applicant comes from an underrepresented community, such as one of Michigan's many rural communities throughout northern Michigan, southern Michigan, up in the Upper Peninsula, or if the applicant is an athlete.

I think it is important to emphasize there is a category where there are certain points that are given and you can either be given points as an athlete or points for racial diversity or points for other kinds of categories—not all of them but one. Certainly, there are a number of factors that are considered in this process to create a balanced student body for the university.

The university considers a long list of factors, including if the applicant is a child of an alumni or if he or she has written a terrific essay. So there are many factors.

All of these factors help the University of Michigan select a diverse, well-rounded student body that is not just racially diverse but economically and geographically diverse as well.

· · ·

This debate is much greater than the admissions policy of one university. This is about whether we are going to have equal opportunity for all Americans. This is about whether we support policies that help provide the opportunity for Americans of all backgrounds to have a chance at the American dream regardless of where they live, regardless of their ethnic background and their religious background, or whether they are male or female, whether they are an athlete or not a good athlete—a wide variety of factors that go into making those decisions. And shouldn't all young people have the opportunity?

· · ·

President Bush's decision to try to dismantle the University of Michigan's admissions policy comes at a very tough time for our nation's minority community. Over the past month, the Republican Party has undergone a makeover—a change in leadership. But it would be very unfortunate if it is a change in style and not of substance.

· · ·

Unfortunately, this administration seems to be all talk and no action. We need to come together in a bipartisan way to act and not just to talk. On the one hand, the president talks about the importance of expanding opportunities to all Americans. And we all talk of that, and that certainly is something with which I agree, but the administration's policies do not back up this rhetoric.

There is still time for the president to file a brief in the Supreme Court case—one that supports the University of Michigan's admissions policy. I urge him to do so. Now is the time for us to come together and work together to make sure there is opportunity and access to our great institutions of higher learning in this country and that educational opportunities are available to every young person and to every American. I urge the president to reconsider the course that he appears to be taking and to join with us who understand the policy of the University of Michigan and to understand the importance of every young person having the opportunity to go to college.

The Congressional Record. January 15, 2003: S336–S337.

HATE CRIMES

Hate crimes are motivated by bias, prejudice, or hatred toward an individual based on his or her race, religion, color, nationality, gender, or sexual orientation. Hate crime legislation began in 1999 with the heinous attack on Matthew Sheppard in Laramie, Wyoming. Former president Clinton urged Congress to formulate a federal hate crime law that would prevent these gruesome acts from happening again. If these acts were repeated, they would entail a much harsher punishment than the normal legal code allowed.

Rep. Nancy Pelosi (D-CA) argues that federal hate crime legislation is long overdue. Rep. Pelosi argues that enhancing the preexisting punishment for hate crimes will serve as a deterrent for hate crimes. Since the victims of hate crimes were attacked for more than personal reasons, legislation should be expanded to protect them from these heinous crimes. Strong hate crime laws will send a message to the violators that their actions will not be tolerated and punished more severely.

Rep. Clifford Stearns (R-FL) opposes hate crime legislation due to the fact that he believes that it is actually discriminatory. He believes that by allowing hate crimes to be punished more severely than regular crimes, we could lead the nation to a time when hate thoughts could also be banned, thus taking away First Amendment rights. While he does not say that state hate crime laws should not exist, he is opposed to federal hate crime laws. He believes wholeheartedly that federal hate crime legislation is discriminatory and counteracts the Bill of Rights.

Conservative Viewpoint

Clifford Stearns (R-FL). First, the argument could certainly be made that "hate crimes" do not belong on a National Defense Authorization bill. This is incredibly important legislation, and it does not deserve to get bogged down over such a controversial and nongermane provision.

I also oppose the notion of hate crimes in general, especially at the federal level. The fact of the matter is that a crime is a crime no matter what motivates it. If two men are brutally murdered, one for his race and the other for his money, are we telling the latter's family that their father's death, or their husband's death, or their son's death, is somehow worth less in the eyes of the law?

I would also contend that the very concept of hate crimes is divisive and tends to Balkanize America. During the Civil Rights movement, black Americans strove to be treated the same as white Americans. Theirs was a noble cause. Yet hate crimes betray the cause of those who fought against segregation by emphasizing our differences, rather than our common concerns.

I am also concerned that if we have laws which punish more severely offenders who are motivated by certain beliefs, it increases the risk that we will try to criminalize the actual beliefs themselves.

There is no need for hate crime legislation. Federal hate crimes prosecute property crimes, assault and battery and murder against the special victims. Yet all of these underlying offenses are already illegal in all fifty states and they are already prosecuted by the states with great effectiveness. I am not aware of any of these types of offenses being inadequately investigated or negligently prosecuted. And let's face it: few criminals are likely to be deterred by an additional penalty for a crime that is already unlawful.

Another reason why I oppose federal hate crimes in general and this Motion specifically is because the prosecution of crimes has largely always been an issue left to the states. The continued federalization of criminal law requires a tremendous expansion in the size and scope of federal law enforcement, federal prosecutors, and frankly, federal power. For too long, Congress has used the Constitution's Commerce Clause to expand the federal government's reach in what was traditionally the jurisdiction of the states. However, the U.S. Supreme Court recently struck down two federal statutes in *U.S. v. Lopez* (1995) and *U.S. v. Morrison* (2000) because they violated our traditional constitutional divisions of authority. I would not be surprised if the Court one day declared unconstitutional other far-reaching federal crime measures, including federal hate crimes.

There is another constitutional problem with giving sexual orientation special treatment. Current characteristics which are classified as hate crimes under federal law include race, ethnicity, sex, national origin, religion, and disability. All of these characteristics—except religion—are what the Supreme Court has called "immutable." That is, if a person is black, or a woman, or from Pakistan, or paralyzed from the waist down, it is not of their choice. It is beyond their control, they cannot change. Therefore, if their characteristic is immutable it cannot, for lack of a better description, be held against them.

Now, good people can disagree about this issue, but the fact remains that homosexuality is not necessarily a trait with which someone is born. In other words, this type of sexual orientation is not immutable, but to a large degree it is chosen. The Supreme Court has certainly never considered sexual orientation to be an immutable characteristic. Why should we?

Mr. Speaker, I believe that violent crimes against any American are despicable. They should be punished swiftly and severely, to the fullest extent of the law. But we should not give special treatment to certain victims, we should not penalize citizens for their beliefs, and we should not federalize hate crimes.

The Congressional Record. September 30, 2004: E1743–E1744.

Liberal Viewpoint

Nancy P. Pelosi (D-CA). Madam Speaker, hate crimes have no place in America. I think we can all agree to that. All Americans have a right to feel safe in their communities. Yet FBI statistics continue to demonstrate a high level of hate crimes in our country. Federal hate crimes prevention legislation is the right thing to do, and it is long overdue.

Some opponents argue that there is no need for federal hate crimes prevention legislation because assault and murder are already crimes. However, when individuals are targeted for violence because of their race, sexual orientation, religion, national origin, gender or disability, the assailant intends to send a message to all members of that community. The message is, you are not welcome.

When violence is visited upon people because of who they are, the color of their skin, how they worship and who they love, we all suffer. When this happens to one of us, it happens to all of us.

We all will remember very sadly the brutal murders of James Byrd in Texas, Matthew Shepard in Wyoming, Waqar Hasan in Texas, and Gwen Araujo in my own state of California.

Current law limits federal jurisdictions to "federally protected" activities such as voting and does not permit federal jurisdiction over violent crimes motivated by bias against the victim's sexual orientation, gender, or disability.

The gentleman from Michigan (Mr. Conyers), our distinguished ranking member on the Committee on the Judiciary and a great leader in civil liberties and protecting the American people and public safety, has introduced H.R. 4204, the Local Law Enforcement Hate Crimes Act, to expand federal jurisdiction to include hate crimes. Along with 175 of my colleagues, I am proud to cosponsor his bill; and I commend the gentleman from Michigan (Mr. Conyers) for his untiring leadership and commitment to this and so many other issues. Thank you for your leadership.

When state and local law enforcement do not have the capacity to prosecute hate crimes, this bill would permit federal prosecution regardless of whether a federally protected activity is involved.

This legislation would increase the ability of local, state, and federal law enforcement agencies to solve and prevent a wide range of violent hate crimes. Numerous law enforcement organizations, including the International Association of Chiefs of Police, support the need for federal hate crimes legislation.

Four years ago, both Houses of Congress supported the hate crimes prevention provisions on a bipartisan basis as part of the defense authorization bill, only to see those provisions stripped by the conference committee. We cannot let that happen again.

This June the Senate, the other body, adopted an amendment to include language identical to H.R. 4204 in its version of the defense authorization bill on a strong bipartisan vote.

Today we have the opportunity to put the House on record in favor of federal hate crimes prevention provisions. We must not allow the provisions to be stripped in conference again. We must continue to fight for justice, hope, and freedom by ensuring that hate crimes prevention provisions are enacted into law. That would be a true and fitting memorial to James Byrd, Matthew Shepard, Waqar Hasan, Gwen Araujo, and so many others who have died because of ignorance and intolerance.

The Congressional Record. September 28, 2004: H7689–H7698.

SELECTED READING

Gay Marriage

"Area Bishop Pushes Anti Gay Marriage Message on Parish." *The Daily Cardinal.* www.dailycardinal.com/news/area-bishop-pushes-anti-gay-marriage-message-on-parish.html.

Bidstrup, Scott. "Gay Marriage: The Arguments and the Motives." www.bidstrup.com/marriage.htm.

Norton, Rictor. "Taking a Husband: A History of Gay Marriage." www.infopt.demon.co.uk/marriage.htm.

"Senate Defeats Anti-Gay Marriage Amendment Without Really Saying Why." www.civilliberty.about.com/b/a/257518.htm.

"Should Same Sex Marriages Be Legalized?" www.balancedpolitics.org/same_sex_marriages.htm.

Equal Rights Amendment

Boles, Janet. "The Politics of the Equal Rights Amendment: Conflict and the Decision Process." *Western Political Quarterly* 33:3 (September 1980), 424–25.

"Chronology of the Equal Rights Amendment." National Organization for Women. www.now.org/issues/economic/cea/history.html.

Francis, Roberta. "Why We Need the Equal Rights Amendment." www .equalrightsamendment.org/why.htm.

"Iowa Women against the Equal Rights Amendment." sdrc.lib.uiowa.edu/iwa/ findingaids/html/IAWomenAgainstERA.htm

"The Equal Rights Amendment: Guaranteeing Equal Rights for Women under the Constitution." U.S. Commission on Civil Rights. June 1981. www.thelizlibrary .org/suffrage/eracom.htm.

Affirmative Action

Biskupic, Joan. "Justices Debate Race, College Admissions." *USA Today*. April 1, 2003. www.usatoday.com/news/washington/2003-04-01-michigan-court_x.htm.

Cohen, Carl. "Race Preference in College Admissions." The Heritage Foundation. April 29, 1999. www.heritage.org/Research/Education/HL611.cfm.

Davenport, David. "The Dilemma of Race in College Admissions." *San Francisco Chronicle*. June 12, 2002. aad.english.ucsb.edu/docs/ddavenport.html.

"Debating Racial Preference." 2006. www.debatingracialpreference.org.

Lewin, Tamar. "Race Preferences Vote Splits Michigan." October 31, 2006. www .nytimes.com/2006/10/31/us/31michigan.html?ex=1319950800&en.

Weisman, Dennis L. "Racial Preferences in College Admissions." March 2005. www .k-state.edu/economics/weisman/papers/Racial%20Preferences%20in%20 College%20Admissions%20March%202,%202005.pdf.

Hate Crimes

Lockyer, Bill. "Reporting Hate Crimes." The California Attorney General's Commission on Hate Crimes. caag.state.ca.us/publications/civilrights/reportingHC.pdf.

Morsch, James. "The Problem of Motive in Hate Crimes: The Argument against Presumptions of Racial Motivation." *Journal of Criminal Law and Criminology* 82:3 (Autumn 1991), 659–89.

Rozeff, Michael. "The Case against Hate Crime Laws." www.lewrockwell.com/rozeff/ rozeff95.html.

"U.S. Hate Crimes: Ethical and Civil Rights Concerns." www.religioustolerance.org/ hom_hat5.htm.

Wright, Debbie. "Hate Crimes." International Encyclopedia of Justice Studies. www .iejs.com/Law/Criminal_Law/Hate_Crimes.htm.

10

Global Issues

On most global issues, liberals and conservatives are largely in agreement. Most believe that global terrorism must be fought vigorously through military action and information gathering. Liberals and conservatives tend to agree that globalization is mostly a good thing that should be promoted through legislative action. Both generally believe that the American government has some role to play in protecting Americans from disease as well as other international threats. And both want some level of control over immigration while nonetheless agreeing that immigrants play a vital role in the economic and cultural advancement of the United States.

Still, there are significant differences between liberals and conservatives on global issues. On economic issues, conservatives tend to believe more in allowing the free market to develop on its own. On issues of global trade, for example, conservatives are more likely to support reduced barriers. Liberals, in contrast, believe that American industries need some level of protection from foreign competitors. Moreover, they argue that the free flow of unregulated capital can lead to American wages dropping, such as by American companies outsourcing work to other countries or moving factories overseas. While conservatives acknowledge these issues, they argue that free trade lifts entire economies so that in the long run and in general, American industries and American workers are better off with unregulated trade.

Second, conservatives tend to be more traditional on cultural issues than liberals. When issues such as immigration are dealt with, they are more likely to be concerned that a new population will shift America away from its core values. Similarly, when dealing with foreign aid, they are more likely to be concerned about issues like limiting abortion. In sharp contrast, liberals welcome cultural diversity and generally do not want to impose their own cultural values on other countries. While conservatives often want stipulations when giving funding to other countries, liberals are more likely to oppose these measures.

Finally, conservatives are more likely to support the use of military force. Liberals and conservatives alike supported the attack on Afghanistan, for example, but liberals are far less likely to agree with the war against Iraq. Besides human rights issues, liberals believe that military conflict is more likely to produce instability, breeding even more costly conflict in the future. In sharp contrast, conservatives are more likely to believe that demonstrations of strength deter others from taking aggressive action against the United States and its interests.

THE GLOBAL SPREAD OF HIV

One policy area of serious contention is how to battle the global spread of HIV, or human immunodeficiency virus. HIV can lead to AIDS, acquired immunodeficiency syndrome, a condition in which the person's immune system becomes unable to fight off even the weakest diseases. AIDS was discovered in 1981 by the Centers for Disease Control (CDC) in the United States in a small group of homosexual men in Los Angeles. It was originally dubbed GRID, or gay-related immune deficiency, but researchers soon discovered that its common victims included intravenous drug users and hemophiliacs. These researchers changed the name of the syndrome to AIDS and concluded that it was being spread primarily through the blood. Within the next few years, researchers discovered the virus causing AIDS and eventually called it HIV.

Already in the early 1980s, scientists at the CDC warned that AIDS could become an epidemic killing a high percentage of Americans. Many AIDS activists criticized the Reagan Administration for not acting sooner—President Reagan did not mention the disease in public until September 1985—and claimed that this conservative administration was ignoring a serious health crisis because its primary victims were groups with little status in American society. The disease spread, but without leading to the worst fears. Nonetheless, thousands of Americans have died, and some estimate that a quarter of a million young Americans are infected but unaware of it. Globally, the infection is spreading rapidly. The vast majority of the millions killed by HIV lived in sub-Saharan Africa, and the disease is moving quickly through Asia. In India, for example, the number of infected people is estimated to double every fourteen months.

By the end of the Clinton Administration, the United States had been the largest funding source for the global fight against HIV. Nonetheless, the greatest jump in this commitment was made by the Bush Administration in

2003. Pledging $15 billion, the President's Emergency Plan for AIDS Relief, or PEPFAR, aimed to provide medication, care, and support to millions of HIV-infected individuals, as well as prevent millions of new infections. The controversy focused on the prevention aspect of the policy. Thirty-three percent of these funds had to be spent on abstinence-only programs. Because this fund included a range of related programs, such as prevention of mother-to-child transmission and HIV testing, in reality. two-thirds of the money meant to curb the spread of sexually transmitted diseases had to promote abstinence. Conservatives justified this approach by arguing that abstinence is the only reliable approach to stopping the sexual transmission of disease. Liberals countered that this approach is unrealistic and, moreover, that the administration was imposing its Christian values on other cultures.

GLOBALIZATION OF PRODUCTION

Globalization is the idea that the world is becoming more integrated and interdependent. In economic terms, globalization is about the opening and integration of markets, including the dropping of trade barriers. This creates a situation in which products produced cheaply in a third-world country could be then assembled and sold in the United States. Similarly, software companies have found it much cheaper to have their software development outsourced to Indian companies, which some argue has increased the profits of these companies at the same time that salaries for American developers have dropped. In the United States, the primary legislative step toward the globalization of production has been trade agreements, like NAFTA, the North American Free Trade Agreement. Proglobalization policies are also promoted by the World Trade Organization, which sets rules for international trade, and the World Bank, which lends money to struggling countries. Both are believed to be heavily influenced by the American government.

Proponents and opponents of globalization do not fall neatly into the liberal and conservative categories. As president, Bill Clinton was a strong proponent of globalization and free trade, for example, as is George W. Bush. Many liberals argue against free trade with the claim that it undermines American workers and worsens the widening income gap in America. When a corporation can build its products far cheaper in a third-world country because of much lower labor costs, the American worker loses that job, and American companies can threaten to leave the United States if its unions do not accept reduced wages or fewer benefits. Social conservatives worry about this as well, and they are also concerned that the United States might lose its identity in a giant global economy.

Proponents of globalization argue that these changes will drive up the entire world economy and in the process push up the American standard of living. Moreover, they argue that globalization is inevitable and therefore arguments against it are pointless.

IMMIGRATION

Immigration has become a more pointed political issue in the past few years for two main reasons. The first is that the number of illegal immigrants from Mexico has increased significantly since the United States entered the NAFTA agreement with its North American neighbors. Second, the terrorist attacks of September 11, 2001, have increased American concerns about all immigrants. The Bush Administration has addressed this issue by proposing what it calls comprehensive immigration reform. One step in that proposed reform is to increase border security. The Bush Administration has significantly increased spending on border security and it signed the Secure Fence Act into law, which authorizes the building of a seven-hundred-mile fence along the Mexican border. Another aspect of comprehensive immigration reform is a proposed guest worker program, in which U.S. employers could sponsor noncitizens for three years of labor. After that period is complete, that person has to leave the country if he or she has not received a green card. Republicans in the House of Representatives have gone further, passing the Border Protection, Antiterrorism, and Illegal Immigration Control Act of 2005 (H.R. 4437), which drastically increases the penalties for aiding illegal immigrants and would end the common "catch and release" policy by requiring the federal government to take all undocumented aliens into custody. The bill has not been voted on by the Senate.

The current debates on immigration also do not fall neatly along liberal and conservative lines. Hispanic groups and others have become particularly vocal in their opposition to the House bill, arguing that making illegal immigration into a felony would severely hurt people already in a vulnerable position. Proponents argue that the borders are now far too porous, that immigration is causing a rapid increase in the American population in ways that significantly stretch social services. They also argue that during a war on terror, the government needs to be particularly vigilant about controlling the flow of undocumented visitors. At the same time, conservatives are divided about the Bush Administration's guest worker proposal. While many support it, others argue that it simply creates legitimacy for a system that must be stopped. Liberals are also divided. Some see it as a flawed but better alternative to a current situation in which undocumented immigrants are at the mercy of their employers and others, but others consider the Bush proposal as a way to create cheap labor for businesses, which would further reduce the wages of the American working class.

THE PATRIOT ACT

The PATRIOT Act is a shorthand name for the USA PATRIOT Act, which is an acronym for the Uniting and Strengthening America by Providing Appropriate Tools Required to Intercept and Obstruct Terrorism Act of 2001. The act was written in reaction to the terrorist attacks of 2001, and it passed Congress with overwhelming support from both the House of Representatives and the Senate. Despite this official support, the PATRIOT Act remains highly controversial. Much of the controversy centers on Section 215, which permits the FBI to gather information about people under investigation for possible terrorism involvement without showing probable cause or even reasonable grounds to believe that the person has been or might be involved in a terrorist act. It also allows the FBI to require anyone to turn over information, including about others, as long as the request is part of an authorized terrorism investigation, and it disallows that person from disclosing that FBI request to anyone. In sum, it significantly increases the government's ability to conduct secret searches.

The PATRIOT Act was renewed in 2006, and some of the more controversial aspects were modified, though critics argue that the main problems remain. Liberals and some conservatives argue that the act violates basic civil rights. They argue that it violates the Fourth Amendment to the Constitution because it allows the government to conduct searches without showing probable cause or getting a warrant. They also assert that it violates people's First Amendment rights. For example, Section 215 could be used to access people's library records or gather information about the websites they visit. Supporters of the bill argue that these provisions are necessary to adequately fight terrorist groups.

GLOBAL GAG RULE

The global gag rule, also known as the Mexico City Policy, requires non-governmental organizations (or NGOs) receiving U.S. funds to agree not to perform abortions or actively promote abortion as a method of birth control. The Reagan Administration announced this policy in Mexico City in 1984. The Clinton Administration rescinded this policy almost as soon as it took office in January 1993, and the Bush Administration quickly reinstated it when it took over the White House in January 2001.

The global gag rule remains a highly controversial policy, and that controversy has largely echoed the abortion debate. Liberals have argued that the U.S. government is infringing on women's rights to control their bodies and choose when they are ready to have another child. They also stress that this policy affects NGOs providing critical services in poor regions where pregnant women and girls often face dangerous circumstances. Conservatives counter that the fetus is a living human that needs protection, and moreover that the American government should not be financially supporting a procedure that many Americans find highly objectionable.

TERRORISM

Finally, much of American global policy has been heavily influenced by the War on Terror. The first major terrorist attack on U.S. soil occurred in 1993, when militants attempted to destroy the World Trade Center by parking a truck full of explosives in the garage under Tower One. This attack did not produce its intended goal of causing the first tower to collapse onto the second and killing thousands of people. The second attack on the World Trade Center as well as the Pentagon, in 2001, was far more successful, leading to thousands of deaths. It also produced a shocked reaction throughout the United States and led to a rally-around-the-flag effect, when a president's public support rises after a significant national event.

Other than a small percentage of antiwar protestors, the initial response to the September 11 attacks by the Bush Administration was generally supported by the public. Most Americans, liberal and conservative, agreed with the attack on Afghanistan to capture or disrupt the leadership of al-Qaeda and oust the Taliban government, which gave the terrorist organization a safe haven. From this point, liberals and conservatives have become deeply divided in how to fight global terror. The Bush Administration chose to attack Iraq and remove the government of Saddam Hussein, claming that he was stockpiling weapons of mass destruction and supporting terrorist organizations. Liberals argued that this was a war of convenience, claiming that the war squandered critical resources, including troops, money, and the goodwill that America had gained after the September 11 attacks. They believe that more resources needed to be spent on preventing terrorist attacks at home, such as by taking more steps to protect the American transportation system.

CONCLUSIONS

When it comes to global issues, liberals and conservatives are often largely in agreement. However, the same divisions that drive debate on domestic issues tend to influence global issues as well. But, the specifics matter a great deal. For example, liberals who tend to oppose military intervention generally supported the Clinton Administration's involvement in the Yugoslavian civil war, since it was a way to end ethnic cleansing as well as promote stability in the Balkans. Many conservatives opposed this measure, seeing it as a misuse of the military. Conversely, liberals were generally quite opposed to the attack of Iraq while conservatives supported the bold move. In general, liberals and conservatives are not simply anti- and promilitary or pro- and antigovernment intervention.

THE GLOBAL SPREAD OF HIV

Acquired immunodeficiency syndrome (AIDS) was first discovered in 1981 and since then has claimed more than twenty-five million lives worldwide. Despite many improvements in technology and in antiretroviral drugs, AIDS continues to be one of the most destructive pandemics in history. Sub-Saharan Africa continues to be the region that is most affected by the disease, but statistics are rising in most parts of the world.

President Bush has proposed significant increased spending for HIV/AIDS programs worldwide. In addition, Bush has focused his efforts on decreasing the price of medication for HIV/AIDS patients. Furthermore, he has studied the already successful programs within the African continent and has looked to them for leadership assistance. President Bush fully believes in the good of the American people and their contribution to fight this global disease.

The Democrats are also greatly concerned about the HIV/AIDS epidemic, and they criticize the Bush Administration for standing still. Liberals such as Rep. Barbara Lee (D-CA) have questioned the Bush Administration's rhetoric and their true beliefs. Although President Bush has claimed to increase HIV/AIDS funding, many countries and organizations have not received any financial assistance from the U.S. government. Much of the Democratic concern lies within the Bush budget, which does not allow for appropriate funding to combat the HIV/AIDS epidemic and does not look at prevention at all.

Conservative Viewpoint

President George W. Bush. Today, on the continent of Africa alone, nearly thirty million people are living with HIV/AIDS, including three million people under the age of fifteen years old. In Botswana, nearly 40 percent of the adult population—40 percent—has HIV, and projected life expectancy has fallen by more than thirty years due to AIDS. In seven Sub-Sahara

African countries, mortality for children under age five has increased by 20 to 40 percent because of AIDS.

There are only two possible responses to suffering on this scale. We can turn our eyes away in resignation and despair, or we can take decisive, historic action to turn the tide against this disease and give the hope of life to millions who need our help now. The United States of America chooses the path of action and the path of hope.

Since January 2001, America has increased total spending to fight AIDS overseas by nearly 100 percent. We've already pledged more than $1.6 billion to the Global Fund to Fight AIDS and other infectious diseases. It is by far the most of any nation in the world today. And last year, I launched an initiative to help prevent the transmission of HIV from mothers to children in Africa and the Caribbean.

These are vital efforts, and they're important efforts. But we must do far more. So in January, I asked the House and the Senate to enact the Emergency Plan for AIDS Relief. With the approval of Congress, this plan will direct $15 billion to fight AIDS abroad over the next 5 years, beginning with $2 billion in 2004. We will create comprehensive systems that diagnose, to treat and to prevent AIDS in 14 African and Caribbean countries where the disease is heavily concentrated. We won't diminish our other efforts that are now ongoing. We will continue the funding that is in place, but we'll focus intensely on fourteen ravaged countries to show the world what is possible.

· · ·

We also know that AIDS can be treated. Antiretroviral drugs have become much more affordable in many nations, and they are extending many lives. In Africa, as more AIDS patients take these drugs, doctors are witnessing what they call the Lazarus effect when one patient is rescued by medicine, as if back from the dead. Many others with AIDS seek testing and treatment, because it is the first sign of hope they have ever seen.

Many past international efforts to fight AIDS focused on prevention at the expense of treatment. But people with this disease cannot be written off as expendable. Integrating care and treatment with prevention is the cornerstone of my Emergency Plan for AIDS Relief, and we know it works.

· · ·

In sub-Sahara Africa, just 1 percent of the more than 4 million people needing immediate drug treatment are receiving medicine. That's about fifty thousand people. The Emergency Plan for AIDS Relief is designed to put major resources behind proven methods of care and treatment and prevention and multiply these goods—good works many times over.

That's what we're going to do. The resources will be managed carefully, with flexibility by a new global AIDS coordinator. And this coordinator will help us utilize and further develop successful clinical networks. These networks link urban medical center staff by specialist physicians and nurses with rural clinics, where HIV tests can be preformed and medications distributed.

And because so much of the health care in sub-Sahara Africa is provided by facilities associated with churches and religious orders, we must ensure that the legislation provides the greatest opportunity for faith-based and community organizations to fully participate in helping a neighbor in need.

Our experts believe that the Emergency Plan for AIDS Relief will, in this decade, prevent seven million new HIV infections, treat at least two million people with life-extending drugs, and provide humane care for millions of people suffering from AIDS and, as importantly, for children orphaned by AIDS.

Confronting the threat of AIDS is important work, and it is urgent work. It is a moral imperative for our great nation. In the three months since I announced the Emergency Plan, an estimated 760,000 people have died from AIDS, 1.2 million people have been infected, more than175,000 babies have been born with the virus. Time is not on our side.

So I ask Congress to move forward with speed and seriousness this crisis requires. But Africa, the Caribbean, and the United States cannot succeed by ourselves. I urge all nations and will continue to urge all nations to join with us in this great effort.

Fighting AIDS on a global scale is a massive and complicated undertaking. Yet, this cause is rooted in the simplest of moral duties. When we see this kind of preventable suffering, when we see a plague leaving graves and orphans across a continent, we must act. When we see the wounded traveler on the road to Jericho, we will not—America will not pass to the other side of the road.

Public Papers of the President: George W. Bush. April 29, 2003: 497–499.

Liberal Viewpoint

Barbara Lee (D-CA). And last year we came very close to reaching a compromise on H.R. 2069, the Global Access to HIV/AIDS Prevention, Awareness, Education and Treatment Act which is a comprehensive global AIDS bill that passed the House in December of 2001 and which the Senate modified and passed in July of 2002. Yet there is still a tremendous amount of work for us to do, particularly now that the President has finally decided to support a significant boost in spending for our international AIDS programs.

But what has the President really proposed and how does this proposal translate into action within the fiscal year 2004 budget which we received early last month? The President has said that the goal of his initiative is to prevent seven million new infections per year and to provide treatment to over two million people who are infected with HIV, and to provide care for ten million HIV-infected individuals and AIDS orphans. But where is the money for this proposal? Certainly it is not contained within the President's recent budget request to the Congress. In fact, the President only requested $450 million for his initiative in this coming year and a total of $1.8 billion for the entire international HIV/AIDS, TB and malaria portfolio. This is barely an increase of $400 million over the fiscal year 2003 budget of $1.4 billion and is far below the figure of $2.6 billion that the Congress was targeting for fiscal year 2004. Yet at the State of the Union address, the President described an immediate need for treatment for four million individuals infected with AIDS, individuals who, as the President described, have been told by their local hospitals, "You've got AIDS. We can't help you. Go home and die."

What does the President say to these same people within his budget request? Additionally, the limited focus of the President's plan to just 25 percent of the forty-eight sub-Saharan countries is really very shortsighted. This kind of policy would neglect millions of individuals who are equally in need of assistance. But the most disconcerting portion of the President's proposal is his level of commitment to the global fund to fight AIDS, TB and malaria. Under the President's proposal, the global fund would receive only $200 million per year for the next five years. Yet at this moment, the fund is nearly bankrupt and has projected that it will require an additional $6.2 billion through 2004 to meet the increasing number of grant requests that the fund is expecting.

As a point of comparison, we recently approved $350 million in the fiscal year 2003 budget for the global fund. The AIDS authorization bills that we were working on last year would have provided between $750 million to $1 billion in fiscal year 2003. Clearly the congressional commitment to the fund exists. This was a bipartisan effort. It is especially critical that we provide funding now, given the recent election of Health and Human Services Secretary Tommy Thompson as chair of the executive board of the fund, in effect, making him the chief fund-raiser for the global fund.

Despite these issues, I believe there is ample hope that the United States will make a substantive commitment to fighting the global AIDS pandemic.

The Congressional Record. March 5, 2003: H1623–H1629.

GLOBALIZATION OF PRODUCTION

The Dominican Republic–Central America Free Trade Agreement (CAFTA) is a trade agreement between several Central American countries and the

United States. The trade agreement eliminates tariffs and promotes free trade between the participants. Currently, countries such as Guatemala, El Salvador, Honduras, Nicaragua, and Costa Rica have begun to implement the trade agreement's policies, while negotiations are still pending with other countries.

The Bush Administration has been in strong support of CAFTA since the beginning. In fact, President Bush made CAFTA one of his top priorities when he took office. President Bush believes that free trade is a win-win situation for all parties involved. The free trade model will stimulate economic growth and promote full employment. Sen. James DeMint (R-SC) believes that CAFTA will eliminate many tariffs that are currently in place for American goods. In turn, it will make it easier for American businesses to compete within the region. In addition to economic growth, Sen. DeMint believes that CAFTA will stabilize democracy in countries previously under authoritarian dictatorships and promote security. By promoting free trade, President Bush believes that the widening global income gap will close.

Even though the promotion of democracy and security are top priorities for Democrats as well, many oppose the trade agreement. Democrats believe that CAFTA prematurely opens up markets in other countries and brings in subsidized goods from the United States. As a result, the local economy is severely damaged because the local industry cannot compete. Sen. Edward Kennedy (D-MA) argues that the agreement is detrimental to American jobs because it further encourages outsourcing. Sen. Kennedy provides numerous statistics about the current state of the U.S. economy and argues that the passing of CAFTA will make it worse. In addition to domestic concerns, Sen. Kennedy points out the difficult working conditions faced by Central American workers and the lack of legislation within the agreement that adequately addresses the concerns. Furthermore, this trade agreement will only widen the global income gap because it will disadvantage Central American economies.

Conservative Viewpoint

James W. DeMint (R-SC). Mr. President, I rise to speak in favor of S. 1307, the CAFTA Implementation Act, because it advances America's economic and security interests. As someone who spent over twenty years in business before entering public service, I continue to be amazed by those in Washington who support outdated policies that make it harder and harder for American businesses to compete. Excessive taxation, regulation and litigation are driving American employers out of their minds and American jobs overseas. Yet too many politicians continue to support higher taxes, junk lawsuits, and trade barriers that effectively put signs on our beaches that say: Go do business somewhere else.

If we are going to have the best jobs in the world, we must make America the best place in the world to do business. This starts by reforming our complicated Tax Code, reducing mindless Government regulations, and eliminating frivolous lawsuits that, together, add mountains of needless costs on our businesses. Creating a pro-business environment in the United States also means we must open international markets to American exports so our workers can compete on a level playing field. CAFTA, for example, would expand the market for U.S. goods with forty-four million consumers in Costa Rica, El Salvador, Guatemala, Honduras, Nicaragua, and the Dominican Republic.

Nearly 80 percent of goods from the six CAFTA countries currently enter the United States duty-free. Yet American exports are taxed virtually across the board when they enter CAFTA markets.

On U.S. motor vehicles and parts, CAFTA countries levy an average tariff of 11 percent, while the U.S. rate is zero. On vegetables, fruits, and nuts, the CAFTA region's average is 16.7 percent, again compared with zero in the United States. On grains, it is 10.6 percent to zero; and on meat products, it is 14.7 percent, while the U.S. rate is just 3 percent. CAFTA would eliminate these disparities.

The agreement would level the playing field by eliminating 80 percent of the tariffs on American exports immediately, with the remaining tariffs phased out over 10 years. This would help exporters in my home State of South Carolina like BMW, Caterpillar and General Electric, as well as farmers and ranchers raising soybeans, peaches, pork, and poultry. The American Farm Bureau Federation estimates CAFTA could expand U.S. farm exports by $1.5 billion a year. Manufacturers would also benefit, especially in sectors like information technology products, agricultural and construction equipment, paper products, pharmaceuticals, and medical and scientific equipment.

According to a recent economic impact study conducted by the U.S. Chamber of Commerce, in the first year alone CAFTA would increase output in South Carolina by $167 million and create over 900 new jobs. In 9 years, the study shows a potential increase in output across all industries of $701 million and the creation of over six thousand jobs. The South Carolina State Ports Authority has told me CAFTA will contribute to greater economic development in South Carolina by stimulating commerce and the shipment of freight through the Port of Charleston. In 2004, Central America represented $359 million of the total value of the Port's business. In fact, Charleston's exports to Central America have grown faster than the average export growth. Most exporters agree: CAFTA is a great deal for South Carolina business.

.   .   .

Yet there is a small group in the textile industry whose opposition poses a threat to this step forward. They say CAFTA will allow China to exploit a "loophole" in the agreement. But they fail to recognize that without CAFTA there will be no loop at all—just one giant hole that China will use to destroy our industry. The truth is that a vote against CAFTA is a vote for China. Garment factories in Central America purchase large amounts of American fabric and yarn. In fact, the region is the second-largest world market for U.S. textile fabrics and yarns.

Under CAFTA, these garments made in the region will be duty-free and quota-free only if they use U.S. fabric and yarn. In fact, more than 90 percent of all apparel made in the region will be sewn from fabric and yarn made in the United States, thereby supporting U.S. textile exports and U.S. textile jobs. This is especially important for South Carolina workers. In 2004, South Carolina's exports of fabric mill products to the CAFTA region were valued at $180 million, more than half of the State's total exports to the region.

If we going to continue to have these exports and not lose the business to Asia, we must pass CAFTA. The American Apparel and Footwear Association made this point in a recent letter to President Bush where it said, if CAFTA "is not enacted soon, U.S. apparel and footwear companies will place more of their business outside this hemisphere." And the National Council of Textile Organizations recently endorsed CAFTA, saying, Central America "is a very important part of the domestic industry's supply chain and we need (CAFTA) to ensure that the U.S. textile industry can remain competitive against China."

The elimination of quotas on Chinese textiles has eroded the partnership the U.S. has with the Central American region. Our existing partnership is also weakened by burdensome documentation requirements and by the fact that it will expire soon. All of these factors reduce the incentive to make clothing in the region using U.S. inputs. CAFTA, however, will solidify and stabilize this partnership by making the current program broader, easier to use, more flexible, permanent, and reciprocal. The agreement will create new sales opportunities for U.S. textile and apparel products by providing permanent incentives for the use of U.S. yarns and fabrics in textile articles made in the region. And it will also give us new advantages over our competitors by promoting duty-free access for U.S. textile and apparel exports to local markets in the region.

I also thank the president and his administration for their efforts to make the agreement even stronger. Specifically, I have worked closely with U.S. Trade Ambassador Rob Portman to strengthen provisions dealing with textile pocketing. On May 9 of this year, Ambassador Portman wrote me about his desire to use the agreement's amendment mechanism to include pocketing in the rule of origin. He wrote: "I assure you that USTR will utilize this mechanism, working closely with our textile industry, to seek an amendment to the CAFTA so that pocketing would have to originate in one of the signatory Parties." This is very important to textile manufacturers in South

Carolina who make pockets and want to have a strong partnership with the CAFTA region.

It is time to stop saying no to every trade agreement, regardless of the benefits. We must stop acting like we are operating in the business environment of fifty years ago. We must stand up and fight for a better deal today. We can't build a wall around our country and expect to remain competitive. And we can't keep sticking our heads in the sand. Instead, we must fight back with new agreements that knock down barriers and create new markets. We must fight back and win because that is what Americans do. We have the best workers in the world and we can compete with anyone in the world.

CAFTA also provides a unique opportunity to promote democracy, security, and prosperity in a part of the world that was once characterized by oppression and military dictatorship. This agreement is critical to the economic and political stability of these young democracies, and it is a signal of our nation's commitment to democracy and prosperity in this hemisphere. As we continue to fight the war on terrorism, America has a vested interest in making sure these countries do not turn their backs on freedom.

I had the opportunity to personally meet with the presidents from the CAFTA countries earlier this year, and many of them are taking significant political risks to promote economic freedom. We need to stand with them. We must stand with them and pass this agreement. The benefits of CAFTA are clear. The agreement will strengthen our economic ties with our democratic neighbors, it will promote opportunity and prosperity in the United States and the region, and it will strengthen our security at home by promoting democracy and prosperity in our hemisphere. This agreement is a forward strategy for freedom, and I encourage my colleagues to support it.

The Congressional Record. June 29, 2005: S7598–S7605.

Liberal Viewpoint

Edward M. Kennedy (D-MA). I support free trade. I have long voted for trade agreements that truly leveled the playing field for our country and for our workers.

Free trade removes unfair barriers to American goods and world markets and creates a fair playing field for competition between American workers and workers abroad. Free and fair trade creates jobs and strengthens our economy. But this Central American agreement is not free trade. I urge the Senate to reject this unfair agreement.

Especially at this time when American workers are deeply concerned about their jobs being outsourced overseas, the Bush administration is wrong to negotiate an agreement that refuses to protect them. I am coming back to that in a moment. It allows participating countries to use labor practices that fail to meet international standards. It means that American workers, the best in the world, will be forced to compete with countries whose workers are abused and exploited. That is not fair trade.

I am for progress and economic development in Central America, dating back to President Kennedy's Alliance for Progress. But this agreement does nothing to improve labor rights for the workers in the CAFTA nations. All it asks is that they enforce their existing laws. It does nothing to create a community of nations that respects the basic rights and dignity of workers.

Most CAFTA nations give their workers no real rights such as an eight-hour day, overtime pay, or protection against discrimination. Laws in some CAFTA nations are even hostile to organized labor. Workers in El Salvador, Nicaragua, and Honduras can be fired for joining a union or even intending to organize a union. In Nicaragua, strikes are prohibited without government permission. Even where laws do exist, violations often cannot lead to fines or sanctions.

Those working conditions are not just what I have to say. There is an excellent study that was commissioned by the Department of Labor to review the working conditions among these countries that would be affected by this agreement. When the results came in, what did the administration do? They tried to hide the report. They went out and pulled all the paper that the study had been written on. What the study showed very clearly—and I will read the excerpts. The Government-paid study concludes: "Countries proposed for free trade status have poor working environments and fail to protect workers' rights." The department instructed its contractors to remove the reports from its web, ordered it to retrieve paper copies before they could be made public, banned the release of the new information from the reports, and even told the contractor it could not discuss the studies with outsiders. The working countries are so bad in those countries that the administration's own independent report stated so. Do we have anything in this particular agreement that will do anything about it? Absolutely not.

Have we at other times tried to do something about the conditions in these other countries? We certainly have. The agreement which stands out is the Jordanian agreement. In the Jordanian agreement they have very clear understanding about what the Jordanians were going to do to try to realize the international labor standards. Number one, they were going to eliminate slave trade; number 2, they were going to make advances moving ahead on child labor; number 3, they were going to permit the organizing of various labor organizations with real enforcement going in there, and penalties and sanctions if there were a violation. In other words, under the labor provisions in the Jordanian agreement that was passed by this body, we were moving forward, upward, to meet the international labor conditions. That is what ought to be in this agreement.

But is it in this agreement? Absolutely not. Were there any provisions in this agreement that, as a result of this agreement, American workers would get some kind of compensation for loss of their jobs as we have done at other times? Absolutely not. That proposal was defeated in the Finance Committee.

In other words, we are leaving American workers out there, high and dry, and are asked to go ahead and pass this without any serious effort to provide at least some protection for workers in those countries where there are going to be profits that will certainly not trickle down to the workers in that country and where real American workers will pay with the loss of their jobs because of this agreement.

CAFTA does not just ignore international standards for Central American workers; it also fails to include the aid for American workers likely to be displaced. When the Senate Finance Committee debated this agreement, it recommended that CAFTA include aid for displaced American workers, but the White House ignored the bipartisan recommendation. The president effectively abused his power and presented Congress and the American people with a take-it-or-leave-it plan. We know it can be better and we should reject this defective agreement, send it to the White House and go back to the drawing board.

Although CAFTA is the administration's top trade priority, it actually does very little to reduce the nation's growing overall trade deficit. Trade in the region accounts for less than 1.5 percent of total U.S. trade. It will barely lead to any improvement in GDP, an increase of only one-tenth of 1 percent. Instead of a policy to reduce our trade imbalance with China and deal with its currency manipulations and WTO violations, the administration has spent more than a year on this trade agreement that will do embarrassingly little to improve jobs and the economy. It is out of touch with sensible trade priorities for this country and ignores the needs of American families.

I want to take a few moments to show the pressure American families are under and why they are wondering why we are considering this legislation that provides no protection even for the workers in those countries and why it will accelerate additional pressures on American workers. Look what is happening in this country. More than thirty-seven million Americans, 28 percent of the workforce, work more than 40 hours a week.

Nearly one in five workers work more than fifty hours a week. More than 7.4 million Americans are working at two or more jobs, and three hundred thousand have two full-time jobs. Americans' work hours have increased more than in any other industrialized nation. American workers are working longer, are doing better, are increasing their productivity. Is there any recognition and respect for this extraordinary achievement? I certainly do not see it.

.   .   .

This president is the first president since Herbert Hoover to lose private sector jobs. These are the figures: 2001, 111,622,000 were working in the private sector. Now we are 111,598,000 in May of 2005. We have seen the reduction of jobs that are available in the private sector. There has been some growth, but it has all been in the public sector, not the private sector.

. . .

It does not have to be this way. We ought to be able to have a program that is going to be fair to American workers, uplift the working conditions of those countries around the world, and also be something that all members of this Senate would be proud to support. That is not this legislation. It is heavily flawed. As a result, there will be not only enormous numbers of people in that region that are going to be exploited, but we will pay for it with the price of American workers.

The Congressional Record. June 30, 2005: S7647–S7695.

IMMIGRATION

When Congress passed new immigration laws in 2006, protests all over the country erupted. The new law would classify anyone crossing the U.S. border or anyone aiding illegal immigrants as a felon. Much of the immigration reform has focused around illegal immigration. Illegal immigration has been a continuous problem for the United States, especially along the Mexico–U.S. border. Although it is problematic to account for the exact number of illegal immigrants in the United States, figures range around twelve million people. Statistics indicate that the United States accepts more immigrants than any other country in the world.

In 2004, President George W. Bush proposed a temporary guest worker program that would allow migrant laborers to enter the United States legally. For those already in the United States, the plan would grant the workers a temporary guest worker pass and allow them to stay in the country legally for up to six years. President Bush's plan was not met with much enthusiasm, not even from his own party. Rep. Virginia Foxx (R-NC) clearly outlined the Republican stance on immigration when she talked about immigration reform. Securing American borders, increasing law enforcement to curb immigration, making employers accountable for their labor force and encouraging legal immigration are all part of the Republican strategy.

The Democrats are criticizing the Bush Administration for not doing enough to protect the U.S. borders or create an efficient and feasible immigration solution. Democrats such as Sen. Harry Reid also accuse President Bush of politicizing the issue for the upcoming election. The Democrats argue that the Bush plan does not support U.S. citizenship for those that are already in the country. Furthermore, the plan has been called a "blanket amnesty program" because it allows anyone who wants to enter the United States to do so under the temporary guest worker program.

Conservative Viewpoint

Virginia Foxx (R-NC). Mr. Speaker, last week, House Republicans outlined five principles that we want included in any immigration reform legislation before it is sent to the president. They are:

- Republicans want to put a premium on border security and provide the resources necessary to strengthen our Border Patrol.
- Republicans want to strengthen the enforcement of immigration laws and stiffen the penalties for those who break those laws.
- Republicans want to hold employers who knowingly hire illegal aliens accountable and strengthen the penalties on them.
- Republicans oppose any and all efforts to reward those who break our immigration laws.
- And last, Republicans believe that immigrants must come here legally, obey our laws, and assimilate into American society by learning English.

Mr. Speaker, House Republicans passed a bill last December that incorporated these principles. Unfortunately, some of our colleagues in the Senate are pushing for legislation that would actually weaken our borders.

Mr. Speaker, this is neither what the American people need nor want.

The Congressional Record. June 28, 2006: H4686.

Liberal Viewpoint

Harry M. Reid (D-NV). Mr. President, it is so interesting that here it is five days before we are set to adjourn, six weeks before an election, and this border fence bill has been brought forward. The majority and the president have had five years since 9/11 to secure our borders, but they basically ignored, for five years, this issue of national security. Now, with the elections looming, suddenly they want to get serious about protecting America. If they want to have this debate, I am happy to join in it.

First of all, we can build the tallest fence in the world, and it will not fix our broken immigration system. To do that we need the kind of comprehensive reform that the Senate passed earlier this year. We have been waiting for months for the majority to appoint conferees so we can move forward on this bill, but they have not done that.

. . .

We need a bill that combines strong and effective enforcement of our borders, tough sanctions against employers who hire undocumented immigrants, a temporary worker program, and an opportunity for undocumented immigrants currently in this country to have a pathway to legal immigration. They need to work hard, pay their taxes, learn English, and stay out of trouble. Only a combination of these elements will work to get our broken immigration under control.

President Bush says he supports comprehensive reform, but he has a strange way of showing it. I heard my friend, who is one of the Senate's lawyers. Rarely does he come to the Senate floor unless he has an element of the law on which to speak. One of the things he talked about, last year they apprehended a little over a million people coming across the borders. However, that is down 30 percent from the time President Bush took office until now. Prior to that, we were picking up close to two million. We have a system that just does not work.

. . .

For years, we have had procedures and laws in place to secure our borders—not well but certainly better—and they have been virtually ignored. The September 11 Commission told the president he should work with other countries to develop a terrorist watch list that our border patrol agents could use to check people coming in. Did he do that? No. The September 11 Commission gave him a failing grade.

In the 9/11 Act—we all remember that—Congress provided for two thousand new Border Patrol agents. Guess what. Like so many things, they are authorized but not paid for. We have been unable to get the president and the Republican Congress to pay for these new Border Patrol agents. We authorized them and do not pay for them.

We did not oppose the sensible fence on the border. Almost all of us voted for a 370-mile fence as part of the comprehensive bill. If I am not mistaken, it is the senator from Alabama who moved forward to have the fence paid for. That is good. Now we have an amendment to build seven hundred miles of extremely expensive fencing—some estimate it will cost as much as $7 billion—with no plan to fix our broken immigration system.

. . .

Among the measures included in the package is a provision making the twelve million undocumented immigrants subject to arrest and detention. This provision has long been opposed by State and local law enforcement authorities who already are stretched thin and do not want to jeopardize the policing efforts in immigrant communities.

This is clearly an effort to sneak the controversial criminalization provisions of the House enforcement-only bill through the back door. I strongly oppose this illegitimate maneuver. If the Republicans want to move forward on these provisions, they should have agreed to a conference on immigration bills that each Chamber passed.

Enforcement measures alone will not secure our border. It is crucial we get control of our border. That is without any question. But, like many of my colleagues on the other side of the aisle, and like President Bush, I believe we can only secure our border through comprehensive reform. No amount of grandstanding will change that.

This is a rehash of a battle we already have fought. The Senate has spoken and profoundly disagrees with the House. The Senate is ready to sit down with the House and work out a real solution. We need the president and the majority leader to help find the solution. We have offered practical, workable, fair solutions to solve our immigration systems. The president and the majority leader said they supported what we were trying to do, but it does not appear they are interested in real solutions, just political posturing at this stage.

The Congressional Record. September 20, 2006: S9739–S9776.

THE PATRIOT ACT

After the terrorist attacks of September 11, 2001, all parties called for a comprehensive review of intelligence and national security. The USA PATRIOT Act, or Uniting and Strengthening America by Providing Appropriate Tools Required to Intercept and Obstruct Terrorism, was introduced in hopes of securing America's freedom. The argument made by the president was that giving up a few civil liberties in exchange for security is a small price to ask. He claimed that the USA PATRIOT Act was necessary to ensure security and for quick identification and removal of terrorists.

Many groups, including the American Civil Liberties Union (ACLU), complained about the law's infringement on the Constitution. The USA PATRIOT Act was passed with most senators and congressmen having never read the legislation. The legislation allows for search and seizure without warrants, secret courts, and the possibility that the government can obtain warrants without any burden of probable cause. It also calls for the immediate deportation of all who have overstayed their student or travel visa. As more and more Democrats read over the legislation under the strong suggestion of the ACLU, they began to take issue with it. The first chance that legislators had of repealing the USA PATRIOT Act was in 2005 when a long and arduous battle over each of the merits of the USA PATRIOT Act ensued. While the president and the Republicans claim that we cannot fight terror without the USA PATRIOT Act, Democrats continuously argue that the USA PATRIOT Act takes away too many freedoms and does not allow for oversight of the Department of Homeland Security and intelligence agencies. No final decision was able to be made, so the USA PATRIOT Act is currently on a six-month continuum until it is debated in Congress again.

Conservative Viewpoint

President George W. Bush. I'm going to sign—in a few moments, I'll be signing—the USA PATRIOT Improvement and Reauthorization Act. This is a really important piece of legislation. It is a piece of legislation that's vital to win the war on terror and to protect the American people.

The law allows our intelligence and law enforcement officials to continue to share information. It allows them to continue to use tools against terrorists that they used against—that they use against drug dealers and other criminals. It will improve our nation's security, while we safeguard the civil liberties of our people. The legislation strengthens the Justice Department so it can better detect and disrupt terrorist threats. And the bill gives law enforcement new tools to combat threats to our citizens from international terrorists to local drug dealers.

•   •   •

America remains a nation at war. The war reached our shores on September the 11, 2001. On that morning, we saw clearly the violence and hatred of a new enemy. We saw the terrorists' destructive vision for us when they killed nearly three thousand men, women, and children.

In the face of this ruthless threat, our nation has made a clear choice: We will confront this mortal danger; we will stay on the offensive; and we're not going to wait to be attacked again. Since September the 11, 2001, we have taken the fight to the enemy. We've hunted terrorists in the mountains of Afghanistan, cities of Iraq, in the islands of Southeast Asia, and everywhere else they plot, plan, and train. Our men and women in uniform have brought down two regimes that supported terrorism. We liberated fifty million people. We've gained new allies in the war on terror.

As we wage the war on terror overseas, we're also going after the terrorists here at home, and one of the most important tools we have used to protect the American people is the PATRIOT Act. The PATRIOT Act closed dangerous gaps in America's law enforcement and intelligence capabilities, gaps the terrorists exploited when they attacked us on September the 11th.

The PATRIOT Act was passed with overwhelming bipartisan support. It strengthened our national security in two important ways. First, it authorized law enforcement and intelligence officers to share vital information. Before the PATRIOT Act, criminal investigators were often separated from intelligence officers by a legal and bureaucratic wall. The PATRIOT Act tore down the wall. And as a result, law enforcement and intelligence officers are sharing information, working together, and bringing terrorists to justice.

Secondly, the PATRIOT Act has allowed agents to pursue terrorists with the same tools they use against other criminals. Before the PATRIOT Act, it was easier to track the phone contacts of a drug dealer than the phone contacts of an enemy operative. Before the PATRIOT Act, it was easier to get the credit card receipts of a tax cheater than trace the financial support of an Al Qaeda fundraiser. The PATRIOT Act corrected these double standards, and the United States is safer as a result.

Over the past four years, America's law enforcement and intelligence personnel have proved that the PATRIOT Act works. Federal, state, and local law enforcement have used the PATRIOT Act to break up terror cells in Ohio, New York, Oregon, and Virginia. We've prosecuted terrorist operatives and supporters in California and Texas, New Jersey, Illinois, Washington, and North Carolina.

The PATRIOT Act has accomplished exactly what it was designed to do. It has helped us detect terror cells, disrupt terrorist plots, and save American lives. The bill I sign today extends these vital provisions. It also gives our nation new protections and added defenses.

This legislation creates a new position of Assistant Attorney General for National Security. This will allow the Justice Department to bring together its national security, counterterrorism, counterintelligence, and foreign intelligence surveillance operations under a single authority. This reorganization fulfills one of the critical recommendations of the WMD Commission. It will help our brave men and women in law enforcement connect the dots before the terrorists strike.

This bill also will help protect Americans from the growing threat of methamphetamine. Meth is easy to make. It is highly addictive. It is ruining too many lives across our country. The bill introduces commonsense safeguards that would make many of the ingredients used in manufacturing meth harder to obtain in bulk and easier for law enforcement to track.

For example, the bill places limits on large-scale purchases of over-the-counter drugs that are used to manufacture meth. It requires stores to keep these ingredients behind the counter or in locked display cases. The bill also increases penalties for smuggling and selling of meth. Our nation is committed to protecting our citizens and our young people from the scourge of methamphetamine.

The PATRIOT Act has served America well, yet we cannot let the fact that America has not been attacked since September the 11th lull us into the illusion that the terrorist threat has disappeared. We still face dangerous enemies. The terrorists haven't lost the will or the ability to kill innocent folks. Our military, law enforcement, homeland security, and intelligence professionals are working day and night to protect us from this threat. We're safer for their efforts, and we'll continue to give them the tools to get the job done.

And now, it's my honor to sign the USA PATRIOT Improvement and Reauthorization Act of 2005.

Public Papers of the President: George W. Bush. March 9, 2006: 423–425.

Liberal Viewpoint

Edward M. Kennedy (D-MA). Mr. President, America deserves laws that protect both their security and their civil liberties. This conference report does not. After years of doubt about the PATRIOT Act, this morning Americans woke up to more startling reports. For the past three years, the administration has been eavesdropping on hundreds of calls without warrants or oversights. These are the newspapers: "Bush Authorized Domestic Spying." "Bush Lets U.S. Spy on Callers Without Courts."

Well, the administration is not responding to the article, but they tell us: Trust us. We follow the law. Give me a break. Across the country and across the political spectrum, no one is buying it anymore.

This administration feels it is above the law, and the American people and our Constitution pay the price. There is no accountability. There is no oversight. The president continues to ignore history.

In the 1970s, Big Brother spied on its citizens, and the American people stood up and said no. President Nixon's program, the COINTELPRO, allowed broad spying on law-abiding American citizens. We stopped Big Brother then by establishing the FISA court to ensure proper oversight and protections. Now this administration believes it is above even those protections. This is Big Brother run amok. With these new developments, we must take a step back and not rush the PATRIOT Act, further risking our civil protections.

The entire world is watching to see how we strike the balance between intelligence gathering and the Constitution. We cannot protect our borders if we do not protect our ideals. We need a bipartisan consensus that protects both our security and our liberty while restoring the public trust.

Our country is at a new low. Not since Watergate has there been such a lack of openness and honesty in our Government. Americans deserve better. The leaking of a CIA agent's identity is the prime example. The president promised he would clean house of anyone in the White House who had anything to do with the leak in the Plame case or the cover-up. It has been suggested that the president himself may know the identity of the source, and I urge him to set the record straight.

The president needs to answer three questions: One, what did he know and when did he know it? Two, did he tell the special prosecutor, Fitzgerald, the whole story? And, three, who else knows the facts? Cheney? Gonzales? Ashcroft? If Novak knew and the president knew, then the American people should know, too.

Mr. President, answer these questions.

In the last few days, we have heard a lot about whether America will be safer if the Senate approves the PATRIOT Act conference report this week.

Let's set the record straight—our national security will not be jeopardized— at all—if existing laws stay in place for three more months. These surveillance methods will expire only if the Republican leadership refuses to negotiate—even with members of their own party.

We have unfinished business on the table. The conference report fails to do all we can to improve intelligence-gathering capabilities and legislative oversight. Americans deserve a law that protects both their security and their liberties, and this bill does not.

We need to preserve the basic powers created by the PATRIOT Act, but we also need to improve the safeguards that are indispensable to our democracy. Civil liberty protections are a continuing source of our country's strength—not just fringe benefits to be abandoned in time of crisis.

We all agree on the need for law enforcement and intelligence officers to have strong powers to investigate terrorism, to prevent future attacks, and improve information-sharing between federal, state and local law enforcement.

In the wake of the tragic events on September 11, Congress, the administration, and the country faced the urgent need to do everything possible to strengthen our national security and counterterrorism efforts, and the original PATRIOT Act was our response to that need.

Even at that time, many of us had concerns about whether the law went too far. In November 2001, Nancy Talanian and a small group of neighbors in western Massachusetts came together to launch the Bill of Rights Defense Committee—what has now become a nationwide movement to protect the Bill of Rights.

This small Massachusetts group encouraged similar community discussions across the country. Seven states and hundreds of local governments engaged in vigorous public debate on the scope of the PATRIOT Act. As of this week, four hundred resolutions have been passed.

These efforts can't be casually dismissed because the administration claims there have not been any "verified abuses" of the PATRIOT Act.

The Republican leadership tells us that time has run out and this legislation must be passed without further debate. We are told that enough oversight has taken place.

But it took two years—*two* years—for the Department of Justice to respond to questions from the Senate Judiciary Committee about the use of the PATRIOT Act tools. We didn't receive the significant written answers until after the committee approved its bill.

We then learned that the federal government has only reported three instances in which a U.S. person was informed of a search because there was no national security interest in keeping it secret. Only three times has the Attorney General notified a United States person that they have been searched.

Yet we read more newspaper stories about FBI mistakes. The FBI says it averages about 10 mistakes a year. As a result of litigation, the FBI has admitted publicly that unauthorized electronic surveillance has gone on for months before mistakes were caught.

Now, I don't doubt that the FBI is trying to do a good job—but how many mistakes does it take to count as an abuse?

This administration tells us to disregard such mistakes because the information is being collected only about individuals linked to terrorism. Clearly, that is not the case.

I know personally about mistakes in the war on terror. Not long ago. I was on the no-fly list, and had to make a number of calls to clear up the resulting confusion.

Countless others have had a similar experience. I received a letter from a man in California. He had gone to the airport with his family to begin a vacation to Disneyland. Arriving at the airport, they encountered an unexpected surprise. His nephew, Liam Collins—at that time just seven years old—was on the government's no-fly list. Seven years old and on the no-fly list.

Liam and his family convinced airport officials it was a "mistake." Liam made it to Disneyland but he sent me a picture about his experience—which had become a memorable part of the trip.

Since then, Liam hasn't traveled by plane, so no one knows whether the "mistake" has been fixed. What about other mistakes? The Justice Department tells us that the so-called libraries provision has never even been used to search a library.

That may be just a clever way of saying that it is happening in a different way. In 2002, Attorney General Ashcroft told Congress that "national security letters" would be the better tool for library searches anyway.

Maybe Ashcroft was right. The so-called libraries provision has only been used thirty-five times—but over thirty thousand national security letters have been issued, according to the Washington Post. The public doesn't know if that number is accurate, because the administration refuses to confirm it.

The conference report will require public reporting on the use. It will also require the Inspector General to audit their use.

But under these authorities, the Government is not required to obtain a court order. Your local library has no clear right to challenge demands for computer records in court. For consumers, there is zero protection—much less notice—if your records are taken by mistake. The recipient of a national security letter is barred forever from talking about it—even if the need for secrecy no longer exists.

On these national security letters, the conference report has two major shortcomings. One of the most glaring omissions is the failure to include a sunset provision for national security letters, which would be consistent and logical given the new reporting and auditing provisions contained in the conference report. Without doubt, it is more meaningful to have a sunset on a provision used thirty thousand times than one that is used thirty-five times.

What we anticipated four years ago is abundantly clear now: four-year sunsets are the only means to ensure adequate congressional oversight of controversial law enforcement and counterterrorism activities. In addition, recipients of these orders should have a meaningful right to judicial review. The administration's acquiescence in giving recipients the right to consult an attorney is not a meaningful concession. The Justice Department has already taken that position in litigation. The conference report does not advance civil liberties on that point. In fact, it makes it harder to win in court. Under the conference report, banks, phone companies, and libraries challenging these authorities will have to overcome an even higher threshold in court, and companies may have to turn over records even where there is not even an individualized suspicion of terrorism.

The federal government should focus on whether the country is doing enough to protect citizens from another terrorist attack, and is providing adequate safeguards to protect fundamental civil liberties.

What Americans want and deserve is responsible legislation. Our Senate bill included the necessary assistance for law enforcement, while maintaining fundamental protections in accord with the Bill of Rights. As a result, it received unanimous approval of the entire Senate.

At the first and only meeting of this conference, I urged my colleagues to support the Senate bill, keeping in mind the recommendations of the bipartisan 9/11 Commission, which made clear that the executive branch has the burden of proof to justify why a particular governmental power should be retained—and Congress has the responsibility to see that adequate guidelines and oversight are made available.

On the two most contentious surveillance methods, the executive branch has failed to meet the 9/11 Commissioners' burden of proof—much less the burden of persuasion. The American people are not convinced that these methods achieve the right balance between our national security and protection of our civil liberties.

This conference report, however, failed to meet the 9/11 Commissioners' recommendations. It is especially alarming that the Commissioners' report card gave five failing grades in key areas of need. Obviously, America is not as safe as it should be.

Snooping on library computers is no substitute for strong and effective steps to prevent terrorist attacks.

With this conference report, some harsh provisions were deleted, but other abusive provisions were added. Debate about extraneous provisions took priority over improvements in the core provisions. It appears that the PATRIOT Act can't get better without also getting worse.

The administration wants to get this bill done—but the American people want it done right.

The Congressional Record. December 16, 2005: S13708–S13735.

GLOBAL GAG RULE

The Mexico City Policy, also known to Democrats as the global gag rule, was a policy first initiated by President Ronald Reagan. President Reagan believed the United States should not use its federal aid money to further abortion practices worldwide. The policy was in effect until 1993 when President William J. Clinton rescinded it.

The Mexico City Policy was reclaimed by President George W. Bush during his second day in office. Like many predecessors before him, President Bush has strong religious beliefs against abortion. Since he believes that abortion is murder, President Bush does not see a reason to continue funding this practice overseas. These U.S.-imposed restrictions mandate that no U.S. family planning assistance can be provided to foreign NGOs that use the funding to perform abortions or lobby to make abortion legal within that country.

Many Democrats continue to be appalled at the Administration's position. The effects of this funding loss have been significant. Cutting off funding to crucial and sometimes sole health providers in many regions is unethical. Many Democrats believe that there is no positive correlation between the Mexico City policy and abortion rates overseas. Some even believe that this policy has the opposite effect. By limiting access to contraception and health information, many believe that the Mexico City policy is actually increasing the number of abortions overseas.

Liberal Viewpoint

Lynn Woosley (D-CA). Mr. Speaker, I rise to express my extreme disappointment that the global gag rule has been imposed on U.S. assistance to international family planning programs once again. On his second full day in office, President Bush reinstated this Reagan-era restriction, gagging foreign private organizations from using their own funds to educate women and families about their full range of reproductive choices.

For decades, U.S. aid to family planning organizations overseas has helped these groups provide invaluable services for women around the world. Our nation has a history of helping women educate themselves and to providing access to needed reproductive health services. I assure my colleagues that piling on restrictions to censor what foreign organizations can and cannot do with their own private funds is nothing to be proud of.

Each year in the developing world, nearly six hundred thousand women die from pregnancy-related complications. That is why our support for a full range of reproductive health services, including contraception, health workshops, counseling and maternal care becomes more important every day.

By imposing the gag rule, President Bush is taking away a woman's right to make decisions, decisions that affect her reproductive health, her emotional and physical security, and her family's future. President Bush is imposing his own values on foreign groups, and he is limiting these groups to providing only the services that get his seal of approval.

The truth is that family planning programs reduce the need for abortion. They promote safe motherhood and they increase child survival. Denying women birth control and counseling creates more unwanted pregnancies, more abortions, and more suffering. It is also a fact that more than seventy-five thousand women die each year due to unsafe abortion. Without access to safe and affordable services, abortion will be less safe and will put more women's lives in danger.

I know that the women of this House are more committed than ever to protect the rights of women around the world. We have a responsibility to work to reduce the rate of unwanted pregnancy and improve the lives of women and children at home and abroad. Implementing a global gag rule is not the way to meet this goal.

The Congressional Record. January 30, 2001: H89.

Conservative Viewpoint

President George W. Bush. The Mexico City Policy announced by President Reagan in 1984 required nongovernmental organizations to agree as a condition of their receipt of federal funds that such organizations would neither perform nor actively promote abortion as a method of family planning in other nations. This policy was in effect until it was rescinded on January 22, 1993.

It is my conviction that taxpayer funds should not be used to pay for abortions or advocate or actively promote abortion, either here or abroad. It is therefore my belief that the Mexico City Policy should be restored. Accordingly, I hereby rescind the "Memorandum for the Acting Administrator of the Agency for International Development, Subject: AID Family Planning Grants/Mexico City Policy," dated January 22, 1993, and I direct the Administrator of the United States Agency for International Development to reinstate in full all of the requirements of the Mexico City Policy in effect on January 19, 1993.

· · ·

Let me start with the latter. That violated the one-question rule, but—I said we're not going to use taxpayers' money to fund abortion. And we're going to make sure, before we spend taxpayers' money, that we're not funding abortion.

Public Papers of the President: George W. Bush. January 29, 2001: 219–230.

TERRORISM

When nineteen terrorists hijacked four planes on September 11, 2001, the world suddenly changed. Many believe that the United States received a wake up-call that even the most powerful country in the world is susceptible to violence. Following the attacks, many laws, including the PATRIOT Act, were passed in Congress to give enforcement agencies more power.

As a result of 9/11, President Bush has made over seventeen hundred speeches about terrorism. In addition, since the beginning of the War on Terror, President Bush has launched many domestic and international initiatives. Domestically, hundreds of people were detained, arrested, or questioned in regard to terrorism. Additionally, President Bush created the Department of Homeland Security to help coordinate homeland security efforts. President Bush also increased military spending dramatically to ensure that the U.S. military had sufficient resources abroad.

Many Democrats have been critical of the Bush Administration's inability to deal with the War on Terror as well as their blatant scare tactics used against the American people. Rep. Marcy Kaptur urges the American public to look past the detrimental Bush rhetoric and instead focus its energy on the root causes of terrorism. These causes include poverty, American foreign policy, intolerance, and the Israel/Palestine conflict. Rather than labeling everyone a terrorist, Rep. Kaptur suggests that education and self-analysis will serve a greater purpose toward solving terrorism.

Conservative Viewpoint

President George W. Bush. This war on terror arrived on our shores on September 11th, 2001. Since that day, the terrorists have continued to kill in Madrid, Istanbul, Jakarta, Casablanca, Riyadh, Bali, Baghdad, London, and elsewhere. The enemy remains determined to do more harm. The terrorists kill indiscriminately but with a clear purpose. They're trying to shake our will. They want to force free nations to retreat so they can topple governments across the Middle East, establish Taliban-like regimes in their place, and turn the Middle East into a launching pad for attacks against free people.

The terrorists will fail. Because we are fighting their murderous ideology with a clear strategy, we're staying on the offensive in Iraq, Afghanistan, and other fronts in the war on terror, fighting terrorists abroad so we do not have to face them here at home. When terrorists spend their days and nights struggling to avoid death or capture, they're less capable of arming and training and plotting new attacks on America.

We're also spreading the hope of freedom across the broader Middle East, because free societies are peaceful societies. By offering a hopeful alternative to the terrorists' ideology of hatred and fear, we are laying the foundations of peace for our children and grandchildren.

In the war on terror, our troops are serving with courage and commitment, and their bravery is inspiring others to join them. All of our services met or exceeded their active duty recruitment goals last month, and the troops closest to the fight continue to reenlist in impressive numbers. The Army, Navy, Air Force, and Marines are all on track to meet or exceed their reenlistment goals for the year. Our troops know the stakes of this war, and Americans can have pride and confidence in our All-Volunteer Forces.

In recent days, we have seen again that the path to victory in the war on terror will include difficult moments. Our nation grieves the death of every man and woman we lose in combat, and our hearts go out to the loved ones who mourn them. Yet, even in our grief, we can be confident in the future, because the darkness of tyranny is no match for the shining power of freedom.

The terrorists cannot defeat us on the battlefield. The only way they can win is if we lose our nerve. That will not happen on my watch. Withdrawing our troops from Iraq prematurely would betray the Iraqi people and would cause others to question America's commitment to spreading freedom and winning the war on terror. So we will honor the fallen by completing the mission for which they gave their lives, and by doing so, we will ensure that freedom and peace prevail.

Public Papers of the President: George W. Bush. August 13, 2005: 1285–1286.

Liberal Viewpoint

Marcy Kaptur (D-OH). Mr. Speaker, President George Bush, in creating fear about terrorists in the American people rather than understanding, often says, "If we don't fight terrorists over there, we will have to fight them right here." He never bothers to explain in detail who the terrorists are or what motivates them or how his policies are creating more of them. The president's explanations are too simplistic, and they are wrong.

The president tried to convince us if we got Saddam Hussein and brought him to justice the battle for peace in the Middle East would take a favorable turn. Indeed, the opposite has happened as Iraq descends into chaos. Indeed, despite the military firmness and bravery of our soldiers, the Iraq war has actually failed politically by failing to win the hearts and minds of the people.

. . .

The president's own White House was forced this week to declassify an intelligence report that I am going to put in the Record. This is a summary, called "Trends in Global Terrorism, a National Intelligence Estimate," and this report says the Iraq war is shaping a new generation of terrorists.

Anyone who knows anything about what is causing rising levels of hatred against the United States in the Middle East would have anticipated this eventuality. The key question the president and we must address and face is, why do his policies yield more and more terrorists who want to harm us, and harm us in many places beyond the boundaries of Iraq and Afghanistan?

The complete story will show terrorists will continue to plot ways to harm America because more than wanting to come here, although some of them are capable of doing that, they want America and American influence out of their countries and regions. They want us out of there more than they want to come here.

Rather than striking fear in the American people, the president ought to do more to explain the forces creating this anti-American and anti-Western sentiment across those troubled regions. Which American interests have caused this antagonism to our nation? An important question to answer. In what countries has this hatred been fomented? Another important question to answer. And what is the face there of America that is hated more and more?

Let me suggest part of that face involves U.S. oil alliances in cahoots with some of the most repressive and brutal regimes and leaders who hold down the potential of their own people. There is not a democracy over there, and we are totally reliant on all of those oil kingdoms.

Let me suggest that the presence of U.S. military bases that ensure the status quo of those repressive regimes doesn't help.

Let me suggest America is hated more because we are not viewed as being evenhanded at arriving at fair and just peace settlements between Israel and the Palestinians and their neighbors. We need to do a better job of cultivating evenhanded diplomacy in the region.

Let me suggest our U.S. popular culture and many of its excesses are regarded as abhorrent to the fundamentalist legions that have gained even greater ascendancy after the disgusting and outrageous behavior by Americans at Abu Ghraib.

Let me suggest the U.S. now is being viewed by the multitudes of Muslims as fighting a religious war against Islam. President Bush made a huge blunder at the start of the Iraqi war by calling it a Crusade hearkening back to the Christian wars. His battle cry gaffe echoed across the Muslim world and became a rallying point for the opposition.

How tragic and inappropriate.

Let me quote from a wise American voice who tries to enlighten about the roots of terrorism, rather than strike fear in our people: Robert Baer, author of best selling book See No Evil, is a decorated CIA agent who put his life on the line for our nation for three decades. He tries to build understanding about the conditions giving rise to terrorism. He defines our problem as larger than just a few men—like Bin Laden and Hussein—and their followers. He argues the reason animosity is growing against the U.S. is the result of much larger forces spanning several decades.

· · ·

Understanding the forces that generate terrorism is fundamental for solving it. The National Intelligence Report summarizes some of the essential steps our nation must take to broaden our understanding of what it will take to break our dependence on oil regimes, resolve peace settlements that have been let languish, and form alliances that are broadly representative and democratic in their focus. The world needs more understanding, not fear, to counter terrorism.

The Congressional Record. September 26, 2006: H7490–H7491.

SELECTED READING

The Global Spread of HIV

Beck, Eduard J., Nicholas Mays, Alan W. Whiteside, and Jose M. Zuniga. *The HIV Pandemic: Local and Global Implications.* 1st ed. (New York: Oxford University Press, 2006).

Garrett, Laurie. "Staggering Trend: HIV Pandemic Worsening among African, Asian Youth." November 24, 1998. www.aegis.com/news/newsday/1998/ND981101 .html.

Haffner, Debra W. "The HIV Pandemic Still Deserves the Best from U.S." *Siecus Report.* December–January 1998. www.findarticles.com/p/articles/mi_qa3781/is_ 199712/ai_n8764163.

Pindborg, J. J. "Global Aspects of HIV Pandemic." July 1995. adr.iadrjournals .org/cgi/reprint/9/2/146.pdf.

Wildman, Sarah. "New Threats to HIV Funding: The Bush White House Is Pledging to Send Billions to Fight HIV/AIDS around the World. Is It Turning Its Back on Those Infected in the U.S.?" *The Advocate.* March 1, 2005. findarticles.com/p/ articles/mi_m1589/is_2005_March_1/ai_n13813029.

Globalization of Production

"CAFTA-DR." The White House. 2006. www.whitehouse.gov/infocus/cafta.

"CAFTA Facts." Office of United States Trade Representative. February 2005. www .freetradeforamericas.org/caftapdf/case percent20for percent20cafta.pdf.

Engler, Mark. "The Trouble with CAFTA." *The Nation.* January 16, 2004. www.thenation .com/doc/20040202/engler.

"House Narrowly Approves CAFTA." *CNN.com.* July 28, 2005. www.cnn.com/ 2005/POLITICS/07/28/house.cafta.

"U.S.-CAFTA-DR Free Trade Agreement: How Can US Companies Benefit?" U.S. Government Export Portal. 2006. www.export.gov/fta/complete/CAFTA.

Immigration

"Homepage." Federation for American Immigration Reform. 2006. www.fairus.org/site/ PageServer.

Murray, Shailagh. "Conservatives Split in Debate on Curbing Illegal Immigration." *Washington Post.* March 25, 2005. www.washingtonpost.com/wp-dyn/articles/ A64179-2005Mar24.html.

Papademetriou, Demetrios G. "Critical Issues in the U.S. Legal Immigration Reform Debate." Department of Labor. January 1990. www.sscnet.ucla.edu/issr/paper/ issr516.pdf.

Schorr, Daniel. "The Immigration Debate: Reform vs. Enforcement." *Christian Science Monitor.* March 31, 2006. www.csmonitor.com/2006/0331/p09s02-cods .html.

United States Citizenship and Immigration Office. 2003. www.uscis.gov/portal/ site/uscis.

The PATRIOT Act

"Congress Needs to Hear about PATRIOT Renewal." The Center for Democracy and Technology. 2006. www.cdt.org/publications/policyposts/2006/1.

Mac Donald, Heather. "Hearing on the Patriot Act." Manhattan Institute for Policy Research. April 19, 2005. www.manhattan-institute.org/html/mac_donald04-19-05 .htm.

Phillips, David J. "Cell Phones, Surveillance, and the State: Monitoring Daily Life." *Dissent* 51(2).

"President Bush Pressed Congress to Renew the Patriot Act." *National Review.* July 4, 2005. www.findarticles.com/p/articles/mi_m1282/is_12_57/ai_n14793401.

"USA PATRIOT Act." American Civil Liberties Union. 2006. action.aclu.org/ reformthepatriotact.

Winkler, Claudia. "Who's Afraid of the PATRIOT Act?" *The Standard.* April 28, 2004. www.weeklystandard.com/content/public/articles/00.

Global Gag Rule

"European Parliament Votes to Fund Abortions Overseas." February 14, 2003. www.cwnews.com/news/viewstory.cfm?recnum=19931.

"Introduction." Population Action International. 2006. www.populationaction.org/resources/publications/globalgagrule/index.htm.

"Memorandum." White House. January 22, 2001. www.whitehouse.gov/news/releases/20010123-5.html.

Stevens, Allison. "Bush Extends Global Gag Rule to AIDS Funds." February 25, 2003. www.womensenews.org/article.cfm/dyn/aid/1233.

"The Bush Global Gag Rule: Endangering Women's Health, Free Speech and Democracy." Center for Reproductive Rights. June 2003. www.crlp.org/pub_fac_ggrbush.html.

Terrorism

Abramowitz, Michael. "Democrats Focus on Terrorism Report in Attacks on Bush." *Washington Post.* September 26, 2006. www.washingtonpost.com/wp-dyn/content/article/2006/09/25/AR2006092501310.html.

"Clarke's Take on Terror." *CBS News.* March 21, 2004. www.cbsnews.com/stories/2004/03/19/60minutes/main607356.shtml.

"House Democrats' Anti-Terrorism Spending Push Defeated." *CNN.com.* November 28, 2001. archives.cnn.com/2001/ALLPOLITICS/11/28/rec.antiterror.bill.

Mazzetti, Mark. "Spy Agencies Say Iraq War Worsens Terrorism Threat." *New York Times.* September 24, 2006. travel2.nytimes.com/2006/09/24/world/middleeast/24terror.html?adxnnl=1&adxnnlx=1162795572-DmtX9sjODipdODaQ9Ue37g.

"News Analysis: War on Terrorism Helps Bush Win Re-Election." *People's Daily News.* November 4, 2004. english.people.com.cn/200411/04/eng20041104_162668.html.

Sammon, Bill, and Jerry Seper. "Bush Says Terrorism on the Run." *Washington Times.* September 11, 2003. www.washtimes.com/national/20030911-120003-9003r.htm.

Index

About the Authors

Gardenia Harris, Ph.D., MSW, is assistant professor at Illinois State University, where she teachers social welfare policy and field practicum courses. Her research interests include racial disparities in the provision and outcomes of social services, the differential impact of child welfare policies on minorities, the effectiveness of drug treatment courts, and HIV among middle-aged African American women. She began her career working as an in-home family therapist, and later served as a manager of an adolescent residential treatment facility. Subsequently she was employed as an academic skills counselor at a private college.

Bernard Ivan Tamas, Ph.D., is assistant professor of politics and government at Illinois State University. Professor Tamas has been a Fulbright scholar to the Central European University in Budapest, Hungary, a postdoctoral fellow at the Harvard-MIT Data Center, a visiting scholar at Harvard's Center for Basic Research in the Social Sciences, and a visiting professor at both Brandeis University and Williams College.

Nancy S. Lind is professor of politics and government and associate department chair at Illinois State University. Her specializations include public administration and policy as well as bureaucracy and the American presidency. She has four edited books including *Violence and Its Alternatives*, *Presidents from Reagan through Clinton*, *Controversies of the George W. Bush Presidency*, and *Comparative Public Administration*.